The Politics of Economic Leadership

# The Politics of Economic Leadership

## THE CAUSES AND CONSEQUENCES OF
## PRESIDENTIAL RHETORIC

*B. Dan Wood*

PRINCETON UNIVERSITY PRESS

PRINCETON AND OXFORD

Copyright © 2007 by Princeton University Press
Published by Princeton University Press, 41 William Street,
Princeton, New Jersey 08540
In the United Kingdom: Princeton University Press, 3 Market Place,
Woodstock, Oxfordshire OX20 1SY

All Rights Reserved

ISBN-13 (cl.): 978-0-691-12977-8
ISBN-13 (pbk.): 978-0-691-13472-7

British Library Cataloging-in-Publication Data is available

This book has been composed in Sabon

Printed on acid-free paper. ∞

press.princeton.edu

Printed in the United States of America

10  9  8  7  6  5  4  3  2  1

*To Joy and Piney*

# Contents

# Illustrations

# Tables

# Preface

THIS BOOK examines the causes and consequences of presidential efforts to lead the economy through words. Presidents have been using their words for this purpose at least since Franklin Roosevelt and the Great Depression. In his first inaugural address, President Roosevelt focused his remarks exclusively on the economic decline that had engulfed the nation for over three years. Many people remember the famous quotation from that address: ". . . let me assert my strong belief that the only thing we have to fear is fear itself—nameless, unreasoning, unjustified terror which paralyzes needed efforts to convert retreat into advance." The fear that Roosevelt was referring to was that of continued economic decline. We often credit these and other inspirational words by President Roosevelt with lifting the American spirit from the depths of the Great Depression. The impact of presidential words, however, is actually an empirical matter that can be addressed by scientific research.

Unless there is an international crisis, modern presidents talk more about the economy than any other issue. Thus, one set of empirical research questions addressed in this book concerns the causes of presidential rhetoric on the economy. No modern president has faced an economic crisis of the same magnitude as that faced by President Roosevelt. Yet recurrent economic rhetoric has been a dominant feature of every presidency from that of Truman through George W. Bush. Are presidential remarks on the economy mere politics? Do presidents respond to particular political conditions, such as their approval ratings, public opinion, or election-year incentives? Is presidential rhetoric on the economy a response to particular economic conditions, such as economic growth, unemployment, inflation, or the federal deficit? What determines the intensity and tone of presidential remarks about the economy through time? More generally, do modern presidents, like President Roosevelt, attempt to lead the economy through rhetoric that can spark economic optimism and potentially alter economic outcomes?

Another set of empirical research questions addressed in this book concerns the consequences of presidential rhetoric on the economy. Does presidential rhetoric become lost in the continuous stream of "noise" characterizing the American system? Or, does the presidents' economic rhetoric have actual impacts? For example, do presidential remarks affect people's assessments of economic conditions such as economic growth, unemployment, or inflation? Do presidential remarks about the economy affect consumer confidence? If so, what are the implications of presidential words for actual economic behavior such as saving, borrowing, and spending? Do the presidents' economic remarks have political implications? For example, do they alter people's assessments of how well the president is doing as an economic leader? Do presidential remarks about the economy alter people's assessments of presidential leadership generally?

All of the preceding research questions are addressed empirically in this book using a dataset consisting of every unique sentence spoken publicly by the president about the economy from World War II through the first George W. Bush administration. Collecting such a dataset was a formidable task, requiring both technology and human effort. I owe a considerable debt to those who helped with this endeavor.

I had worked with presidential rhetoric earlier when I studied agenda setting and the causes of issue attention in the American system (Edwards and Wood 1999; Wood and Peake 1998; Wood, Flemming, and Bohte 1999). From this earlier work I developed a strong interest in how presidents affect the political system.

The data for the earlier work were collected in the very rudimentary manner of using human coders and the tedious parsing of indices of consecutive paper editions of *Public Papers of the Presidents*. In January 2001, however, I attended a seminar focusing on PERL and the machine coding of text documents. The seminar was conducted by Phil Schrodt of the University of Kansas. In the months and years after the seminar, I developed PERL programs for manipulating text from large documents, which enabled the coding of an electronic version of the entire *Public Papers of the Presidents*. This methodological innovation was used in this current project to create a dataset that comprises all presidential remarks about the economy since World War II. For introducing me to PERL, I sincerely thank my friend Phil Schrodt.

There are several others who were influential of this project. George C. Edwards III, my colleague at Texas A&M, was important in encouraging me to explore the "causes" side of the work. Without the incentive of presenting a paper at his Conference on Researching the Public Presidency in February 2004, I would probably never have moved in this direction. George was also very helpful with assorted advice along the way on both sides of the project. Thanks, George, for always having an open office door.

Jeffrey Cohen of Fordham University read and commented on various convention papers that later became chapters. Jeff also read the entire manuscript when it neared completion and made numerous helpful suggestions. Richard Curtin of the University of Michigan provided the most recent data from the Survey of Consumers when I was up against deadlines and wanted up-to-date data on consumer attitudes. Also, Richard's papers on the psychological approach to studying consumer behavior

(Curtin 1983; Curtin 2000) became the seed for the theory used on the "consequences" side of the research in chapters 5 and 6.

I am also indebted to those who provided research assistance. The data on the presidents' economic rhetoric were initially machine coded using PERL. Machines are dumb, however, and considerable human effort was required to ensure valid and reliable measures. The bulk of the human effort was supplied by Chris Owens and Brandy Durham over the two-year period from 2001 to 2002. The data were later updated through 2004 and further cleaned by Justin Vaughn, Gilbert Schorlemmer, Daniel Hawes, and Sarah Kessler.

In the interest of future research, I encourage replication of the work reported here, as well as further application of the data. Thus, all of the data on presidential rhetoric reported in the empirical parts of the book are available on my website at Texas A&M University. The web address is currently *http://www-polisci.tamu.edu/faculty/wood/*. A Google search for my name should also find the data.

Chuck Myers of Princeton University Press offered sage advice on how to craft the manuscript. Given my strong methodological leanings, he encouraged me to focus on substance, rather than minor technical questions that might excite those in the methodological community. Chuck was also a pleasure to work with as an editor, especially in securing expert reviewers and in dealing with deadlines that I promised but seldom met. I also thank two anonymous reviewers for numerous insightful suggestions, most of which are implemented in the final manuscript.

Financially, the research was supported by Texas A&M University through a University Faculty Fellowship from 2002 to 2006. I also received a grant from the Center for Presidential Studies at the George Bush School of Government and Public Service. I am also deeply appreciative of my department and university for providing a supportive intellectual environment.

Finally, I want to thank those closest to me for their understanding and support of my career and research. My wife, Patricia, has been steadfast in helping me in every possible way. I dedicate the book to my mother and father, Joy and Piney, who encouraged me to be who I am.

The Politics of Economic Leadership

# CHAPTER 1

# Presidential Words and the Economy

ON JULY 2, 2004, as the election season got underway, President George W. Bush spoke on the U.S. economy from the East Room of the White House. The White House press release for this event was entitled "Over 1.5 Million Jobs Created and 10 Straight Months of Job Gains." In his remarks, President Bush noted that the U.S. economy had been through a lot during his administration, with a recession, national emergency, corporate accounting scandals, and a war. The tone of his remarks on the economy, however, was decidedly positive. He made multiple references to his administration's tax policies, which he claimed were stimulating job growth and the economy. The president also alluded to growing consumer confidence, increasing personal income, record home ownership, improved manufacturing, and a robust job market. He claimed that all of these factors bode well for the future of the U.S. economy. Through this election season speech, the president was obviously trying to foster the notion that his stewardship of the U.S. economy had been good during his first term.

Various surveys released shortly after the president's speech provide a reality check on the president's remarks. They suggest that the president may have been singing to a deaf audience. In separate polls conducted by CBS News/New York Times and the Associated Press, around 57 percent of survey respondents viewed the nation as "on the wrong track," and a majority of survey respondents "disapproved" or "strongly disapproved" of the president's handling of the economy. The monthly ABC News/ Money Magazine poll of American attitudes about the economy released five days later found that 59 percent of respondents gauged the state of the nation's economy as either "not good" or "poor." Fully 45 percent of survey respondents rated their own personal finances as either "not good" or "poor"; around 58 percent of those same respondents viewed the current time as "a not so good time" or "a poor time to buy the things you want and need." Obviously, there was a disjuncture between the president's words and the perceptions of ordinary citizens.

Of course, the president's speech was only part of a continuing strategy by the administration to use economic rhetoric for political ends. From the 2001 inauguration through January 20, 2005, the president alluded to the economy 3,351 times in various speeches, news conferences, radio addresses, and other public appearances.[1] This was an average frequency of about 70 times per month. In relative terms, over this period the president devoted more public remarks to the economy than any other issue except national security.

The tone of President Bush's economic remarks, however, changed considerably over the course of the administration. During the 2000 election campaign, candidate Bush had promised a large tax cut to his conservative supporters. A large tax cut is ill advised, however, when the economy is "overheated" since it would be inflationary.[2] Indeed, over the two years prior to the 2000 election, the Federal Reserve Board had raised interest rates six times in an effort to cool down the economy. In December prior to the presidential inauguration, the unemployment rate had been a mere 4 percent, and recent economic growth had been robust. Nevertheless, during the 2000 election campaign and after the inauguration the president attempted to justify a reduction in taxes as a move to stimulate the economy. The president seemingly "talked down" the economy to persuade Americans that a tax cut was needed.

Four days after the inauguration a reporter asked the president how he could convince congressional Democrats to go along with his large proposed tax cut. He responded, "I think the evidence is going to become more and more clear that the economy is—it's not as hopeful as we'd like, which I hope will strengthen my case" (Remarks Prior to a Meeting with Bipartisan Congressional Leaders and an Exchange with Reporters, January 24, 2001). Later in early February, the president spoke to Republicans at a congressional retreat. He said,

> It is so important for us to understand some facts. One, the economy is slowing down. And it's important for us to combine good monetary policy with good fiscal policy. . . . I come from the school of thought that by cutting marginal rates for everybody who pays taxes is a good way to help ease the pain of what may be an economic slowdown. I'm going to make that case over and over and over again until we get a bill through. (Remarks at the Republican Congressional Retreat in Williamsburg, Va., February 2, 2001)

The president was true to his words to congressional Republicans. Over the next three years, he repeatedly pounded home the message that the U.S. economy was doing poorly and that tax cuts were needed to stimulate jobs and economic growth. Between the inauguration and September 2001, the president made an average of twelve pessimistic comments about the economy each month. During September, the month of the terrorist attacks, the president alluded to poor U.S. economic performance seventeen times.

As it turned out, economic growth did slow in 2001. The National Bureau of Economic Research (NBER) determined that a recession had occurred between March and November.[3] Whether the slowdown was a self-fulfilling prophesy or simply a matter of chance, the first Bush tax cut came at an opportune time. The Economic Growth and Tax Relief Reconciliation Act of 2001 (PL 107–16) reduced taxes by roughly $1.3 trillion over the next 10 years. It reduced the estate tax, cut the top four income tax rates, shifted the tax burden away from upper-income groups, and carved out a new 10 percent tax bracket from part of the existing 15 percent bracket. The president had achieved the largest tax cut in U.S. history, thereby keeping a campaign promise to core partisan supporters.

The president, however, did not achieve all he had promised during the 2000 election campaign. Therefore, he continued the same strategy over the next two years to push for even more tax cuts. In response to the president's efforts, in March 2002 Congress passed the Job Creation and Worker Assistance Act (PL 107–147), which provided tax relief for businesses and an extension of benefits for unemployed workers. According to the NBER, at this point the economy was no longer in recession. A year later when the economy was obviously no longer in recession, the president signed yet another piece of tax legislation that gave the third largest tax cut in U.S. history. The Job and Growth Tax Relief and Reconciliation Act of 2003 (PL 108–27) provided an additional $350 billion in tax cuts for the nominal purpose of stimulating economic growth and producing more jobs.

Over three years the president had accomplished three large tax cuts to produce the sharpest reduction in federal revenues in U.S. history. Large federal budget deficits resulted that are projected to last through the next decade. The largest beneficiaries of the Bush tax cuts were upper-income groups and investors. The tax-cutting campaign was purported by the Bush administration to be in response to what the National Bureau of Economic Research classified as the mildest recession since World War II (Nordhaus 2002).

During this period, the president was more pessimistic about the economy than any past president. There was also an obvious increase through this period in consumer pessimism. Between the 2000 election and early 2003, the University of Michigan's Index of Consumer Sentiment, a measure of consumer confidence, declined by around 40 percent. As the introductory vignette suggests, most Americans were skeptical about the economy and the president's economic leadership. This economic pessimism among citizens may have related somehow to the president's continuing pessimism.

In early 2004, public opinion about the president's economic leadership did not bode well for reelecting the president. Accordingly, during the election season the president became increasingly optimistic, assuming the role of cheerleader for administration policies and the economy. The president touted the three tax cuts as responsible for turning around a weak economy. Unemployment had fallen to 5.4 percent by August. There was little evidence of inflation, and economic growth averaged around 3.5 percent. The president needed to produce a perception of effective economic leadership to bolster the upcoming reelection effort, so he claimed credit for a set of economic statistics that were less positive than when he took office. Interestingly, the optimistic tone of President Bush's remarks dropped precipitously immediately after his 2004 reelection.

## WHY DO PRESIDENTS TALK SO MUCH ABOUT THE ECONOMY?

President Bush talked more about the economy during his first term than about any topic except national security. This pattern of continuous presidential attention to the economy is typical of modern presidents. Unless there is an international crisis, they talk more about the economy than any other issue. A core research question addressed in this book is "Why?" Why do modern presidents feel so compelled to emphasize the economy in their public remarks?

Of course, presidential remarks about the economy have not always been so intense. President Truman alluded to the economy in a public setting about 2,124 times in his roughly eight years in office, or an average of about twenty-three public comments about the economy each month. This relatively low level of presidential attention continued through the Eisenhower administration, but increased gradually for the Kennedy through Nixon administrations. During the stagflation era of the 1970s, the frequency of presidential remarks on the economy increased sharply. President Ford mentioned the economy in a public setting 3,799 times in about two and a half years. This was over five times as often as Presidents Truman and Eisenhower. During the Clinton administration, which adhered to the mantra "It's the economy stupid!" presidential attention to the economy increased sharply again. President Clinton mentioned the economy in a public setting 12,798 times in eight years, or around 133 times per month. This was about six times as often as Presidents Truman and Eisenhower. As noted earlier, this pattern of elevated presidential attention to the economy continued through the George W. Bush administration.

Modern presidents are on a permanent campaign (Blumenthal 1982; Gergen 2000; Ornstein and Mann 2000), and emphasis on the economy is a major part of that campaign. "Going public" has become an important dimension of governing in America, with presidents from Richard Nixon through George W. Bush devoting an increasing amount of White House resources to public relations (Jacobs and Shapiro 1995a, 1995b; Kernell 1997). A major component of the permanent campaign is a focus on the president's stewardship of the economy. Thus, a simplistic answer to the question of why presidents talk so much about the economy is that contemporary presidents believe it is a useful public relations ploy.

The introductory vignette suggests, however, that presidential rhetoric has no real impact on public opinion. If this is true, then this motivation is questionable. If presidential rhetoric is ineffective, then presidential attention and energy would be better spent behind the scenes building coalitions to address a range of pressing issues such as health care, Social Security, education, or the environment. Thus, the research reported in this book serves a practical purpose in informing scholars and presidents alike as to the efficacy of presidential efforts at rhetorical leadership.

More generally, this work intends to increase the body of scientific knowledge about the public presidency. I specifically want to explore what factors determine variations through time in the intensity and tone of presidential remarks about the economy. Are presidential remarks on the economy mere politics, as suggested by the economic rhetoric of George W. Bush? Are presidential remarks on the economy a response to political conditions, such as approval ratings, public opinion, or election year incentives? Is presidential rhetoric on the economy a response to the economy? If so, what is the nature of that response? More generally, do presidents attempt to lead the economy through rhetoric that can spark economic optimism and potentially alter economic behavior?

## THE INSTITUTIONAL CONTEXT

As noted, the frequency of presidential remarks about the economy has increased through time. Some of this increase may be due to the changing nature of the presidency as an institution. The presidency generally has become more rhetorical through time. For example, Tulis (1987) describes the rise of the rhetorical presidency from the early days of the Republic through modern times. He argues that presidents beginning with Theodore Roosevelt and Woodrow Wilson increasingly used rhetoric to place the presidency at the center of the political system. Similarly, Edwards (1983) describes the development of the public presidency whereby presidents increasingly use public relations to influence Congress, the media, and public opinion. Hart (1989) documents these changes further by analyzing presidential speechmaking from Truman through Reagan and concludes that modern presidents have spoken more and more through time, but may actually say less. Similarly, Hinckley (1990) describes the rise of the symbolic presidency, as presidents have increasingly used rhetoric to play on the media stage to shape public images.

The evolution of the public presidency may be important to an increasingly rhetorical style of presidential leadership. It does not explain, however, why presidents have focused so much of their rhetorical attention on the economy. Rather, we must also consider the particular economic institutions that have emerged to understand increasing presidential attention to the economy. Through time, multiple institutions have evolved, culminating in a modern presidency that is now the chief economic policy-making actor in the United States.

The evolution of presidential responsibility for the economy began with the Great Depression.[4] The despair and devastation of massive unemployment, lost wealth, and widespread poverty produced a cry for help from the federal government. The cataclysmic economic downturn altered citizen expectations about the role of the central government in promoting a strong national economy. With the Great Depression also came an intellectual shift which recognized that "laissez-faire" markets could no longer be trusted, and that the national government should be a mechanism for addressing market failures (Heilbroner and Singer 1999, 261–87).

The response was the election of President Franklin Roosevelt in 1932. The first Roosevelt administration achieved few concrete policies to remedy the depression. Indeed, the United States was still experiencing severe economic hardship during the second Roosevelt administration up to World War II. Nevertheless, Roosevelt was a dynamic rhetorical leader who spoke optimistically about the future (Burns 1956; Schlesinger 1960). Through weekly radio addresses and speeches, he directed attention to himself to inspire confidence that prosperity would return. The president's chief accomplishment was to alter the political culture surrounding public expectations for government management of the economy (Cohen 2000).

Following World War II, a feared return of high unemployment and the rise of Keynesian economics led Congress to pass the Employment Act of 1946 (PL 79–304). This legislation formally institutionalized an activist role for the president, charging government with promoting "maximum employment, production, and purchasing power." From this point forward, presidents were required to make an annual Economic Report to Congress detailing the current and future state of the economy, as well as the administration's plans and recommendations for promoting these goals. The president also received an advisory staff within the Executive Office of the President through the creation of a Council of Economic Advisors.

During the economic upheavals of the 1970s, the mandate for the president to promote a sound economy expanded through passage of the Humphrey-Hawkins Act of 1978 (PL 95–523). This legislation was a response to the era of "stagflation," which combined high inflation and high unemployment. It formally established a goal of full employment for the U.S. economy. The president was required each year to set numerical goals for key economic indicators over the subsequent five years. The president was also required to report, with the annual budget, projections of federal spending and revenues that were consistent with maintaining full employment. Presidents since Carter have generally ignored the mandate to set specific numerical targets (Frendreis and Tatalovich 1994, 37–38). Nevertheless, the reinforced mandate from the Humphrey-Hawkins Act placed responsibility for U.S. economic performance squarely on the shoulders of the president.

Saddled with these responsibilities, presidents responded by expanding White House institutions for economic policy-making and advice (Frendreis and Tatalovich 1994, 66–69). Presidents Truman and Eisenhower had a single economic policy advisor, the Chairman of the Council of Economic Advisors, to coordinate economic policy and provide guidance to the president. Presidents Kennedy and Johnson used a troika system that involved discussions among the president, Council of Economic Advisors, Bureau of the Budget, and Treasury Department. President Nixon centralized the budgetary function by reorganizing the Bureau of the Budget into the Office of Management and Budget. Since President Ford, there has continuously been an organizational unit under various names within the White House for the purpose of coordinating economic policy and advising the president on economic matters.[5] President Clinton established the current office called the National Economic Council by Executive Order 12835 (of January 25, 1993). President George W. Bush has continued this office to the present.

The evolution of institutions imposing obligations on the presidency for the economy means that modern presidents are continually immersed in economic affairs. Presidents receive frequent briefings on the state of the economy and participate in the formulation and implementation of plans for the economy. As a result, the economy is omnipresent in the president's routine. This institutional immersion is a continuing incentive for presidents to talk publicly about the economy.

The evolution of economic policy-making institutions also means that people hold the president accountable for the economy. Undoubtedly, few Americans are aware of the specific legal mandates on the president or the details of presidential plans for the economy. Nevertheless, citizens are concerned about the economy and alter their opinions about the president when the economy changes.

Since 1946, the Gallup poll has asked "What do you think is the most important problem in this country today?" In general, economic problems have dominated people's responses, except when the nation has been at war or in crisis. Responses to the "most important problem" question correlate strongly with actual macroeconomic performance, suggesting that people are very attentive to how the economy is doing.

Americans hold the president accountable for U.S. economic performance by changing their approval of the president's job performance. While the president does not directly control economic growth, unemployment, or inflation, people tend to personalize presidential responsibility for these outcomes (Sigelman and Knight 1985). Indeed, numerous studies show that the public's approval of the president's job performance depends strongly on macroeconomic performance (Beck 1991; Bloom 1975; Brody 1991; Chappell and Keech 1985; Clark and Stewart 1994; Edwards, Mitchell, and Welch 1995; Erikson, MacKuen, and Stimson 2002; Fiorina 1981; Haller and Norpoth 1994; Hibbs 1987; Kinder and Kiewiet 1979; Kinder and Kiewiet 1981; MacKuen 1983; MacKuen, Erikson, and Stimson 1992; Markus 1988; Monroe 1978; Mueller 1970; Norpoth 1996; Ostrom and Smith 1993; Tufte 1978; Wood 2000). Variously, these studies show a relationship between unemployment, inflation, economic growth, and consumer expectations about the future of the economy and presidential job approval ratings. The current understanding in this literature is that expectations about the economic future are most important in determining the president's standing with the public (Erikson, MacKuen, and Stimson 2002).

The institutionalization of presidential responsibility for the economy has also meant that presidents must achieve certain policy ends in order to be considered effective stewards of the economy. Presidents, however, are constrained in their ability to implement economic policy. They must usually obtain approval from Congress to make policy changes.[6] This means that presidents must persuade others about the efficacy of their plans for the economy. Presidents lobby members of Congress directly in attempting to pass their economic plans. They have also increasingly used the strategy of "going public" through the media and mass public to build support (Kernell 1997). Thus, modern presidents often speak publicly about the economy while acting as advocates for their economic policy proposals.

In his influential book *On Deaf Ears*, George C. Edwards III (2003, chap. 1) argues persuasively that presidents and other political actors believe that public approval is important to achieving policy success in Congress. Substantial scholarly evidence supports these beliefs, even if the effects are sometimes only marginal (Bond, Fleisher, and Wood 2003; Brace and Hinckley 1992; Edwards 1980, 1989, 1997; Ostrom and Simon 1985; Rivers and Rose 1985). When presidential approval is declining or low, the president is less successful in promoting policy ambitions in both domestic and foreign policy arenas. Thus, presidents wanting to maintain economic policy leadership must maintain high approval ratings. One component of doing so is projecting an image of strong economic stewardship through public rhetoric.

Perceptions of effective stewardship of the U.S. economy also affect the electoral success of the president and the president's party. There are numerous studies showing that the electoral success of the president and president's party depends on public perceptions of U.S. economic performance through time (Erikson 1989; Erikson, Bafumi, and Wilson 2001; Fair 1978; Fiorina 1981; Kiewiet and Rivers 1985; Markus 1988; Rosenstone 1983). Indeed, virtually all forecasting models for presidential elections include variables that measure economic performance (e.g., see Lewis-Beck and Rice 1992, table 6.1). These forecasting models typically show that a lagging economy diminishes the prospects of reelection for the president or the president's party, while a strong economy covaries strongly with reelection success.

Moreover, it is easy for presidents and others to observe what has happened to incumbent presidents perceived as poor economic managers. President Carter left office in 1980 after a single term during an era of rampant inflation and high oil prices that the president seemed powerless to control. President Reagan was easily reelected in 1984 as the economy showed improvement following the 1982–83 recession. President George H. W. Bush failed in his reelection bid following the 1990–91 recession amidst the perception that he was a weak economic leader. President Clinton easily won reelection in 1996 during a period of robust economic growth. In every presidential election since 1960, when the unemployment rate was declining the incumbent or incumbent's party won the presidential election; but when the unemployment rate was stable or increasing, the incumbent or incumbent's party lost the presidential election (Lewis-Beck and Rice 1992). Therefore, presidents who value reelection for themselves and their political party should want to produce a public perception of strong economic leadership.

These various incentives mean that modern presidents talk regularly about the economy in their public appearances. Political scientists, however, know little about variations in this behavior. What determines how often presidents talk about the economy? When do presidents talk about the economy? Are there systematic variations across presidencies in propensity to talk about particular dimensions of the economy such as unemployment, inflation, or the federal deficit? Are there systematic variations within and across presidencies in the tone of presidential rhetoric on the economy? How do economic conditions and political incentives affect the intensity and tone of presidential remarks about the economy?

True economic leadership implies that presidents should attempt to create a favorable climate for economic activities, both through policy and by instilling confidence in the economic system. Therefore, presidential rhetoric should do more than simply mirror prevailing economic conditions. Presidents should speak often and optimistically about the economy to encourage economic activity. Which presidents have spoken more often and more optimistically about the economy after controlling for economic conditions, public approval, and political incentives? What variations in presidential optimism have occurred within presidencies and why? The research reported in this book addresses all of these questions with empirical data.

## Do Presidential Remarks Matter?

A second core research question addressed by this book is whether presidential remarks about the economy matter. If presidential rhetoric does not matter, then, from a practical standpoint, we should question why presidents spend so much time talking about the economy. On the other hand, if we can show that presidential rhetoric does matter, it would suggest strategies of presidential leadership that do not depend on other institutions or people.

For example, a major part of the president's permanent campaign is presumably to secure and maintain high public approval ratings. Scholars, however, generally depict presidents as limited in ability to alter their own approval ratings. The standard textbook explanation of presidential approval is that there is a pattern of long-term secular decline (Edwards and Wayne 2006, 112–23; Pika and Maltese 2006, 79). Presidents faced with high public expectations rarely live up to those expectations. However, if presidential rhetoric matters, then this suggests that presidents can alter the pattern of declining approval through image manipulation. Presidents who successfully project an image of strong economic leadership should better maintain the public's approval.

Another major part of the president's permanent campaign is to secure favored public policies. With respect to economic policy leadership, the president is constrained by the need to obtain cooperation from Congress, the courts, and the bureaucracy. Yet, the president needs no permission from Congress, the courts, or the bureaucracy to be a cheerleader for the economy or to tout ongoing programs. If presidential rhetoric matters, then expressing confidence about the economy may have impacts on economic behavior and economic performance. Thus, presidential rhetoric, becomes a unilateral tool of economic leadership for use without delay or impediment.

Furthermore, if the president can successfully project an image of economic leadership through rhetoric, then this provides at least a partial answer to the first question of why presidents talk so much about the economy. Presidents view economic rhetoric as a tool for bolstering their public approval ratings and achieving economic policy ends. On the other hand, if citizens remain largely oblivious to the president's economic rhetoric, as suggested by the introductory vignette, then this suggests a presidential credibility problem. Under these conditions, presidential words are wasted.

In addressing the general question of whether presidential words matter, I also consider several more specific questions. Do presidents *directly* affect their own public approval ratings by projecting an image of economic leadership? Do presidents *indirectly* affect their public approval ratings by altering public perceptions about the economy? Much of the past research on public approval has ignored presidents as a factor in determining the public's approval of presidents' job performances.

Other specific questions addressed in this book concern whether presidential rhetoric affects actual economic outcomes. Do presidential remarks alter consumer perceptions about the health of the economy? Do presidential remarks affect perceptions by other economic actors such as investors, savers, or borrowers? Do presidential remarks *directly* affect economic behavior, such as personal consumption, business investment, or borrowing? If so, what are the mechanisms for these effects? Prior research has not addressed these questions.

Of course, presidents obviously believe that their remarks are important or they would not speak so often about the economy. Edwards (2003, chap. 1) provides a plethora of anecdotal evidence supporting the thesis that presidents believe their public remarks matter. He argues that modern presidents engage in a permanent campaign because they believe that their efforts can persuade or even mobilize the public.

White House communications advisors to Presidents Reagan and Clinton generally fostered this notion. For example, Gergen (2000, 348) stated that Ronald Reagan turned television "into a powerful weapon to achieve his legislative goals." Similarly, Blumenthal (1982, 284) suggested that Reagan had "stunning success in shaping public opinion" and used it to achieve policy goals. Similarly, Jacobs and Shapiro (2000) conducted interviews during the 1990s with White House and congressional staff. Interviewees typically expressed great confidence in the president's ability to lead public opinion.

Yet, scholarly research on how presidential rhetoric affects public opinion arrives at mixed conclusions. A literature exists on the ability of the president to alter their public approval ratings through speeches and political drama. The early work in this genre (MacKuen 1983; Ragsdale 1984,

1987) found that presidents succeed in manipulating their approval ratings through speeches, but the effects are very short-lived. Presidents also receive a brief bump in public approval from dramatic events such as military interventions and foreign policy trips. Those bumps, however, tend to last only one or two months. Moreover, such manipulations tend to be serendipitous and not fully within the control of the president.

In contrast, other studies cast doubt on the president's ability to manipulate public approval ratings through speeches. Various work by Simon and Ostrom suggests that political and economic environments are the main determinants of the president's approval ratings (Ostrom and Simon 1985, 1988, 1989; Simon and Ostrom 1985, 1988, 1989). Thus, presidents are rarely able to manipulate their own approval ratings through speeches and dramatic events. Consistently, Edwards (2003) examined presidential approval before and after major speeches, from Presidents Reagan through George W. Bush, and found only a random pattern of changes. Additionally, when increases in presidential approval did occur following major speeches, these gains tended to be brief. Therefore, the current scholarly understanding is that presidents are not very successful in manipulating their approval ratings through individual speeches.

Another scholarly literature examines the relative success of presidential efforts to exert policy leadership. The evidence from this literature is also mixed. Early experimental research shows that if the president's name is attached to specific policy proposals, then some members of the public are more likely to support that proposal (Conover and Sigelman 1982; Sigelman 1980b). Subsequent experimental research, however, suggests that identification of the president as supporting particular policies can fail to increase support, and may even diminish public support (Sigelman and Sigelman 1981). These contradictory findings have been construed to mean that support for the president on particular policies depends on presidential popularity or credibility (Mondak 1993).

The work on aggregate public opinion lends some support to this conclusion. For example, Page and Shapiro (1985; see also Page, Shapiro, and Dempsey 1987 ) found that presidents can produce small effects on aggregate public opinion by going public, but only when the president is popular. This effect is probably bipolar, though, since those who approve of the president are more likely to approve of the president's policies relative to those who disapprove (Kernell 1984; Sigelman 1980a).

On the other hand, Edwards (2003, chaps. 2 and 3) examined public opinion polls on a variety of domestic and foreign policy issues before and after major presidential addresses. He found little or no evidence that the president had been successful in moving public opinion during either the Reagan or Clinton presidencies. If any presidency should have been successful in moving public opinion, it should have been these, since

Reagan and Clinton were both highly acclaimed as effective communicators and recognized for their strong standing with the public. Therefore, Edwards (2003, 241) concludes, "[P]residents typically do not succeed in their efforts to change public opinion. Even 'great communicators' usually fail to obtain the public's support for their high-priority initiatives."

If the president has difficulty altering public opinion on specific policy issues, can the president at least affect what issues people are paying attention to? Again, past research arrives at mixed conclusions. Cohen (1995) examined annual State of the Union messages to find that increased presidential attention to economic, foreign, and civil rights policy leads to increased public attention to these same issues. Hill (1998), however, observed that Cohen's work ignored potential reverse causality associated with presidential rhetoric and public attention. In other words, presidential rhetoric may be a response to preexisting public attention, rather than a cause. In his reanalysis, Hill's results suggest that the relationship is two-way for economic and foreign policy attention, but one-way for attention to civil rights.

In contrast, Wood and Peake (1998) and Edwards and Wood (1999) used weekly time-series data to cast doubt on the extent to which presidential rhetoric leads media attention to various policy issues. They examined six issues, three in a foreign policy domain and three in a domestic policy domain. While they did not evaluate economic issues, the results for both domains, after controlling for other factors, suggest that presidential attention follows, rather than leads, media attention.

Thus, some prior research casts serious doubt on the president's ability to influence public sentiment through words. Past studies suggest that individual presidential speeches do not systematically change the president's public approval ratings, and when they do, the effects are brief. Past studies also suggest that major speeches do not systematically alter the public's views on specific policy issues. Even the president's ability to alter what issues the public is attending to appears limited. Therefore, the weight of empirical evidence from prior research should make us skeptical about presidential efforts to lead the public through words.

## WHY SHOULD PRESIDENTIAL REMARKS ON THE ECONOMY BE ANY DIFFERENT?

Why should results from this study, with its specific emphasis on the presidents' economic rhetoric, differ from those of earlier studies? Zaller (1992) has argued that moving public opinion is strongly conditional on whether a message is received by the public. For a message to be received, the potential receiver must be attentive and the message must be well transmitted. Consistently, I argue that people are very attentive to economic issues because such issues can have personal effects. Additionally, the transmitter of the message, the president, is someone to whom people are attentive. Thus, this study of presidential effects on public opinion should produce different results for several reasons.

First, economic issues are more salient than other domestic policy issues. Most prior research has studied presidential rhetoric generally by focusing across a range of issues. This current research, however, focuses intently on a single issue that has high salience with the public. Using Gallup's Most Important Problem Surveys, around 44 percent of respondents since World War II have, on average, listed some dimension of the economy as the most important problem facing the nation. Note also that this most important problem series correlates strongly with actual macroeconomic performance. When the economy is in recession, or when inflation or unemployment is high, there is an increase in the proportion of respondents listing these as important problems. This suggests that people are highly attentive to the economy.

Second, the president's remarks on the economy should matter because the president's economic message is a sustained message. Presidents talk about the economy more than any other single issue, and through a variety of forums. Much of the scholarly work on the public presidency has examined the impact of *single* presidential speeches on public support across a range of policy issues. Many presidential speeches address specific policy issues, but there is no subsequent sustained presidential attention to the issue. Edwards (2003) even isolated his focus to the effect of single presidential speeches on public support immediately before and after a speech. While this approach is useful for expanding understanding of the short-term effects of presidential rhetoric, it may not provide a true reflection of the dynamic time path of presidential rhetoric and public opinion.

Modern presidents have engaged in a continuous effort to shape public perceptions of their leadership of the economy. In this effort, they have used a variety of forums including speeches, interviews, economic reports, press conferences, press releases, town meetings, and other forms of communication. Information from all of these sources flows into the news stream. As a result, a single speech may have little or no impact since it is just one of many cues received by citizens. A sustained public relations campaign, however, may well have a strong impact that spreads more slowly and evolves more dynamically over time. It may be that a single presidential speech has only a brief effect on public opinion, but a continuous message about the economy produces effects that build gradually through time to produce changing attitudes and behavior. In short, presidents help establish a climate for economic perceptions that does not flow from a single speech but from a stream of messages through different sources. As a result, dynamic measures and research methods are required to reveal fully the effect of presidential rhetoric on public attitudes and behavior.

Third, presidential remarks about the economy should make more of a difference because the president is an authoritative source of information on the economy. As noted above, the president is institutionally responsible for formulating a fiscal policy consistent with maintaining full employment and stable economic growth. Public law and public expectations impose strong obligations on the presidency for providing economic leadership. As a result, the president is the most visible and important economic actor in the U.S. system.[7] Presidents are assumed by virtue of their role and supporting expertise to have more information about the economy than other actors. They have a large support staff on the economy, including the National Economic Council, Council of Economic Advisors, Office of Management and Budget, Departments of Treasury, Commerce, and Labor, and Bureau of Economic Analysis. Experts in these institutions provide the president with economic advice, plans, and assessments that enable authoritative economic leadership. The credibility of these institutions filters over to the presidency, making for an authoritative voice on the economy.

Furthermore, the media broadly publicize presidential remarks on the economy. Most Americans get most of their information about the nation and world from the news. The president features prominently into this scheme of information collection. The chief executive is the most visible and important political and economic actor in the United States. As such, virtually every television newscast has at least one brief segment on the president and/or the administration. Regardless of topic, whether it is the president's pets, health, scandal, foreign policy, or the economy, the media covers the presidency broadly and intensely. Given their public salience, the president's remarks about the economy receive special attention from a news media hungry for an audience.

These three conditions provide the optimal context for a critical test of whether the president's public remarks should ever make a difference. The economy is highly salient to most Americans. The president gives sustained attention to the economy. The president is authoritative so that the news media provide intense coverage of administration remarks on the economy. The president's message is well transmitted and should be received by an audience that is attentive. If the president's remarks do not make a difference under these circumstances, then we can rest assured that they will not matter under the less optimal conditions that characterize other issues.

## Conclusion

In this introductory chapter, I have laid out the research questions and objectives that guide the work reported in this book. Specifically, I seek to explain why presidents talk about the economy. I also seek to explain whether presidential words about the economy make a difference.

A core theoretical emphasis is to resolve the contradiction between practical politics and academic scholarship on the public presidency. On the one hand, presidents, presidential advisors, the popular press, and mass public believe that presidential words are powerful instruments that can change public opinion. Seemingly, presidents talk about the economy because they believe their words make a difference. On the other hand, a significant body of scholarly research on the public presidency suggests that presidential words do not matter. Various studies cited earlier report that single presidential speeches across a range of issues have had no lasting impact on the president's public approval ratings. Other studies show that presidential words have had no impact on people's attitudes about particular policy issues. Thus, past scholarly research has produced great skepticism about the importance of presidential words. This work seeks to clarify which perspective is correct.

It is also useful to highlight the interconnections among the various research concepts examined in later chapters. Most relationships are potentially multi-directional. That is, the president's economic rhetoric can both cause and be caused by various political and economic factors. For example, this research explores the determinants of presidential rhetoric on the economy. It also explores whether presidential remarks about the economy produce changes in other indicators such as public approval, the economic news, consumer confidence, personal consumption, business investment, borrowing, and interest rates. It may be, however, that presidential rhetoric on the economy is both a response to and a cause of these indicators. Presidents may alter the intensity and tone of their remarks about the economy as the economy worsens. The intensity and tone of presidential remarks about the economy may alter the psychology of economic and political behavior, resulting in altered outcomes. Thus, a challenge for this study is tracing the paths of causal influence between the president's economic rhetoric and economic and political outcomes.

If we are to conduct a critical test of theories about the president's permanent campaign and disentangle patterns of causal influence, we require a source of empirical data that accurately reflects presidential remarks on the economy through time. The next chapter discusses the data sources for measuring these concepts and their method of collection.

# CHAPTER 2

# Measuring the Intensity and Tone of Presidential Rhetoric about the Economy

> Every day is election day in the permanent campaign. Such campaigning is a nonstop process seeking to manipulate sources of public approval to engage in the act of governing itself. American governance enters the twenty-first century inundated with a campaign mentality and machinery to sell politicians, godly policies, and everything in between.
>
> (Heclo 2000, 17)

IF WE ARE TO UNDERSTAND the causes and consequences of the president's economic rhetoric, then we need a systematic source of data to capture the intensity and tone of the president's rhetoric through time. We could, as has been done in past research, simply focus on single presidential speeches (Cohen 1995; Edwards 2003; Hill 1998) or use a case study approach to explore why presidents speak and whether a response occurs. Case studies, however, are subject to interpretation and may suffer from myopic causal judgment. Therefore, we should prefer a more global approach that allows generalization across multiple presidencies and enables systematic analysis through time.

Accordingly, this study focuses on the larger context for presidential remarks about the economy. Do presidents *generally* vary the intensity of their remarks as a function of how well the economy is doing? Does the tone of presidential remarks *generally* change as a function of economic performance? If so, how does it change? Is presidential rhetoric on the economy *generally* just political rhetoric intended to bolster electoral perceptions of economic leadership or to accomplish partisan political ends? Or do presidential remarks on the economy sometimes reflect economic leadership independent of economic performance and political ends?

Rather than focusing on single presidential speeches or events, this study employs a continuous time perspective to measure the *flow* of presidential remarks and gauge the responses of economic and political actors. Presidents maintain an extensive public relations apparatus for transmitting a continuous stream of messages through various means. They transmit their economic messages using multiple mechanisms, including speeches, radio addresses, group appearances, news conferences, town meetings, policy briefings, news releases, and other public appearances (e.g., see Edwards and Wayne 2006, chap. 5). As presidents engage in a permanent campaign, they create a continuous stream of stimuli intended to produce a sustained message about the economy.

For example, the discussion in the introductory chapter suggests that the message of the first three years of the George W. Bush administration was that the economy was not doing well, and we needed to reduce taxes to deal with this problem. Similarly, we shall see later that if we focus on virtually the entire Clinton administration, the sustained message was that the economy was doing very well and people had reason to be optimistic about the economic future.

A response to these continuous presidential messages can be immediate, or it can be delayed and evolve dynamically over time. Economic and political actors may require time to receive and absorb fully the president's message. Citizens are limited in their cognitive abilities and may require multiple stimuli to hear fully the president's message (Berelson, Lazarsfeld, and McPhee 1954; Campbell et al. 1960; Stimson 1999; Zaller 1992). As a sustained presidential message occurs, the response sometimes can develop immediately after the message. The response can also require time to develop. Limited cognition also implies that citizens need time to translate the president's message into a response. Once the stimulus from a sustained presidential message is received, the response may be realized within a single time period, or it can be distributed over multiple time periods. Therefore, we shall focus on the impact of a sustained presidential message from diverse outlets, and consider the possibility that the response to the message develops dynamically over time.

Given these requirements, we need measures of the president's economic rhetoric that extend over a long time frame, with sufficient temporal resolution to evaluate the dynamics of presidential messages and subsequent responses. Accordingly, this study uses monthly time-series measures of the president's economic rhetoric extending from the first day of the Truman administration through the last day of the first George W. Bush administration.

The stimuli transmitted by the president generally occur daily, and may even occur hourly. Use of such finely divided data, however, would produce noise when combined into a time series of presidential rhetoric. Presidential rhetoric can be sporadic and clustered within or across days. Therefore, I smooth the flow of presidential messages by aggregating them into longer monthly time intervals. Specifically, I measured the aggregate monthly intensity and tone of *all* public presidential remarks across multiple dimensions of the economy from April 12, 1945, to January 20, 2005.

The measures used in this study capture both a general and more specific dimension of the president's economic rhetoric. Presidents often speak in very general terms about "the economy" or "our economy" without going into much detail. For example, they may tout a strong economy without reference to specific details to bolster perceptions of economic leadership. They may also speak of the need for stimulating the economy without mentioning various economic statistics. One could argue that these simple messages, free of technical discussion, are the easiest for the intended audience to understand.

At other times, presidents speak about specific dimensions of the economy such as the employment situation, prices, or the government's fiscal status. While some economic actors may have difficulty assimilating the details of the president's message about unemployment, inflation, or the deficit, these messages do contain information. A specific message coming from the president may be important by itself, and may also reinforce other messages about the economy coming from other outlets such as the news media.

For each of these dimensions of the president's economic rhetoric, we can isolate at least two concepts: intensity and tone.

*The intensity of presidential rhetoric refers to the relative frequency with which presidents mention the economy or its specific dimensions.* As discussed in the introductory chapter, the intensity of presidential rhetoric about the general economy has been increasing through time. Recent presidents talk more about the economy than did earlier presidents. There may also be systematic variations *across* presidencies in their focus on specific dimensions of the economy, as well as variations *within* presidencies that depend on economic and political factors. For example, controlling for actual levels of unemployment, some presidents may talk more about unemployment relative to others. There may also be variations within presidencies in the tendency to talk about unemployment. We shall explore these more systematic variations across and within presidencies for each dimension of presidential rhetoric in the next chapter.

*The tone of presidential rhetoric is defined as the relative optimism of presidential remarks about the economy and its specific dimensions.* Through their relative optimism presidents help establish a climate for the national economy. Of course, presidents do not singularly determine the economic climate of the country, since a plethora of events, economic reports, and ongoing economic processes are very important. Presidential remarks, however, do help economic actors interpret those processes and in so doing affect economic confidence. The president is an important economic actor in this role, since he has responsibility for the economy and receives intense scrutiny from the media. To assess this dimension of presidential leadership of the economy, I developed measures of the relative optimism of presidential remarks from the Truman administration through the first George W. Bush administration.

## CONSTRUCTING THE MEASURES

The data source for the measures of the intensity and tone of presidential rhetoric on the economy was *Public Papers of the Presidents*. This serial set is compiled and published by the Office of the Federal Register, National Archives and Records Administration. It was established in 1957 in response to a recommendation of the National Historical Publications Commission. Noting the lack of uniform compilations of messages and papers of the presidents before this time, the commission recommended establishing an official series containing presidential writings, addresses, and other public remarks.

Volumes covering the administrations of Presidents Hoover, Truman, Eisenhower, Kennedy, Johnson, Nixon, Ford, Carter, Reagan, George H. W. Bush, Clinton, and George W. Bush are included in the *Public Papers* series. President Roosevelt's papers are not part of the series, but were published privately. Currently, volumes are published approximately twice a year, and each volume covers roughly a six-month period. Each *Public Papers* volume contains the papers, speeches, and public remarks of the President of the United States that were issued by the Office of the Press Secretary during the specified time period. The appendices to the *Public Papers* contain additional materials previously published in the *Weekly Compilation of Presidential Documents*. A companion to the *Public Papers* series, the *Weekly Compilation* was begun in 1965 to provide a broader range of presidential materials.

The *Public Papers* comprises a massive amount of text containing all public remarks by twelve presidents over a time span of sixty-three years. It would be a near impossible task for a single researcher to read and code variables from this massive amount of text. Indeed, the task would require many years, even with research assistance and sufficient monetary resources. Not wishing to undertake such an effort with human resources alone, I used a computer-assisted approach to coding the *Public Papers*.

First, an electronic file was created containing the entire *Public Papers of the Presidents* from April 12, 1945, through January 19, 2005. The file was constructed by extracting the ASCII text from a CD-Rom marketed commercially by Western Standard Publishing Company (2000). This medium contained the entire *Public Papers* through 1999, including appendices that contain supplemental materials from the *Weekly Compilation*. To complete the electronic file through January 2005, the remaining years' materials were downloaded from the web through OriginalSources.com. The resulting electronic file for content analysis of the president's public rhetoric consisted of around 360 megabytes of ASCII text.[1]

Even with the electronic file, it was impractical to use conventional word processor search and find techniques to identify and code the president's remarks on the economy. Conventional word processors cannot handle files that are 360 megabytes in size. For example, it required roughly thirty minutes just to open the electronic *Public Papers* file using Microsoft Word. Once opened, the program was extremely slow in searching the document. Given that there were tens of thousands of presidential remarks about the economy since World War II, dealing with a document this size required a more advanced technology.

Initially, various content-analytic software packages such as the General Inquirer were considered. These programs performed adequately when the goal was simply to count the frequency of presidential remarks about the economy. They performed poorly, however, in actual analysis of the presidents' words. For example, using human coding of a sample of sentences as a benchmark and the canned dictionary in the General Inquirer, roughly three out of five sentences coded electronically were incorrect for the presidents' economic optimism. Similarly, other content-analytic software produced generally poor results. While it would have been quick and systematic to employ a "canned" content-analysis software package, the conclusion from these initial tests was that they are not very good at discerning the subtle nuances of the English language. Therefore, I used a combination of machine and human coding to construct the measures for the study.

In implementing this process, the Practical Extraction and Report Language (PERL) was used to manipulate the text contained in the electronic file. PERL is a public domain open-access code software package for logical manipulation of text. It is a high-level programming language derived from the ubiquitous C programming language and to a lesser extent from sed, awk, the Unix shell, and at least a dozen other tools and languages (Schwartz, Olson, and Christiansen 1997). A full description of PERL, as well as various user support functions, is available at *http://www.perl .com*. PERL can be downloaded free from a link on this website.

Prior research has focused on entire presidential speeches as a unit of analysis. The research presented here, however, focuses on *each unique sentence* within presidential speeches and other public remarks. Why focus on sentences, rather than entire speeches or rhetoric from other public events? Focusing on sentences enables a natural weighting scheme that transcends particular events. For example, one could rightly argue that the State of the Union message should be more important than a speech to the Chamber of Commerce in Poughkeepsie, N.Y. However, remarks made in Poughkeepsie that repeatedly mention high unemployment and low economic growth may be picked up by the news media and actually be more important than a State of the Union message that mkes little or no mention of these conditions. For example, President Carter's 1980 State of the Union message focused almost entirely on the U.S. response to the Iran Hostage crisis, even though inflation was at record levels. The president expressed this economic concern through a plethora of other public remarks and other outlets.

Focusing on sentences provides a natural weighting scheme by highlighting the relative emphasis in the presidents' rhetoric on particular economic issues and the economy. The more a speech or other event emphasizes the economy, the more sentences there should be on the economy. In contrast, a speech that mentions the economy only in passing will have fewer sentences dealing with the economy and its various dimensions.

In implementing the electronic searches, I first developed a PERL program to extract from the *Public Papers* every sentence spoken publicly by the presidents containing keywords relevant to the presidents' economic rhetoric. To reflect a general dimension of the presidents' economic rhetoric, a separate file was created containing all sentences from April 12, 1945, through January 20, 2005, in which the presidents used the phrases "the economy" or "our economy." Other possible keywords were considered, but an analysis of the sentences extracted with an expanded set of keywords revealed that it was rare that the president spoke of the economy without using these core phrases. Therefore, the phrases "the economy" and "our economy" formed the basis for extracting a general measure of the presidents' economic rhetoric.

I also extracted sentences reflecting the more specific dimensions of the presidents' economic rhetoric: unemployment, inflation, and the federal deficit. I chose presidential rhetoric on unemployment because this is a highly visible and personal dimension of the economy for most people. On average since World War II, roughly 11 percent of respondents to the Gallup "most important problem" survey have listed unemployment as the most important problem facing the nation. Unemployment statistics are also the focus of frequent media reports. High job losses mean reduced income for some Americans, and produce greater economic uncertainty for the population. Presidents should care about unemployment because this is perhaps the most visible manifestation of U. S. economic performance for most voters. Therefore, presidential remarks on unemployment should be externally motivated and have economic and political importance.

For unemployment, I extracted every sentence in which the president used the word "unemployment." Again, I considered adding more keywords and phrases for the *Public Papers* search. For example, the word "unemployed" could have been added to the unemployment dimension.

However, a check by human coders again showed that there were few instances where the president used the secondary word that were not captured by the primary word.

Presidential rhetoric on inflation was also included in the analysis. Contrary to intuition based on recent experience, inflation has actually been the most salient dimension of the economy since World War II. The Gallup Most Important Problem Series shows that since 1946, roughly 17 percent of Americans have viewed inflation as the most important problem facing the nation. Of course, since the mid-1980s inflation has been relatively invisible to most people while remaining at low levels. Recent presidents have regularly mentioned low inflation rates, but only in passing. However, during the era of stagflation, when the inflation rate peaked at almost 15 percent, it was a focus of intense presidential attention. Between July 1972 and June 1983 more than 50 percent of Americans viewed inflation as the most important problem facing the nation. On average between 1946 and 1986 roughly one-fourth of citizens surveyed viewed inflation as an important public problem. As a result, inflation should have been a major concern of the presidency through this period.

For inflation I extracted every sentence in which the president used the word "inflation." Again, I considered adding more keywords and phrases for the *Public Papers* search. For example, the phrase "higher prices" could have been added to the inflation search. A check by human coders again showed, however, that there were few instances where the president used the secondary phrase that were not captured by the primary word.

The final specific dimension of the presidents' economic rhetoric was attention to the federal deficit. On average, citizens since World War II have viewed the federal deficit as the third most important economic problem facing the nation. While the number of respondents in the Gallup most important problem series who viewed the deficit as an important problem is much smaller than that of those who cited unemployment and inflation (roughly 3.5 percent), presidents have periodically focused much attention on the federal deficit. As the budget was continuously out of balance between 1970 and 1997, political rhetoric intensified on the efficacy of the government's fiscal policy. Indeed, President George H. W. Bush threw support behind a tax increase to resolve the deficit crisis that emerged during the Reagan era, and this may have cost him the presidency. Resolving the deficit crisis was an even stronger focus of the Clinton administration, which pushed the issue intensely as a means for stimulating the economy.

In measuring presidential attention to the federal deficit, a separate file was created that contained every sentence in which the president used the word "deficit." These sentence files required considerable cleaning, because references to the key concepts were sometimes off topic or devoid of context. For example, the president sometimes spoke about "the economy" of Latin America or other unrelated topics. Similarly, references to unemployment, inflation, and the deficit sometimes referred to other concepts or arenas. Using human coders, I identified all instances in which presidential rhetoric was off topic and excluded these sentences from the measures.

Table 2.1 contains illustrative examples of extracted sentences drawn from the sentence file for the general economic dimension across presidencies from Reagan through George W. Bush. Note that each sentence was identified by year, month, day, paragraph number, and sentence number. This enabled human coders to return to the entire text when there was doubt about coding that arose from the context of the presidents' remarks. After cleaning the files for off-topic remarks and missing context, I had files containing only valid references to the key dimensions of the presidents' economic rhetoric.

These sentence files formed the basis for measuring the intensity and tone of presidential rhetoric on the economy through time. A simple count in a given time period of the total number of sentences by the president referring to the economy, unemployment, inflation, or the federal deficit provides a measure of how much attention the president was devoting to these issues. More sentences in a given time frame imply that the president was more intensely attentive to the economy or its specific dimensions during that time frame. Fewer sentences imply less presidential attention. The resulting four time series measured the intensity of presidential remarks on the general economy, unemployment, inflation, and the federal deficit.

Beyond measuring the intensity of presidential attention to the economy, I also measured the tone of presidential remarks on the economy. Again, tone is defined as the relative optimism of presidential remarks about the economy. Constructing this measure required a dictionary of optimistic and pessimistic words. In developing the dictionary, I first wrote a PERL program to list every unique word in the sentence files. The words were sorted by frequency of use. Then, human coders were used to identify words associated with presidential optimism and pessimism. Specifically, the human coders assessed each word intuitively, and also evaluated the proportion of correct "hits" from the previous sentence files when using the identified words. *Every unique word was evaluated* in developing the dictionary, and every unique word was validated using both machine and human analysis. Based on the frequency of hits, I concluded that the resulting dictionary had high reliability and validity. However, it was still not perfect in evaluating the tone of presidential remarks.

Having developed dictionaries of optimistic and pessimistic words, I used PERL again to extract optimistic and pessimistic sentences from *Public Papers of the Presidents* pertaining to the economy, unemployment,

TABLE 2.1
Example Sentences from *Public Papers of the Presidents* Using PERL

19820819.025.02
I think what they're going to see and what is going to happen, that they are going to be thinking about, is I think the economy is going to continue to improve.

19821106.023.02
As more and more Americans see daylight ahead, our economy will grow stronger.

19830125.007.01
As we gather here tonight, the state of our Union is strong, but our economy is troubled.

19901108.067.06
And we've been enjoying rather robust growth for many years, and now we all know the economy is slower.

19901130.017.02
Our economy, as I said the other day, is at best in a serious slowdown, and if uncertainty remains in the energy markets, the slowdown will get worse.

19910129.041.02
But there are reasons to be optimistic about our economy.

19920219.025.05
I think people feel that the economy is poised for recovery.

19940518.006.02
Our economy is the strongest in the industrialized world.

19991001.004.01
Today, our economy is strong, incomes are up, and poverty is at the lowest rate in 20 years.

20010124.012.02
And I think the evidence is going to become more and more clear that the economy is—it's not as hopeful as we'd like, which I hope will strengthen my case.

20010208.005.05
A warning light is flashing on the dashboard of our economy.

20010228.022.03
Greenspan offered a sober assessment of the current state of the economy through the sharp downturn that's been evident in the last few months.

inflation, and the federal deficit. Some error remained even after validating the dictionary as just discussed. Therefore, human coders were again used to read each sentence to verify that presidential optimism and pessimism were accurately coded. In many cases, the machine failed because of the complex nuances of the English language. Thus, human coders were used to validate the machine coded measures. Based on this repetitive combination of machine and human coding, I obtained near perfect validity in defining the tone of presidential remarks on the economy.

Table 2.1 contains examples of both optimistic and pessimistic sentences across recent presidencies. The first three sentences are from the Reagan presidency during the 1982–83 recession. Note that the first two Reagan sentences are coded as optimistic, while the third Reagan sentence is coded as pessimistic. The fourth through sixth sentences are from the George H. W. Bush presidency during the 1990–91 recession. The fourth and fifth sentences are coded as pessimistic, while the sixth sentence is coded as optimistic. The seventh through ninth sentences are from the Clinton administration. All of the Clinton sentences are coded as optimistic. The tenth through twelfth sentences are from the George W. Bush administration. Sentences ten and eleven were coded as pessimistic, while the last was coded as optimistic.

Having coded the individual sentences spoken by the presidents for each event on each day, the remaining task was to aggregate the sentences into discrete time intervals. The appropriate time interval varied from monthly to quarterly depending on the availability of other data for statistical analysis. In measuring the relative optimism of presidential remarks, the number of pessimistic sentences were subtracted from the number of optimistic sentences in a given time interval. I aggregated the counts of sentences spoken by the presidents on the economy into discrete time intervals from April 1945 through January 2005.[2] The resulting four time series measured the tone of presidential remarks on the general economy, unemployment, inflation, and the federal deficit.

## DESCRIBING THE MEASURES

We can gain a sense of how the intensity and tone of presidential attention to the economy have varied through time by graphing the measures and calculating some descriptive statistics.

### Intensity

Figure 2.1 contains a monthly time series of the intensity of presidential remarks about the economy generally, as well as on unemployment, inflation, and the federal deficit. The vertical scale of figure 2.1 measures the

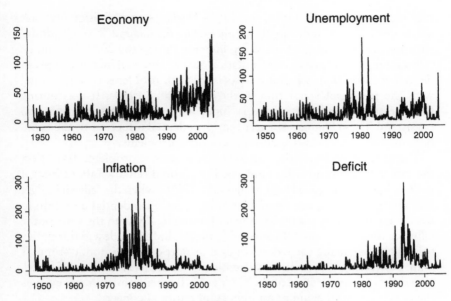

Figure 2.1  Intensity of Presidential Rhetoric on the Economy

count of the number of sentences the president spoke on each of these dimensions during each month. The scales of the four graphs are different to capture the peaks in presidential attention. The four time series, however, are numerically comparable with the average monthly number of presidential sentences on the economy, unemployment, inflation, and the federal deficit at 16.48, 12.80, 20.43, and 14.12 respectively.

There was considerable variation over time in the intensity of presidential remarks for each of the four measures. In particular, the general economy graph shows sharp increases in presidential rhetoric corresponding roughly with the Kennedy, Ford, and Clinton administrations. Another sharp increase in presidential attention to the economy occurred during the presidential election season of the George W. Bush administration. These shifts suggest that there are presidency- and perhaps election-specific factors that determine the intensity of presidential attention to the economy through time.

There are further indications of presidency-specific effects for the unemployment series. Interestingly, the intensity of presidential rhetoric about unemployment increased during the Kennedy, Ford, and Clinton administrations. During the Reagan administration there was also a sharp increase in unemployment rhetoric corresponding with the 1982–83 recession, but talk of unemployment declined sharply after the 1984 election, and even more sharply during the George H. W. Bush administration. The elder Bush spoke little about unemployment, even as the unemployment rate increased sharply during the 1990–91 recession. Additionally, talk about unemployment declined sharply during the George W. Bush administration, again in spite of the sharp increase during the 2001 recession.

Both the unemployment and inflation graphs show an increase in presidential rhetoric that is perhaps associated with problems corresponding with the period of stagflation in the 1970s, and 1980s. It was during this period that inflation was very high, while unemployment was also persistent. These changes suggest that presidential attention to the economy may at times be a response to economic problems.

The deficit time series also suggests that economic problems may affect the intensity of presidential remarks. Presidential remarks about budget deficits initially increased beginning in the 1970s, when the federal budget first began to experience significant imbalances. Presidential attention to the deficit again increased abruptly and dramatically with the start of the Clinton administration. Of course, President Clinton made a major policy priority of balancing the federal budget as part of his economic stimulus plan. Interestingly, presidential attention to the federal budget deficit declined sharply at the start of the George W. Bush administration, even as the deficit emerged again as an important national concern.

We can also better understand how the intensity of economic rhetoric has varied across presidencies by calculating presidential averages for the data shown in figure 2.1. Table 2.2 reports the average number of sentences spoken monthly by each president on the economy, unemployment, inflation, and federal deficit. With some deviations, the results for the general economy in the first column show a clear pattern of increasing presidential attention through time. These averages are consistent with discussion in the introductory chapter, pointing toward increasing presidential engagement in a permanent campaign, and that economic rhetoric is an important part of that campaign.

However, the averages for the more specific dimensions of the presidents' economic rhetoric seem more complex. The pattern in table 2.2 for unemployment suggests a partisan bias in presidential rhetoric on unemployment. After accounting for trends and the outlier Ford presidency, Democrats appear far more likely to talk about unemployment than Republicans. Of course, this is consistent with the concept of presidential responsiveness to core constituencies, since Democrats are widely perceived as more sensitive to demands of working people.

The patterns across presidencies shown in table 2.2 for inflation and the deficit suggest that the intensity of presidential rhetoric has followed the changing severity of these conditions. Presidents Nixon, Ford, Carter, and Reagan discussed inflation far more than other presidents. These presidencies correspond with the era of stagflation in the 1970s and 1980s. Presidents from Ford through Clinton talked more about the

TABLE 2.2
The Average Intensity of Presidential Rhetoric on the Economy, Unemployment, Inflation, and the Federal Deficit, 1948–2004

| President | Economy | Unemployment | Inflation | Deficit |
|---|---|---|---|---|
| Truman | 5.90 | 5.41 | 10.78 | 2.37 |
| Eisenhower | 4.51 | 3.41 | 3.49 | 2.14 |
| Kennedy | 13.65 | 16.24 | 4.68 | 6.06 |
| Johnson | 7.98 | 10.65 | 7.23 | 4.18 |
| Nixon | 6.64 | 7.71 | 20.35 | 1.79 |
| Ford | 23.30 | 29.20 | 61.40 | 12.73 |
| Carter | 11.92 | 26.60 | 75.44 | 9.42 |
| Reagan | 16.57 | 14.73 | 36.95 | 24.22 |
| G.H.W. Bush | 16.17 | 5.94 | 7.19 | 18.29 |
| Clinton | 38.85 | 26.45 | 18.01 | 50.00 |
| G. W. Bush | 47.55 | 4.86 | 3.74 | 5.79 |

*Note*: The numbers in the table are the average number of sentences per month by each president directed at each issue.

deficit than earlier presidents. These presidencies correspond with the emergence of large deficits in the 1970s and subsequent efforts to resolve federal budgetary problems.

## Tone

Figure 2.2 graphs the four monthly time series of the changing tone of presidential remarks about the economy and its specific dimensions. Recall that tone is measured as the aggregate net number of optimistic minus pessimistic sentences spoken by the president during each month.

The graph for the general economy, shown in the first panel of figure 2.2, suggests that President Clinton was far more optimistic about the general economy than other presidents. Beginning with the inauguration in January 1993, the president became ever more optimistic about the economy through time. At the peak month, President Clinton made over forty optimistic remarks net of his pessimistic remarks. There were also numerous months when the president made over thirty optimistic remarks, with more than twenty optimistic remarks per month being common during the last five years of the Clinton presidency.

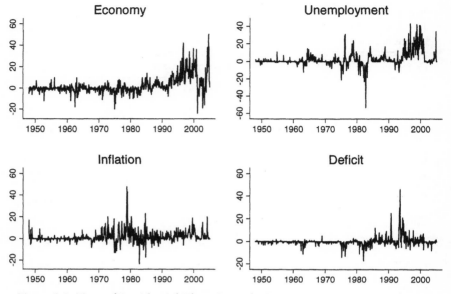

Figure 2.2 Tone of Presidential Rhetoric on the Economy

In contrast, George W. Bush was the most pessimistic president about the general economy. There appear to be four separate breaks in economic optimism during the George W. Bush presidency. Early on, President Bush was extremely pessimistic, perhaps corresponding with the political thrust for the tax cut promised in the 2000 election. There was a second period of economic pessimism, perhaps corresponding with the thrust for the second large tax cut in 2003. Third, President Bush became extremely optimistic about the economy as the 2004 election approached. Finally, note that President Bush's optimism about the economy declined immediately after the 2004 election. Of course, these variations are consistent with the introductory vignette of the first chapter.

The graph in the second panel of figure 2.2 shows that President Clinton was by far the most optimistic president on unemployment. In contrast, President Reagan was the most pessimistic. The Reagan pessimism suggests a response to very high unemployment during the 1982–83 recession. More generally, there are significant variations across presidencies in the tone of presidential remarks on unemployment that suggest a need for further analysis.

The graphs in the third and fourth panels of figure 2.2 for inflation and the deficit show what appears to be a random pattern of variation in the tone of presidential rhetoric through time. However, there is one exception to this pattern. President Clinton was far more optimistic about the

TABLE 2.3
The Average Tone of Presidential Rhetoric on the Economy, Unemployment, Inflation, and the Federal Deficit, 1948–2004

| President | Economy | Unemployment | Inflation | Deficit |
|---|---|---|---|---|
| Truman | −0.58 | 0.25 | 0.53 | −0.32 |
| Eisenhower | −0.09 | 0.16 | −0.16 | −0.22 |
| Kennedy | −2.18* | −0.74 | −0.06 | −1.65* |
| Johnson | −0.15 | 2.61** | 0.32 | −0.02 |
| Nixon | −0.92 | 0.02 | 3.03** | −0.32 |
| Ford | −1.93* | −0.67 | −0.50 | −2.97** |
| Carter | −1.67* | 3.48** | 7.65** | −0.15 |
| Reagan | 1.22* | −0.06 | 0.51 | −0.65 |
| G.H.W. Bush | 1.73* | 0.54 | 1.33 | 1.10* |
| Clinton | 14.36** | 13.78** | 3.90** | 3.51** |
| G. W. Bush | 4.09** | 0.88 | 2.62** | −0.83 |

Note: The numbers in the table are the differences between the number of optimistic and pessimistic sentences each month by each president directed at each issue. * indicates statistical significance at the 0.05 level for the hypothesis that the coefficient equals zero; ** indicates statistical significance at the 0.01 level.

deficit than other presidents during his first term. This may correspond with President Clinton's policy focus on deficit reduction and economic stimulus during the early part of his administration.

We can again refine understanding of how the tone of economic rhetoric has varied across presidencies by calculating presidential averages for the data shown in figure 2.2. Table 2.3 reports the average tone of presidential rhetoric on the economy, unemployment, inflation, and federal deficit for each president from Truman through George W. Bush. The results in the first column show that beginning with Ronald Reagan, presidents have been more optimistic about the economy than earlier presidents. Again, President Clinton was far more optimistic than any other president in his general rhetoric on the economy.

Presidents Johnson, Carter, and Clinton were significantly more optimistic about unemployment than other presidents. This again suggests a partisan bias in presidential rhetoric on unemployment. Democratic presidents are both more likely to talk about and talk optimistically about unemployment than Republicans.

The descriptive statistics in table 2.3 also reveal two other points that are suggestive of presidential leadership. First, President Carter was significantly more optimistic than other presidents on the issue of inflation. Yet, we know that inflation was worse during the Carter presidency than at any other time in modern history. This statistic suggests that President Carter attempted to lead rhetorically on the issue of inflation in spite of the tough economic conditions.

Second, Presidents George H. W. Bush and Clinton were optimistic about the deficit. This corresponds with common perceptions that these presidents undertook the most serious efforts to resolve the growing federal deficit that had emerged in the 1970s and 1980s. These data suggest that both presidents also took a strong rhetorical lead in attempting to address budget imbalances and the growing federal debt that emerged in the 1980s

## CONCLUSION

This chapter has described the measures used for statistical analyses in subsequent chapters of this book. Using an approach involving both machine and human coding, eight time series of presidential rhetoric were constructed. These time series reflect *every* public presidential remark about the economy, unemployment, inflation, and the deficit across eleven presidencies over sixty years. Focusing on such an extended period enables a more general approach than evaluating a single speech or presidential administration. The goal is to produce generalizable knowledge about the causes and consequences of presidential rhetoric about the economy.

I have also provided a cursory and very preliminary descriptive analysis of processes that may underlie the time series measuring the intensity and tone of presidential rhetoric. Again, the intensity of presidential rhetoric about the economy measures the amount of attention that presidents direct toward economic matters. Exploratory analysis of the time series suggests that the intensity of presidential rhetoric may be presidency specific. There are also indications from the graphs that presidential attention may correspond with fluctuations in the economy and its various dimensions. For example, figure 2.2 shows that presidents talked more about inflation and unemployment during the period of stagflation in the 1970s and 1980s.

We should not draw strong conclusions, however, from these preliminary analyses. It is unclear whether these relationships are systematic and can be generalized across presidencies and through time. For example, figure 2.2 also shows that President Clinton talked a lot about the economy, unemployment, and inflation, even as economic conditions were strong and improving. Seemingly, Clinton "talked up" the economy during a period of economic expansion. Furthermore, President George W. Bush talked little about unemployment and the deficit even as these conditions grew worse. Thus, it is unclear that the intensity of presidential rhetoric is systematically related to U.S. economic performance in a simple way.

Again, the tone of presidential rhetoric is measured by evaluating the relative optimism of presidential remarks about the economy. The graphs and tables presented in this chapter suggest that the tone of presidential remarks is also presidency specific. President Clinton was far more optimistic than other presidents across multiple dimensions. In contrast, President George W. Bush was far more pessimistic about the economy generally during the first three years of his administration.

Yet, knowing that presidents differ in the intensity and tone of their public remarks about the economy offers little in the way of new understanding. Thus, in the next chapter I develop a theory-oriented approach to understanding when and why presidents talk about the economy.

# What Determines the Intensity and Tone of Presidential Rhetoric on the Economy?

CBS NEWS POLL

THE ECONOMY, JOBS, AND THE PRESIDENT
AUGUST 11–12, 2003

Do you think George W. Bush is paying enough attention to the economy, or should he be paying more attention to the economy?

| Group Response | All Respondents | Republicans | Democrats | Independents | May 2003 |
|---|---|---|---|---|---|
| Should pay more attention | 70 | 47 | 88 | 74 | 61 |
| Paying enough attention | 25 | 48 | 10 | 20 | 36 |
| Don't know/No answer | 5 | 5 | 2 | 6 | 3 |

IN AUGUST 2003, a public opinion poll released by CBS News showed that a large majority of Americans thought the president should be paying more attention to the economy. This number had increased significantly between May and August 2003. Americans were clearly concerned about the president's economic leadership.

Soon after this poll, the president increased the frequency of his public comments on the economy, and became significantly more optimistic. In the six months prior to the poll, the president mentioned the economy an average of about thirty-three times per month. The tone of presidential remarks during this period was decidedly negative. In the months between the poll and the 2004 election, the intensity of presidential remarks on the economy more than doubled to around eighty-eight comments per month. Furthermore, the tone of the president's remarks became decidedly positive with the president making an average twenty-three optimistic comments each month. What caused this sudden turnabout in the president's economic rhetoric?

The marked shift in the intensity and tone of President Bush's public remarks about the economy following the CBS News poll is suggestive of responsiveness to public opinion. The evidence, however, is only suggestive, since there may have been other reasons for the change. For example, the economy may have shown improvement, resulting in presidential cheerleading. The president's approval ratings were declining, and the president may have talked about the economy to help bolster perceptions of his economic leadership. Also, the upcoming election season may have been responsible for altering the intensity and tone of presidential rhetoric. Reelection generally requires a president to produce a perception of strong economic leadership, and to respond positively to challenger claims about poor economic performance.

Without getting inside White House decision-making processes, we cannot know with certainty the specific reasons for the abrupt turnabout in the president's economic rhetoric. This case, however, does highlight two major research questions. What determines the *intensity* of presidential rhetoric on the economy through time? What determines the *tone* of presidential rhetoric on the economy through time? This chapter focuses on developing systematic and generalizable answers to these questions.

The phrase "systematic and generalizable" means more than making subjective judgments about what might have caused changing presidential rhetoric. Rather, it means providing theory-driven explanations that are empirically true across different presidential administrations and through time, while controlling for diverse economic circumstances.

## A Theory of Presidential Rhetoric on the Economy

Three general factors should be important in explaining the changing intensity and tone of the president's economic rhetoric through time: (1) the president's personal style, (2) institutional prerogatives relating to the economy, and (3) political incentives.

### Personal Style

Differences in personal style should produce variations in rhetoric across presidencies, but not within presidencies. Personal style is a relatively fixed factor that determines a president's innate tendency toward public communication as well as the flavor of that communication. It is determined by psychological orientations combined with the president's distinctive background. Personal style should affect a president's general tendency to speak in public. It should also affect a president's relative optimism when speaking in public. Therefore, personal style is a fixed determinant of how and how much each president talks about the economy.

The concept of personal style used here is related to James David Barber's (1992) concept for evaluating presidential character. According to Barber, "Style is the president's habitual way of performing his three political roles: rhetoric, personal relations, and homework" (5). All presidents must perform each of these roles, since the office requires speaking in public, dealing with others, and making decisions. However, as Barber notes, "[T]here are marked differences in stylistic emphasis from President to President. . . . [O]ne President may put most of himself into rhetoric, another may stress close, informal dealing, while still another may devote his energies mainly to study and cogitation" (5).

The concept of personal style is also related to Fred Greenstein's (2004) notion of a president's leadership style. Greenstein observes differences in leadership style from FDR through George W. Bush along six dimensions: organizational capacity, political skill, vision, cognitive style, emotional intelligence, and public communication. With respect to public communication, Greenstein notes, "Most presidents have not addressed the public with anything approximating the professionalism of countless educators, members of the clergy, and radio and television broadcasters. Roosevelt, Kennedy, and Reagan—and Clinton at his best—are the shining exceptions" (2004, 217).

President Kennedy had a casual manner that made him appear comfortable and confident when speaking to an audience (Silvestri 2000). Greenstein characterized Kennedy's oratory as eloquent and his press conference performances as "intelligent and stylish" (2004, 70). President Reagan was often referred to as the "Great Communicator" (Ritter and Henry 1992). According to Greenstein, Reagan "carried off his rhetorical responsibilities with a virtuosity exceeded only by FDR" (2004, 155). President Clinton, at his best was "an outstanding public communicator." However, at his worst "he was long-winded, unfocused, and 'off message'" (Greenstein 2004, 185). With regard to intensity, President Clinton carried the rhetorical presidency strategy to new extremes, speaking on average 550 times per year and traveling around the country every fourth day (Edwards 2003, 3).

In contrast, other presidents have seemed less adept at public communication, perhaps due to the absence of an effective strategy (Rozell 2003). Early modern presidents such as Truman and Eisenhower lacked a strong public relations apparatus within the White House. Their presidencies occurred before the media and political transformations that made it essential for presidents to attend to their public image. They may also have lacked the natural ability for effective public communications (Greenstein 2004, 39, 54).

Other presidents also seemingly lacked the natural ability to communicate well in public. For example, Greenstein observes that President Johnson's oratory came across as "bombastic and long-winded." During news conferences "he was stiff and defensive . . . revealing little of the vividness that made him memorable in less formal settings" (2004, 87). President Nixon "was patently ill at ease in press conferences, and his formal addresses came across as strained and stilted" (106). President Carter began well as a public communicator, but after the first year his rhetoric suffered because of an absence of organizing principles (140). President George H. W. Bush "seemed to go out of his way to avoid the rhetorical emphasis that led Reagan to be dubbed the 'Great Communicator'" (164). Lastly, President George W. Bush "seemed insensitive [early on] to the importance of public communication in presidential leadership." However, following September 11, 2001, he "became a rhetorical activist, addressing the public regularly, forcefully, and sometimes eloquently" (206).

Of course, the evolution of communications technology has produced expectations that the president be a strong rhetorician. Mass communications and the television age have meant that an inability to speak in public makes it difficult to be elected, and to maintain the public's approval. As political parties have declined as an organizing force in American politics, presidential success while in office has come to depend on the president's ability to get a message out and appeal directly to the public (Brace and Hinckley 1992; Edwards 1983; Kernell 1997). Accordingly, the White House has through time developed a sophisticated communications apparatus (Grossman and Kumar 1981; Hinckley 1990). These developments have meant that recent presidents have spoken more often in a public setting than their predecessors (Edwards 1983; Hart 1989; Tulis 1987). Therefore, the intensity of presidential rhetoric on the economy, while unique for each president, should also have been increasing through time.

The concept of personal style used here also relates to Barber's concept of presidential character. He defines character as "the way the President orients himself toward life—not for the moment, but enduringly" (1992, 5). Underlying Barber's notion of presidential character is the individual's self-esteem and confidence in performing the required tasks of the office. Related to this, personal style encompasses the relative optimism that the president brings to the job.

There is a popular perception that some presidents have exhibited greater optimism than others. For example, many remember President Reagan as "the eternal optimist" (Will 2004). Eulogizing President Reagan, Senate Minority Leader Thomas A. Daschle (D-SD) said he "will be forever remembered for his faith, his optimism and his unwavering commitment to his convictions." Similarly, 2004 presidential candidate John Kerry said, "We lost one of our great optimists. President Reagan's belief in America was infectious" (Associated Press 2004).

In contrast, President Carter's famous "malaise" speech in 1979 labeled him as a pessimist. Reacting to advice from advisor Patrick Caddell that Americans were suffering from a general "crisis of confidence," President Carter mirrored this sentiment by stating, "The solution of our energy crisis can also help us to conquer the crisis of the spirit in our country." The president then asked Americans to join him in adapting to a new age of limits where energy costs would be perpetually rising and energy supplies would be continuously declining.

Initially President Carter's remarks were well received by the public. Perhaps appreciating the president's frankness, the public rewarded him with higher approval ratings in the days after the speech. The media's "malaise" spin on the president's speech, however, highlighted his allegedly pessimistic views on energy and the character of the American public. The word "malaise" was not used by the president, or elsewhere by his staff. Rather, it was an invention of the media. According to Bosch (2002), Ronald Reagan defeated President Carter in the 1980 election by offering Americans a vision of the future that was as optimistic as Carter's was allegedly pessimistic.

Whether Presidents Reagan and Carter were intrinsic optimists or pessimists cannot be determined by referring to popular commentary. Nevertheless, it seems reasonable to assert that personality differences could produce variations across presidencies in the relative optimism of their public remarks. Presidents who are natural optimists should exhibit greater optimism. In contrast, those who lack an inner sense of confidence in themselves and the nation should exhibit greater pessimism.

More generally, a core determinant of the intensity and tone of presidential remarks about the economy should be the person occupying the office. The personal style of each president should affect how frequently the president speaks in public. It should also affect whether the president comes across as an optimist or pessimist when speaking in public. Since personal style is an intrinsic personality trait, intuition suggests that this dimension of presidential rhetoric should be relatively fixed through time for each presidency.

The issue that remains is what determines variations in presidential rhetoric *within* presidencies. Riding on the fixed differences in presidential rhetoric across presidencies should be dynamic variations through time that depend on the other two elements of the theory: institutional prerogatives and political incentives.

## Institutional Prerogatives Relating to the Economy

Institutional prerogatives refer to presidential opportunities to talk about the economy that flow from the president's role as institutional leader. Presidents often speak in fulfillment of various institutional tasks and responsibilities. As noted in the introductory chapter, law charges the president with monitoring the economy and making adjustments to ensure that the nation reaches its economic potential. While not required to do so, they often speak publicly as an authoritative source about newly released economic reports. As chief economic leader, the president is also required to provide an annual economic report and deliver a budget message to Congress. The president may also seek legislation to address the nation's economic problems, and subsequently campaign for passage of that legislation. Each of these institutional prerogatives provides an opportunity for presidents to talk more or less intensely and optimistically about the economy.

Some institutional obligations of the presidency with respect to the economy are laid out by the Employment Act of 1946 (PL 79–304) and the Humphrey-Hawkins Act of 1978 (PL 95–523). These laws charge the president with promoting "maximum employment, production, and purchasing power." The president is required to monitor U.S. economic performance and make plans and recommendations for promoting these goals. The president's plans are often contained in the Annual Economic Report of the President. The Humphrey-Hawkins Act formally established a goal of full employment for the U.S. economy (Frendreis and Tatalovich 1994, 37–38). This legislation reinforced the obligations of the president to monitor and address problems of slow economic growth, unemployment, and inflation, which plagued the United States through the 1970s.

Assisting the president in these tasks is an assortment of agencies that collect and report economic statistics and provide advice to the president. The Department of Commerce's Bureau of Economic Analysis monitors economic growth and issues a quarterly report on various economic conditions. The Bureau of Labor Statistics monitors unemployment and inflation rates, issuing a monthly report on these more specific indicators. Since 1970, the Office of Management and Budget has performed budgetary analysis,[1] which assists the president in formulating economic plans. The Council of Economic Advisors and various organizational units within the Executive Office of the President under different names have assisted the president in interpreting economic indicators and formulating economic policy.

As these various agencies issue economic reports, the president will often comment on them and provide interpretations. These comments often occur in the context of news conferences or the president's frequent interactions with reporters. Commenting on economic reports makes the president appear authoritative and casts an aura of economic leadership. The president sends a message of being in charge. The nature of these comments and interpretations are typically political, not technical. That is, the president is generally not an economist,[2] but a politician who attempts to put the best "spin" on the statistics.

Of course, the political goals of presidents differ, and they have varying personal styles. As a result, there may not be a consistent relationship between the ongoing flow of economic reports and the nature of presidential remarks in response to changing economic conditions. For example, when economic reports are negative the president may choose to downplay them by decreasing the intensity of remarks. On the other hand, under the same conditions another president might increase the intensity of remarks to provide a confident sense of leadership on the economy. Negative economic reports may also lead to greater economic pessimism if the president simply mirrors the report or wants to appear sympathetic. On the other hand, negative economic reports may also lead to greater economic optimism if the president is attempting to lead the economy in a "statesman-like" manner in the mold of FDR. Because of potentially different presidential styles, it is likely that presidents will respond differently to the various economic reports issued by government agencies.

Another institutional prerogative occurs when presidents attempt to alter the direction of the economy by proposing legislation. Presidents periodically propose and promote policies intended to affect economic growth, unemployment, inflation, and the federal deficit. During these periods, we should expect presidential rhetoric on the economy to intensify. Presidents campaign for the initiatives they have proposed or support, leading to more intense rhetoric. It may also be that the tone of presidential rhetoric will change during these periods. One possibility is that presidential rhetoric becomes more pessimistic in an attempt to persuade people of the urgency for change. Alternatively, the president may become more optimistic in painting a rosy economic picture that will result from the proposed policy change.

We can gain a sense of when presidents have pursued economic policy change by observing the major legislative efforts through time directed at the economy. Mayhew (1991) identified all major legislation passed by Congress and the president from 1947 through 1990. Similarly, Edwards, Barrett, and Peake (1997) identified all major legislation that failed to pass Congress from 1947 through 1992. Using Mayhew's methodology, I supplemented both lists to provide a summary of all major economic initiatives pursued or supported by the presidents from World War II through 2004.[3]

Tables 3.1a and 3.1b contain lists of initiatives that were supported by presidents and that sought economic stimulus, jobs programs, inflation legislation, and deficit reduction. Note that some of the initiatives were intended to stimulate the economy generally. Others were intended to address specific economic problems such as unemployment, inflation, or

TABLE 3.1a
Successful Economic Initiatives since World War II

| Initiatives | Issue |
| --- | --- |
| Employment Act of 1946 (PL 79–304) | Stimulus |
| Manpower Development and Training Act of 1962 (PL 87–415) | Unemployment |
| Revenue Act of 1962 (PL 87–834) | Stimulus |
| Economic Opportunity Act of 1964 (PL 88–452) | Unemployment |
| Revenue Act of 1964 (PL 88–272) | Stimulus |
| Excise Tax Reduction Act of 1965 (PL 89–44) | Stimulus |
| Revenue and Expenditure Control Act of 1968 (PL 90–364) | Inflation |
| Employment Security Amendments of 1970 (PL 91–373) | Unemployment |
| Revenue Act of 1971 (PL 92–178) | Stimulus |
| Emergency Employment Act of 1971 (PL 92–72) | Unemployment |
| Comprehensive Employment and Training Act of 1973 (PL 93–203) | Unemployment |
| Tax Reduction Act of 1975 (PL 94–12) | Stimulus |
| Unemployment Compensation Amendments of 1976 (PL 94–566) | Unemployment |
| Tax Reduction and Simplification Act of 1977 (PL 95–30) | Stimulus |
| National Energy Act of 1978 (PL 95–617) | Inflation |
| Crude Oil Windfall Profits Tax Act of 1980 (PL 96–223) | Inflation |
| Economic Recovery Tax Act of 1981 (PL 97–34) | Stimulus |
| Tax Equity and Fiscal Responsibility Act of 1982 (PL 97–248) | Deficit |
| Job Training Partnership Act of 1982 (PL 97–300) | Unemployment |
| Deficit Reduction Act of 1984 (PL 98–369) | Deficit |
| Balanced Budget and Emergency Deficit Control Act of 1985 (PL 99–177) | Deficit |
| Balanced Budget and Emergency Deficit Control Reaffirmation Act of 1987 (PL 100–119) | Deficit |
| Omnibus Budget Reconciliation Act of 1990 (PL 101–508) | Deficit |
| Omnibus Budget Reconciliation Act of 1993 (PL 103–66) | Deficit |
| Balanced Budget Act of 1997 (PL 105–33) | Deficit |
| Economic Growth and Tax Reform Reconciliation Act of 2001 (PL 107–16) | Stimulus |
| Job Creation and Worker Assistance Act of 2002 (PL 107–147) | Stimulus |
| Jobs and Growth Tax Relief Reconciliation Act of 2003 (PL 108–27) | Stimulus |
| Working Families Tax Relief Act of 2004 (PL 108–311) | Stimulus |

Note: Compiled from Mayhew's (1991) list of significant legislation, updated through 2004.

TABLE 3.1b

Failed Economic Initiatives Having Presidential Support, since World War II

| Initiative | Issue |
| --- | --- |
| Unemployment Compensation Overhaul (1961) | Unemployment |
| Youth Employment Opportunities (1961–63) | Unemployment |
| National Service Corps (1962–63) | Unemployment |
| Unemployment Compensation Overhaul (1963–65) | Unemployment |
| Energy Tax Reform (1974–76) | Inflation |
| Countercyclical Aid: recession-targeted aid to state and local governments (1978–79) | Stimulus |
| Real Wage Insurance: wage standards independent of inflation (1978–79) | Inflation |
| $40 Billion Tax Cut (1979) | Stimulus |
| Job Creation Bill (1983) | Unemployment |
| Capital Gains Tax Cut (1989–90) | Stimulus |
| Economic Stimulus Package (1993) | Stimulus |
| Job Corps (1995–96) | Unemployment |
| Estate Tax (2001–2002) | Stimulus |

Note: Condensed from Edwards, Barrett, and Peake's (1997) list of failed significant legislation, updated through 2004.

the deficit. Presidential rhetoric on the successful initiatives in table 3.1a often reflected short campaigns, at the beginning of a presidential term or early in a legislative year, intended to persuade members of Congress and the public.

On the other hand, presidential rhetoric on the failed initiatives in table 3.1b tended to reflect longer-term efforts to jump start legislation that was in trouble. Often the failed initiatives involved legislation that was buried in committee and/or died at the end of a Congress or presidential term. Generally, failed initiatives never come to a floor vote in one or both Houses. Alternatively, failed presidential initiatives may be supplanted by proposals from members of Congress and passed in a different form. In contrast with successful initiatives, it is usually difficult to determine when the president's rhetorical campaign ends due to the extended nature of the failure process, which may cross multiple congressional sessions and years, and even extend across entire presidential administrations.[4]

We should also expect the president's public rhetoric during efforts to pass economic initiatives to be specific to the issue. That is, when attempting to pass an economic stimulus package, the president's rhetoric should pertain more to the general economy. Similarly, when attempting to pass a measure directed at unemployment, inflation, or the deficit, we should expect the president's rhetoric to be directed at these problems specifically.

### Political Incentives

Political incentives refer to those factors affecting what all politicians want, increased political capital and reelection. As politicians, presidents often attempt to bolster their political capital and reelection possibilities through public appearances. They schedule speeches and public remarks to increase their exposure to potential supporters. They often tailor their public remarks for these events to garner support. In these efforts associated with the permanent campaign, the intensity and tone of the president's economic remarks should vary systematically as a function of various political incentives.

One such incentive is the president's public approval ratings. Most presidents sense that their political power depends on the public's approval of their leadership. Edwards (2003, chap. 1) provides a plethora of evidence that presidents and other political actors believe that public approval is important to achieving policy success in Congress. There is also a large body of scholarly evidence to support these beliefs, even if the effects are deemed quite small (Bond, Fleisher, and Wood 2003; Brace and Hinckley 1992; Edwards 1980, 1989, 1997; Ostrom and Simon 1985; Rivers and Rose 1985). Thus, public approval is a source of power for the president that enables the accomplishing of policy ends.

Of course, public approval of the president is strongly dependent on perceptions of the president's economic leadership. Numerous studies of the determinants of public approval show that Americans hold the president accountable for economic performance (Beck 1991; Bloom 1975; Brody 1991; Chappell and Keech 1985; Clark and Stewart 1994; Edwards, Mitchell, and Welch 1995; Erikson, MacKuen, and Stimson 2002; Fiorina 1981; Haller and Norpoth 1994; Hibbs 1987; Kinder and Kiewiet 1979, 1981; MacKuen 1983; MacKuen, Erikson, and Stimson 1992; Markus 1988; Monroe 1978; Mueller 1970; Norpoth 1996; Ostrom and Smith 1993; Tufte 1978; Wood 2000). Thus, presidents should seek to produce a vision of confidence in current and future economic conditions to maintain the public's approval. Through their rhetoric, presidents should inspire confidence in their policies and the economy generally. As the public becomes more confident, public approval should increase accordingly, thereby increasing the president's political capital.

Do presidents talk more about the economy when their public approval is low, or when it is high? Logically, presidents could use either approach to build political capital. We could argue that when public approval is low, presidents should talk more about the economy and in more optimistic terms to bolster perceptions of economic leadership. On the other hand, we could also argue that when public approval is high presidents should talk more intensely and more optimistically about the economy as they "pound their chests" over administration accomplishments. Thus, while public approval is likely to be an important determinant of the intensity and tone of presidential rhetoric on the economy, it is an empirical question as to whether the relationship is *systematic* across presidencies and through time.

Another political incentive that should affect the president's economic rhetoric is public opinion specific to the economy and its various dimensions. The anecdotal evidence in the introduction to this chapter suggests that President George W. Bush responded to public opinion that he was not paying enough attention to the economy. As a democratic leader, it makes sense that the president should respond to public opinion. The president may also respond out of self-interest, since public views on the president's responsiveness should be related to approval of the president's job performance. Thus, when Americans express the opinion that particular problems are pressing, the president should respond by paying more attention to those problems.

There is substantial scholarly evidence from prior research that politicians in general respond to public opinion (Erikson, MacKuen, and Stimson 2002; Hill and Hinton-Anderson 1995; Page and Shapiro 1992; Stimson, MacKuen, and Erikson 1995; Wright, Erikson, and McIver 1987). These studies find congruence between public opinion and policy responses on an assortment of issues at the systemic level. There is also scholarly evidence that presidents in particular respond to public opinion. For example, Cohen (1997) finds that presidents respond to public opinion in selecting what issues to focus on. Brace and Hinckley (1992) find that presidents adjust their activities in correspondence with public opinion. Erikson, MacKuen, and Stimson (2002; see also Stimson, MacKuen, and Erikson 1995) examine the relationship between public opinion and presidential policy activity and find a link between the public's mood and the relative liberalism of policies pursued by the president. Similarly, Wlezien (1996) shows that presidents are responsive to mass public opinion on defense spending proposals. Canes-Wrone and Shotts (2004) find responsiveness in presidential budget proposals across a range of issues, but only when citizens are familiar with the issue area. Studies in foreign policy also suggest that presidents consider public opinion in decisions to engage in military action or economic sanctions (Baum 2004a, 2004b;

Fearon 1994; Jordan and Page 1992; Ostrom and Job 1986). Given this broad range of evidence of presidential responsiveness to the public, we should find presidential rhetoric responsive to public opinion.

Yet another stimulus to presidential rhetoric derives from election-year incentives. Presidents should talk more about the economy during election years, because the economy is a perennial election issue. Presidents also have a strong incentive to "talk up" the economy during election years, because electoral success depends on perceptions of their administrations' economic leadership. In contrast, challenger candidates have a strong incentive to "talk down" the economy to raise questions about the president's economic leadership. Challengers attempt to deride the president's economic leadership to gain favor with voters. In turn, the president or president's party must respond to the challenger by touting the effectiveness of policies and leadership. Therefore, presidents should talk more and more optimistically about the economy during election years.

Of course, there are many studies showing that the electoral success of the president and president's party depend on U.S. economic performance (Erikson 1989; Erikson, Bafumi, and Wilson 2001; Fair 1978; Fiorina 1981; Kiewiet and Rivers 1985; Lewis-Beck and Rice 1992; Markus 1988; Rosenstone 1983). It may be that the public's *perception* of the economy is more important, however, than the actual economic statistics during election years (Hetherington 1996). For example, President Reagan was easily reelected in 1984 at a time when the unemployment rate was a relatively high 7.2 percent (down only slightly from 7.5 percent when he assumed office). In contrast, President Clinton's party was turned out of office in 2000 when the unemployment rate was a very low 3.9 percent (down significantly from 7.3 percent when he assumed office). These statistics suggest that presidential campaigns can manipulate perceptions of the economy through economic rhetoric. If this is true, then we should see presidential efforts to do so during presidential election seasons.

## Data and Measures for Testing the Theory

Is the intensity and tone of the president's economic rhetoric purely a matter of the president's personal style? Does the changing intensity and tone of presidential rhetoric also relate systematically to institutional prerogatives and political incentives? In the following two sections, I report statistical analyses to answer these questions with quantitative evidence. Before we can proceed to a discussion of the statistical analyses, however, we need a brief discussion of the data and measures for the concepts embodied in the theory.

As noted in the previous section, presidential style is a factor that should be fixed within presidencies, but that should vary across presidencies. Consistent with these requirements, this study measured presidential style using indicator variables for each president. A separate indicator variable was created for each president, and coded one for all months of the particular presidency and zero for all other months. For the analysis of the intensity of presidential rhetoric, the base category was Eisenhower. For the analysis of the tone of presidential rhetoric, all presidency indicator variabled were included, with the regression intercept omitted from the analyses. This enabled a statistical test of whether each president was significantly optimistic or pessimistic controlling for other factors.

The presidency-specific indicator variables capture fixed differences in personal style across presidencies. Their "ignorant" nature, however, means that they may also pick up factors acting on particular presidencies not fully captured by other variables in the statistical model. For example, presidents' overall tendency to use rhetoric may change as a function of the major problems of the times that encompass entire presidential administrations. This may have occurred, for example, with the vast inflation of the 1970s or the large budget deficits of the 1980s–90s. Thus, while presidential style underlies a president's rhetorical emphasis, the presidency-specific indicator variables may also pick up change due to these exogenous factors dominating particular eras.

The presidency-specific indicator variables enable capturing differences in intensity and tone *across* presidencies. We can also think of them as providing a base upon which ride the rhetorical dynamics that occur *within* presidencies. The *within*-presidency rhetorical dynamics should be a function of both institutional prerogatives and political incentives.

Two measures are used to capture institutional prerogatives. First, presidential rhetoric on the economy may be a response to the release of various economic and statistical reports. To measure this concept, I included four economic measures: Commerce and Labor Department reports on U.S. economic growth, unemployment, inflation, and the federal deficit.

Economic growth was reported quarterly as the percent change in real Gross Domestic Product (GDP) by the Bureau of Economic Analysis.[5] Unemployment was reported as the monthly change in the civilian unemployment rate by the Bureau of Labor statistics. Inflation was reported as the annualized percent change in the consumer price index for urban consumers by the Bureau of Labor Statistics. The federal deficit was reported as the quarterly federal deficit as a proportion of Gross Domestic Product by the Bureau of Economic Analysis.[6] Each of these variables was lagged one period to give presidential rhetoric time to respond to changing economic conditions.[7]

The second measure for institutional prerogatives was a set of variables indicating the periods during which the president was pursuing economic initiatives that passed Congress as reflected in table 3.1a. I did not include the failed economic initiatives in table 3.1b because of the obvious difficulties in measuring when an initiative failed and presidential rhetoric should end.

Again, table 3.1a contains a list of the significant economic legislation approved by the president as identified by Mayhew (1991) and updated through 2004. Using *Public Papers of the Presidents*, I identified the dates when the president initially proposed or supported legislation. The date that the legislation was signed by the president was also identified. The indicator variables were then coded "one" for all months between the start and end points of public debate over the legislation, and zero otherwise.

The right column of table 3.1a contains the issue domain associated with each enactment. In evaluating the president's general economic rhetoric, I included variables for all four issue domains. This is because all four domains may relate to general economic performance. In evaluating the president's rhetoric on unemployment, inflation, and the deficit, only the variables specific to these issue domains were included in the analysis.

The *within*-presidency dynamics of presidential remarks about the economy may also be a response to various political incentives. Three variables were included in the analysis to capture political incentives. First, the president's average monthly job approval rating as reported by the Gallup survey organization was included in the analyses.[8] This variable was measured in monthly changes, and lagged one period to allow presidents time to recognize changes in their public approval.

Second, the lagged percentages from the relevant Gallup Most Important Problem series were included in the analyses. Since 1946 the Gallup poll on a regular basis has asked a random sample of respondents, "What do you think is the most important problem in this country today?" On average since World War II, around 44 percent of respondents have listed some dimension of the economy as the most important problem facing the nation. The response categories include the economy generally, unemployment, inflation (prices), the federal deficit, trade, and various other economic problems that arise through time.

For the analysis involving the president's general economic rhetoric, the summed lagged response percentages for all categories involving the economy were included. This resulted in a measure of the percentage of Americans who think *some* dimension of the economy is the most important problem facing the nation. For the analyses of the sub-dimensions of the president's economic rhetoric, the respective lagged-response percentages for unemployment, inflation, and the federal deficit were included. If presidential rhetoric on the economy responds to public opinion, then an increased percentage of Americans viewing the economy or some dimension of the economy as important should result in more presidential attention to the economy.

Finally, an indicator variable was included to account for reelection-year incentives. This variable was coded "one" for the first ten months of each presidential election year, and zero otherwise. As discussed earlier, the electoral fortunes of the president and president's party depend on perceptions of macroeconomic performance. Furthermore, the challenger during an election year is likely to question the president's economic leadership, thus spurring more presidential remarks. As presidents attempt to woo economic voters and stave off political opponents, we should see increased presidential remarks about the economy, as well as more presidential optimism.

## EXPLAINING THE INTENSITY OF PRESIDENTIAL RHETORIC ON THE ECONOMY

This section reports a statistical analysis of how personal style, institutional prerogatives, and political incentives affect the intensity of presidential rhetoric on the economy. The dependent variables are the four intensity time series graphed in figure 2.1 and described in chapter 2.

### Statistical Method for the Intensity Analysis

The intensity measures are monthly counts of sentences spoken by presidents about the economy and its various dimensions. Count variables naturally have a minimum of zero. Because the dependent variables consist of discrete integers, theoretically ranging from zero to infinity the analyses should employ a statistical estimator that assumes a variant of the Poisson distribution. Because the dependent variables are time series, the analysis should also use a statistical estimator that also takes into account temporal correlation. Therefore, the Poisson Autoregressive Regression estimator developed by Brandt and Williams (2001) was used for the analyses reported in this section.

### Presidential Style and Intensity

The results for the variables representing presidential style are in table 3.2a. The numbers in the table are coefficients, with z-statistics in parentheses. Since we are using a Poisson-type estimator, interpretation of the

TABLE 3.2a
Presidency-Specific Effects on the Intensity of Economic Rhetoric after Controlling for Other Determinants

| President | Economy | Unemployment | Inflation | Deficit |
|---|---|---|---|---|
| Kennedy | 0.15 | 2.19 | 0.43 | 0.07 |
| | (3.54) | (15.70) | (3.67) | (1.06) |
| Johnson | 0.05 | 1.83 | 0.53 | −0.18 |
| | (1.12) | (14.08) | (4.29) | (−2.83) |
| Nixon | 0.12 | 1.51 | 1.99 | −0.11 |
| | (1.77) | (11.28) | (18.71) | (−1.78) |
| Ford | 1.10 | 2.38 | 2.68 | −0.45 |
| | (3.78) | (18.58) | (25.02) | (−5.07) |
| Carter | 0.79 | 2.55 | 2.83 | −0.07 |
| | (4.89) | (20.31) | (25.13) | (−0.77) |
| Reagan | 1.00 | 1.65 | 2.51 | 1.40 |
| | (7.20) | (13.11) | (24.41) | (19.52) |
| G.H.W. Bush | 1.00 | 1.12 | 0.91 | 1.30 |
| | (7.43) | (8.11) | (7.22) | (17.28) |
| Clinton | 2.03 | 2.67 | 1.97 | 2.94 |
| | (15.99) | (21.73) | (19.08) | (39.56) |
| G. W. Bush | 2.20 | 1.02 | 0.32 | 0.82 |
| | (17.94) | (7.15) | (2.16) | (8.76) |
| Constant | 1.48 | 0.21 | 0.63 | 0.37 |
| | (10.53) | (1.70) | (6.35) | (4.85) |

Note: The numbers in the table are coefficients and $z$-statistics (in parentheses) for each president from the Poisson Autoregressive Regressions further reported in table 3.2b. Eisenhower was the omitted reference category. The numbers in parentheses are $z$-statistics for the null hypothesis that each president did not differ significantly from Eisenhower.

coefficients is in the context of the different metric for Poisson versus linear estimators. Each coefficient must be exponentiated from the base $e$ to be in a linear metric. For example, the constants for the four models in table 3.2a are, respectively, $e^{1.48} = 4.39$, $e^{0.21} = 1.23$, $e^{0.63} = 1.88$, and $e^{0.37} = 1.45$. These numbers represent the expected number of sentences spoken each month by President Eisenhower (the base category) about the general economy, unemployment, inflation, and the federal deficit, during non-election years, when there is no push for significant economic legislation and when all the other variables are at zero. The rhetorical intensity for each president is then considered relative to President Eisenhower. To know a president's average rhetorical intensity, we simply add their coefficient to Eisenhower's coefficient.

With respect to rhetoric on the general economy, President Johnson was statistically indistinguishable from President Eisenhower. President Nixon was perhaps slightly more intense than President Eisenhower, but not at conventional levels of statistical significance. These three presidents talked about the economy at about the same monthly frequency. All other presidents were significantly more intense than President Eisenhower in their rhetoric on the general economy. As observed in the previous chapter, there is a strong pattern of increasing intensity through time extending through the George W. Bush presidency. Controlling for other factors, President Bush was predicted by the analysis to speak 9.03 more sentences each month on the general economy relative to President Eisenhower.

Concerning unemployment rhetoric, all other presidents spoke more often about unemployment than President Eisenhower. However, there is no trend through time in the intensity of unemployment rhetoric. Rather, the pattern for the coefficients suggests a partisan bias. Controlling for other factors, Democratic presidents spoke an average 6.35 more sentences per month about unemployment than Republican presidents.[9] The most intense president on unemployment was President Clinton, who spoke an average of 14.4 more sentences per month than President Eisenhower. This is after controlling for institutional prerogatives and political incentives associated with each presidency. This partisan variation in personal style suggests that Democratic presidents are fundamentally more sympathetic toward working people who constitute a core constituency.

Concerning inflation rhetoric, all presidents were significantly more intense than President Eisenhower. The pattern of the coefficients across presidencies, however, suggests an effect that depends on eras. Controlling for inflation, institutional prerogatives, and political incentives, Presidents Nixon, Carter, and Reagan talked more about inflation than other presidents. Of course, these presidents served during the worst inflationary period of the twentieth century and had strong reason to talk about inflation. It was highly salient to Americans and the most pressing issue of the time. The exception to this pattern was President Clinton, who also talked about inflation about as much as President Nixon. Clinton's emphasis on inflation may have resulted from a stylistic tendency to tout the accomplishments of his administration, which included a prolonged period of inflation-free economic growth.

Presidential rhetoric on the deficit also follows a pattern suggestive of an era effect. Presidents from Kennedy through Carter were either statistically indistinguishable from or less intense than President Eisenhower on the federal deficit. Of course, President Eisenhower was a fiscal conservative who strongly espoused balanced budgets. However, presidents from

TABLE 3.2b

The Determinants of the Intensity of Presidential Rhetoric on the Economy, Unemployment, Inflation, and Deficit, 1953–2004

| Variable | Economy | Unemployment | Inflation | Deficit |
|---|---|---|---|---|
| Economic Growth $_{t-1}$ | −0.01 (−1.41) | | | |
| Unemployment $_{t-1}$ | −0.04 (−0.80) | −0.26 (−3.91) | | |
| Inflation $_{t-1}$ | −0.01 (−2.18) | | 0.04 (6.72) | |
| Deficit $_{t-1}$ | 0.04 (5.61) | | | 0.22 (26.35) |
| President Pushing Significant Economic Legislation | −0.02 (−0.45) | 0.37 (10.62) | 0.15 (3.39) | 0.53 (18.82) |
| Presidential Approval $_{t-1}$ | −0.01 (−4.20) | 0.01 (3.30) | 0.03 (12.18) | −0.01 (−1.78) |
| Most Important Problem $_{t-1}$ | 0.01 (3.93) | 0.02 (19.55) | 0.01 (4.89) | 0.02 (8.37) |
| Election Year | 0.29 (7.74) | 0.48 (17.34) | 0.47 (18.29) | 0.29 (9.86) |
| $\rho_1$ | 0.05 (7.12) | 0.07 (9.00) | 0.23 (14.64) | 0.05 (9.41) |
| $\rho_2$ | | | −0.03 (−3.06) | 0.02 (2.89) |
| Log-Likelihood | −3108 | −3670 | −5133 | −3602 |
| Wald (H0: Poisson) | 49.24 | 79.00 | 216.10 | 97.46 |
| Degrees of Freedom | 600 | 603 | 602 | 602 |

Note: The numbers in the table are coefficients and $z$-statistics (in parentheses) from Poisson Autoregressive Regressions of the monthly frequency of presidential remarks about the economy on the variables in the left side of the table. All regressions also contained indicator variables for each presidency to control for presidency-specific effects as discussed in chapter 2 and observed in table 2.2.

Reagan through George W. Bush talked a lot more about the deficit than earlier presidents. This increase in presidential rhetoric beginning with Reagan corresponds with the period during which the federal budget deficit zoomed out of control. The federal budget was continuously in deficit from 1969 to 1996, but ran a surplus from 1997 to 2000. The deficit, however, grew much larger after passage of the Economic Recovery Tax Act of 1981 (PL 97–34). Table 3.1a shows that seven significant deficit-reducing enactments were passed after 1981 to regain control of the federal budget. The pattern observed in the presidency-specific coefficients in table 3.2a mirrors this increasing concern for the growing federal deficit over time.

## Institutional Prerogatives and Intensity

The results for the variables representing institutional prerogatives and political incentives are in table 3.2b. Because presidents routinely comment on economic reports, the intensity of presidential rhetoric should be responsive to their release. As noted earlier in the theoretical section, however, the response may not be *systematic* through time. On the one hand, when economic reports are poor, presidents may become less intense in their rhetoric to avoid focusing on the negative. On the other hand, when economic reports are poor, presidents may intensify their rhetoric to appear sympathetic and produce the perception that they are on top of things. Due to these ambiguities, it is unclear how the intensity of presidential remarks should respond to the release of various economic reports.

The results in the first four rows of table 3.2b confirm this ambiguity in prior expectations. In the second column, the analysis of rhetoric about the general economy contains all four measures of U.S. economic performance. Only two of the four measures are statistically significant: inflation and the deficit.[10] When inflation is rising, presidents talk less about the general economy (but more about inflation as noted later).[11] When deficits are increasing, presidents talk more about the general economy (but more about deficits as will be noted later). However, there is no statistically significant change in the intensity of presidential rhetoric as a function of economic growth and unemployment. Presidents are equally likely to talk more/less about the general economy when economic growth or unemployment is increasing/decreasing. These results show that the two most important objective indicators of economic performance have no systematic bearing on how frequently presidents mention the general economy.

The story for the more specific dimensions of the presidents' economic rhetoric is also fuzzy. In the third column of table 3.2b, the analysis for unemployment shows that presidents talk less about unemployment when reports on unemployment show it to be rising, and vice versa. This suggests that presidents, as self-interested actors, prefer not talking about bad employment reports, but do like talking about good employment reports. Thus, their more specific rhetoric through time is highly political, emphasizing the positive and downplaying the negative.

On the other hand, the responses in the intensity of presidential rhetoric on inflation and the deficit are precisely opposite from the response on unemployment. As reports on inflation show prices rising, presidents talk more about inflation. This result may be due to presidents attempting to demonstrate being on top of an important issue. It may also be dominated by the low inflation rates before and after the era of stagflation of the 1970s and 1980s (e.g., see figure 2.1). Presidents had little incentive to talk about inflation when the inflation rate was low in the 1940s–60s and later in the 1990s–2000s. Low inflation meant that this was a low-salience issue. In contrast, they had a lot of incentive to talk about inflation during the high inflation era of the 1970s–80s. People were very concerned about inflation, and so presidents during these years talked more about the issue.

Presidents also talk more about the federal budget deficit as the deficit grows worse. The results for the deficit in the last column of table 3.2b show that as the deficit increases (as a proportion of GDP), presidential rhetoric intensifies. Again, presidents as self-interested actors may want to appear active on a political issue that most recognize as important to the economy. Therefore, as the deficit grows worse, presidents become increasingly political by preaching the gospel of fiscal responsibility.

The intensity of a president's economic rhetoric should also increase during periods when the president has proposed and is pushing significant economic legislation. The fifth row of table 3.2b confirms this expectation. The results for economic stimulus legislation in the first column are not statistically significant. Yet during the periods when a president is pushing for unemployment, inflation, or deficit reduction legislation, the intensity of presidential rhetoric for each of these domains systematically increases. Thus, we can conclude that presidential rhetoric intensifies during periods when presidents campaign for economic policy change.

## Political Incentives and Intensity

Now consider how the intensity of the president's economic rhetoric responds to various political incentives. First, the results for presidential approval in the sixth row of table 3.2b show that as public approval declines presidents talk more about the economy generally, but they also become less specific about particular economic problems. A decline in public approval results in significantly more presidential remarks per month on the general economy. The same decline in public approval, however, results in similar declines in presidential remarks on unemployment and inflation. The result for the federal deficit is not statistically significant. Thus, the results here show that presidents *do* try to bolster their approval through increased economic rhetoric. When approval is declining, however, they also hedge about the specific components of economic performance such as unemployment and inflation.

Second, the response to public opinion on the importance of various economic problems shows strong and consistent results for all dimensions. The response of presidential rhetoric to the Gallup Most Important Problem series is contained in the seventh row of table 3.2b. As survey respondents increasingly believe that the general economy, unemployment, inflation, and the deficit are the most important problems facing the nation, presidents respond consistently by increasing the amount of attention devoted to the respective problems. As democratic and self-interested actors, presidents respond systematically to changing public opinion on the economy generally, as well as for specific economic issues.

Finally, the results in the eighth row of table 3.2b show that presidents consistently speak more often about all dimensions of the economy during the presidential election season. The changes in the ninth row represent changes of 7, 9, 9, and 8 percent respectively in the intensity of presidential remarks on the economy during presidential election years. These are modest average changes in the intensity of presidential remarks about the economy. They do show, however, that presidential remarks on the economy increase due to electoral incentives.

## EXPLAINING THE TONE OF PRESIDENTIAL RHETORIC ON THE ECONOMY

This section reports the statistical analysis of the determinants of the tone of presidential rhetoric on the economy. The dependent variables are the four tone time series graphed in figure 2.2 and described in chapter 2.

### Statistical Method for Tone Analysis

Recall from chapter 2 that the tone measures are time-series containing counts of the number of optimistic minus pessimistic sentences spoken by the president during discrete time intervals. Theoretically, the measures can run from minus infinity to plus infinity. In practice, the average tone is near neutral for all series. Because the dependent variables can range from large negative numbers to large positive numbers, Box-Jenkins (1976) time-series regression methods were used to construct the statistical models. These methods provide a strong control for history and autocorrelation.

TABLE 3.3a
Presidency-Specific Effects on the Tone of Economic Rhetoric after Controlling for Other Determinants

| Variable | Economy | Unemployment | Inflation | Deficit |
|---|---|---|---|---|
| Eisenhower | 0.09 | 0.11 | −0.02 | −0.25 |
| | (0.04) | (0.04) | (−0.01) | (−0.10) |
| Kennedy | −1.29 | 0.95 | 0.19 | −1.91 |
| | (−0.67) | (0.27) | (0.05) | (−1.46) |
| Johnson | −0.03 | 1.83 | 0.85 | −0.00 |
| | (−0.01) | (0.77) | (0.40) | (−0.00) |
| Nixon | 1.92 | 1.76 | 4.07 | −0.66 |
| | (0.62) | (0.63) | (3.26) | (−0.18) |
| Ford | 2.02 | 0.97 | 0.82 | −3.39 |
| | (0.49) | (0.43) | (0.41) | (−2.69) |
| Carter | 4.07 | 3.58 | 8.77 | −0.92 |
| | (0.93) | (1.70) | (4.12) | (−0.56) |
| Reagan | 3.84 | 1.00 | 1.42 | −3.51 |
| | (1.36) | (0.39) | (1.45) | (−3.41) |
| G.H.W. Bush | 4.11 | 1.90 | 2.56 | −1.52 |
| | (1.11) | (0.66) | (1.45) | (−1.46) |
| Clinton | 15.56 | 12.71 | 4.32 | 2.00 |
| | (10.39) | (11.63) | (4.14) | (3.35) |
| G. W. Bush | 7.09 | 2.25 | 2.89 | −1.17 |
| | (4.21) | (0.84) | (1.96) | (−0.67) |

Note: The numbers in the table are coefficients and $z$-statistics (in parentheses) for each president from the Autoregressive Regressions further reported in table 3.3b. The constant was suppressed for hypothesis testing purposes. The numbers in parentheses contain $z$-statistics for the null hypothesis that the tone of each president's remarks was zero.

## Presidential Style and Tone

The coefficients for the variables representing presidential style are in table 3.3a, with $z$-statistics shown in parentheses. All categories of the presidency-specific indicator variables are included in the regression, and the regression intercept is excluded from the analysis. This enables a direct interpretation of the presidency-specific coefficients, which represent the average monthly tone of each president's public remarks on the economy after controlling for institutional prerogatives and political incentives.

Controlling for other factors, the analysis of presidential remarks on the general economy show no difference in average tone from Presidents

Eisenhower through George H. W. Bush. All of these presidencies were statistically neutral in their relative optimism.

The coefficient for President Reagan is particularly interesting since he was not much different from Carter or George H. W. Bush. This finding runs counter to the popular perception that Reagan was an "eternal optimist" (Associated Press 2004; Will 2004). Indeed, after controlling for economic conditions and other factors, he was not much different in relative optimism from other presidents during the troubled economic times of the 1970s–80s. Moreover, Presidents Carter and George H. W. Bush were slightly more optimistic in the tone of their remarks than Reagan. We shall discuss the relative optimism of Carter and Reagan at length in the next chapter.

The results also show that President Clinton was far more optimistic than other presidents on the economy generally. He averaged a net 15.56 more optimistic than pessimistic remarks on the economy each month. Clinton's mantra "it's the economy stupid" obviously spilled over into his public remarks.

President George W. Bush was also significantly optimistic. We shall see in the next chapter, however, that this statistic masks significant variations in his optimism. Virtually all of his optimism was confined to the 2004 election season. Thus, stylistically most presidents were on average neither optimists nor pessimists on the general economy, with only Clinton regularly attempting to "talk up" the economy.

Concerning unemployment rhetoric, there was again no difference in optimism for presidents from Eisenhower through George H. W. Bush, also including George W. Bush. All nine of these presidents were statistically neutral in the tone of their public remarks about unemployment. If we use a relaxed standard of statistical significance, then President Carter was optimistic on unemployment. However, the only president who was optimistic on unemployment using the normal scientific standard was Clinton. Controlling for actual levels of unemployment and other factors, he registered 12.71 more optimistic than pessimistic remarks per month on unemployment.

Concerning inflation rhetoric, Presidents Eisenhower, Kennedy, Johnson, Ford, Reagan, and George H. W. Bush were statistically neutral in the tone of their public remarks on inflation. In contrast, Presidents Nixon, Carter, Clinton, and George W. Bush were significantly optimistic.

Interestingly, the results show that two presidents who served during the high inflation period of the 1970s–80s were actually optimists on inflation. President Nixon spoke a net 4.07 more optimistic than pessimistic sentences per month even as oil prices spun higher. Remarkably, President Carter spoke an average 8.77 more optimistic than pessimistic sentences per month during the worst inflationary period of the twenti-

TABLE 3.3b
The Determinants of the Tone of Presidential Rhetoric on the Economy, Unemployment, Inflation, and Deficit, 1953–2004

| Variable | Economy | Unemployment | Inflation | Deficit |
|---|---|---|---|---|
| Economic Growth $_{t-1}$ | 0.00 | | | |
| | (0.01) | | | |
| Unemployment $_{t-1}$ | 0.04 | −6.12 | | |
| | (0.03) | (−5.11) | | |
| Inflation $_{t-1}$ | −0.56 | | −0.30 | |
| | (−1.83) | | (−1.70) | |
| Deficit $_{t-1}$ | 0.11 | | | 0.36 |
| | (0.34) | | | (1.79) |
| President Pushing Significant | −0.29 | −4.37 | 0.89 | 3.88 |
| Economic Legislation | (−0.28) | (−3.26) | (0.63) | (7.53) |
| Presidential Approval $_{t-1}$ | 0.04 | −0.01 | 0.02 | 0.00 |
| | (0.70) | (−0.12) | (0.44) | (0.11) |
| Most Important Problem $_{t-1}$ | −0.01 | −0.07 | 0.02 | 0.09 |
| | (−0.37) | (−1.35) | (0.72) | (2.08) |
| Election Year | 4.37 | 3.19 | 0.46 | −0.94 |
| | (4.47) | (3.21) | (0.70) | (−1.45) |
| $\rho_1$ | 0.39 | 0.49 | 0.26 | 0.32 |
| | (15.23) | (19.04) | (12.73) | (10.64) |
| $\rho_2$ | 0.11 | 0.09 | 0.14 | 0.15 |
| | (3.81) | (3.21) | (4.97) | (7.41) |
| Log–Likelihood | −1929.77 | −1954.68 | −1841.08 | −1631.15 |
| Degrees of Freedom | 605 | 608 | 608 | 608 |

Note: The numbers in the table are coefficients and z-statistics (in parentheses) from Autoregressive Regressions of the average monthly tone of presidential remarks about the economy on the variables in the left side of the table. All regressions also contained indicator variables for each presidency to control for presidency-specific effects as discussed in chapter 2 and observed in table 2.3.

eth century. This finding belies the image of Carter as a pessimist that prevailed during the 1980 election. Carter was significantly more optimistic than any other president on the issue of inflation, even as inflation approached record levels in 1980. We shall discuss his optimism in more detail in the next chapter.

The tone of presidential rhetoric on the deficit shows that all presidents except Clinton were either statistically neutral or pessimistic. Controlling for other factors, Clinton's optimism on the deficit was modest, averaging about 2.00 more optimistic than pessimistic comments per month. His relative optimism is consistent obviously with the successful efforts to rein in the federal deficit during the 1990s. President Reagan was the most pessimistic on the deficit, averaging about 3.51 more pessimistic than optimistic comments per month. Of course, this was during the period after the 1981 tax cut, when the federal deficit ballooned. The Reagan presidency was also associated with four significant legislative enactments intended to address the deficit problem (see table 3.1a). It may be that Reagan's pessimism on the deficit was due to emphasizing the severity of the problem in an effort to support economic initiatives on the deficit.

### Institutional Prerogatives and Tone

Consider next how the tone of presidential remarks has responded through time to institutional prerogatives relating to the economy. First, presidential optimism may change as a function of the release of various economic reports. The results in the first four rows of table 3.3b reflect the predicted ambiguities from our earlier theoretical discussion.

In the second column, the analysis of rhetoric about the general economy contains reports for all four measures of U.S. economic performance. None of the measures is statistically significant. In other words, presidents do not become systematically more optimistic or pessimistic in their general economic rhetoric as a function of the release of various reports on economic growth, unemployment, inflation, or the federal deficit.

Results for the more specific dimensions of presidents' economic rhetoric are mixed. The third column of table 3.3b shows that as unemployment increases, presidents become significantly less optimistic about unemployment. Similarly, when unemployment declines they become more optimistic. Thus, presidential optimism on unemployment simply mirrors the economic reports.

The results for inflation and the deficit in the fourth and fifth columns are not statistically significant. The sign on the coefficient for inflation suggests that higher inflation may lead to more presidential pessimism, and vice versa. The sign on the coefficient for the deficit suggests the opposite. We should not, however, place much emphasis on these nonsignificant results.

More generally, the results reported here suggest little or no systematic relationship between reports on U.S. economic performance and the tone of presidential rhetoric. The tone of presidential remarks on unemployment mirrors economic reports on the issue. Along other dimensions, however, some presidents appear to be optimists when economic indicators are poor, and others appear to be pessimists. We shall further explore the relationship between economic indicators and presidential optimism in chapter 6, using a subset of later presidencies and different statistical methods.

Second, we theorized that the tone of the president's economic rhetoric may change when the president is supporting significant economic legislation. The prediction was that presidents should become more pessimistic during efforts to pass legislation to make the case that the legislation is necessary. We have anecdotal evidence from chapter 1 to this effect in the negativism of President George W. Bush while securing three tax cuts from 2001–2003. The results in the fifth row of table 3.3b, however, do not confirm that this effect holds systematically across presidents and across the various dimensions of the economy.

The second column shows that presidential optimism is generally unresponsive to efforts to pass economic stimulus legislation. The third column shows that presidents do become systematically more pessimistic in periods when the president is seeking unemployment legislation. Presidents obviously talk about the severity of the unemployment problem to convince people of the need for jobs programs. The fourth column shows no relationship between efforts to pass anti-inflation legislation and the relative optimism of presidential rhetoric. Finally, the last column shows an opposite relationship. Presidents are significantly optimistic about the deficit when they are campaigning for antideficit legislation.

## Political Incentives and Tone

Now consider how the tone of the presidents' economic rhetoric responds to various political incentives. First, the results for presidential approval in the sixth row of table 3.3b show that there is no relationship between public approval and the economic optimism of the president along any dimension. Presidents do not systematically become more optimistic or pessimistic about the economy as their approval changes.

Second, the seventh row of table 3.3b shows that presidential optimism about the economy is unresponsive to public opinion on the importance of economic problems for three of the four economic dimensions. The fourth dimension for the deficit yields the nonsensical result that presidents become more optimistic with the increase in the percentage of Americans viewing the deficit as the most important problem.

Finally, the eighth row of table 3.3b shows that presidents do systematically become more optimistic about the general economy and unemployment during presidential election years. Election-year incentives encourage presidents to emphasize leadership on matters important to voters. Perennially, what matters greatly to voters is the strength of the economy and jobs. These are also the issues most often raised by challengers. As challengers raise economic issues, presidents respond by attempting to produce a vision of confidence in the economic future.


CONCLUSION

Modern presidents increasingly focus on the economy in their public remarks. When the nation is not in crisis, modern presidents talk more about the economy than any other single issue. Furthermore, they have generally grown more optimistic through time in the tone of their remarks about the economy. One of the major research questions of this book is why? Why do modern presidents feel so compelled to talk about the economy? Why has the tone of presidential remarks about the economy grown more optimistic through time? More generally, what determines variations through time in the intensity and tone of presidential remarks on the economy?

This chapter developed and tested a theory intended to answer these questions and reveal *systematic* and *generalizable* relationships that hold across all presidencies and through time. The theory posits that variation through time in the intensity and tone of presidential rhetoric about the economy should be a function of a president's personal style, institutional prerogatives relating to the economy, and political incentives. Using data covering a time span from 1953 through 2004, and encompassing ten presidencies, the statistical analyses show that each proposed theoretical component is important to some extent for explaining variations in presidential rhetoric through time.

With respect to the presidents' personal style, the results show clear differences across presidencies in their propensity to talk about the economy and its various dimensions. Controlling for changing institutional prerogatives and political incentives, the results also confirm what seems obvious, that presidential style has grown increasingly rhetorical. Why has presidential style become more rhetorical? It could be because the evolution of media technology has made it a requirement for achieving office. It may also be that presidential success once in office has increasingly depended on skillful use of rhetoric. Moreover, White House institutions have evolved to support a more public presidency, and people have come to expect rhetorical leadership from the president.

Some presidents, however, stand out from the others for their strong emphasis on economic rhetoric. President Clinton was by far the most intense and optimistic on all dimensions of the economy. The statistical analysis shows that he talked about the general economy roughly twice as often as any prior president. He focused on unemployment and the federal deficit more than any other president. He spoke about inflation almost as much as presidents of the stagflation era. On the general economy, he was roughly 2.5 times more optimistic than the next most optimistic president. Using the same benchmark, he was about 3.4 times more optimistic on unemployment. He was the only president who was significantly optimistic on the federal deficit. He was the second most optimistic president on inflation. Clearly Clinton was distinctive in his use of economic rhetoric.

A few other presidents also stand out as distinctive when facing adverse economic circumstances. For example, President Nixon was both intense and optimistic on inflation during a period when inflation was a serious problem. President Carter was also intense and optimistic on unemployment and inflation during a period when they were at levels that for other presidents might have warranted silence and pessimism. This finding belies the image of Carter as a pessimist, as the media portrayed him following the famous "malaise" speech. It is also of interest to note that President Reagan was neither among the more intense presidents in speaking about the economy, nor among the most optimistic. This finding stands in contrast with the popular image of President Reagan as the "eternal optimist."

With respect to institutional prerogatives and political incentives, the analysis shows that some of these variables are effective in explaining the intensity of presidential rhetoric within presidencies. However, they are often ineffective in explaining the tone of presidential rhetoric.

Presidents respond most consistently when talking about reports on unemployment. Systematically, reports of lower unemployment result in increased presidential rhetoric and higher presidential optimism. In other words, it is a regular phenomenon that presidents "pound their chests" as the employment situation improves. In contrast, they become reticent and more pessimistic when the employment situation deteriorates. Thus, presidential rhetoric on unemployment appears highly political.

Presidents generally ignore reports on economic growth, however, and the intensity of their rhetoric tends simply to mirror reports on inflation and the deficit. They talk more about inflation and the deficit when reports are released, but there is no statistically significant relationship between these reports and the tone of presidential rhetoric.

Systematically, when presidents are pushing for significant legislation on unemployment, inflation, and the federal deficit, they talk more about these issues. There is mixed evidence, however, concerning how the tone of presidential rhetoric responds during periods of presidential efforts to pass legislation. Contrary to the anecdotal evidence from the George W. Bush administration, which talked down the economy in seeking tax cuts between 2001 and 2003, there is no evidence that presidents systematically become more pessimistic during these periods. There is also no evidence of increased presidential pessimism when pushing for inflation or deficit reduction legislation. Presidents do tend, however, to become more pessimistic when pushing for unemployment legislation.

With respect to political incentives, the intensity of presidential rhetoric responds systematically to public opinion. As public approval of a president's job performance declines, the intensity of presidential rhetoric on the general economy increases. Yet declining public approval also results in less emphasis on specific economic conditions such as unemployment and the deficit.

The intensity of presidential rhetoric also responds systematically to what the public thinks is an important problem. As the public increasingly gauges the general economy, unemployment, inflation, and the deficit as important problems, presidents respond by increasing the intensity of their rhetoric on these issues. Thus, presidents as democratic and self-interested actors respond in harmony with changing public opinion.

Like clockwork, the intensity and tone of presidential rhetoric changes during presidential election years. These are periods when presidents tout their accomplishments and respond to challengers who question the presidential record on the economy. Presidents become more optimistic during election years on specific economic issues. During election years presidents tend to be more optimistic on the general economy and unemployment, but there is no change in presidential optimism on inflation and the federal deficit.

More generally, the analysis in this chapter shows various empirical regularities about the determinants of the intensity and tone of presidential rhetoric on the economy. However, the results are also complex due to differences in personal style across presidencies. At the core, presidents appear highly political, responding in a self-interested manner to the institutional prerogatives and political incentives that emerge over time. Stylistic differences across presidencies, however, sometimes produce variations in these responses, and the statistical determinants of presidential rhetoric are not always consistent.

Due to these complexities, it is important to explore further the stylistic differences across presidencies. In the next chapter I develop four case studies in presidential rhetoric to provide a more nuanced description of why, when, and how presidents talk about the economy.

# Four Cases of a President's Rhetorical Leadership of the Economy

> For the great majority of mankind are satisfied with appearance, as though they were realities and are often more influenced by the things that seem than by those that are.
>
> (Machiavelli 1517)

THE PREVIOUS CHAPTER used quantitative evidence to explore the *systematic* determinants of presidential rhetoric on the economy. The measures for personal style, however, were indicator variables devoid of substance and context. We also found evidence that all presidents do not respond in the same way to certain institutional prerogatives and political incentives. Differences in personal style may cause presidents to react differently when faced with similar economic and political circumstances. Therefore, if we are to understand the determinants of the intensity and tone of presidential rhetoric on the economy, we must take better account of how presidents have differed in personal style.

This chapter provides case studies of the personal style of four presidencies when using economic rhetoric: those of Carter, Reagan, Clinton, and George W. Bush. The purpose of this chapter is *not* to test the theories of the last chapter in a rigorous way. Case studies are ill suited for this purpose. Rather, it is to provide readers with an intuitive grasp of what presidents have said about the economy under difficult economic circumstances. The chapter is intended to fill the substantive void left by the statistical analyses of the last chapter by giving concrete examples of economic rhetoric for presidents with differing personal styles.

These four presidencies were chosen because, based on the systematic evidence presented in the last chapter, they represent interesting and sometimes divergent cases. Exploring the rhetoric of these particular presidents in some detail enables us to move beyond mere appearance toward a better substantive understanding of how different presidents have used economic rhetoric.

For example, the media characterized President Carter as a pessimist after his famous "malaise" speech, but the statistical evidence from the last chapter showed that he was both intense and optimistic on inflation even as inflation worsened and a push was on to pass inflation-fighting legislation. In contrast, President Reagan is often viewed as the "eternal optimist," but the statistical evidence from the last chapter showed that he was no more intense or optimistic than other presidents on the economy. Indeed, figure 2.2 shows that during the 1982–83 recession, Reagan was more pessimistic than any other president on unemployment. Standing in stark contrast, President Clinton appeared far more optimistic than other presidents across all dimensions of the economy. Finally, President George W. Bush seemed to use economic rhetoric opportunistically to achieve partisan political ends. Are these images flowing from the media or prior analyses correct? This chapter explores whether they have a basis in the flow of actual presidential remarks.

Another reason to examine the rhetoric of these four presidents is that they all served during times of economic crisis. Carter faced the worst non-war inflationary period of the twentieth century.[1] Reagan faced the worst economic recession since the Great Depression. Clinton inherited a budget crisis and the worst federal deficit and debt problem since World War II. President George W. Bush faced a mild recession that could have intensified due to the shock from the September 11 terrorist attacks.

During an economic crisis, rhetorical leadership by the president becomes especially important as others look to the chief executive for economic leadership. Presidential leadership of the economy requires meeting the economic challenges of the time with policies, concern, and confidence. Just as President Franklin Roosevelt met the economic crisis of the Great Depression with reassuring words and calming fireside chats, we should expect presidents of the modern era who are truly economic leaders to inspire confidence through rhetorical leadership.

The case studies in the next four sections allow an evaluation of how well Presidents Carter, Reagan, Clinton, and George W. Bush lived up to this standard.

PRESIDENT CARTER AND INFLATION

President Carter served during the worst inflationary period of the modern era. Figure 4.1 provides a plot of the annualized monthly U.S. inflation rate from 1965 through 1985 to provide a sense of the severity and dynamics of inflation during this period. The heavy vertical lines mark the start and end points of the Carter administration.

The graph in figure 4.1 shows that inflation had been a persistent problem starting with the late 1960s.[2] The Arab oil embargo in late 1973 contributed to a large increase in inflation that peaked in December 1974. By the beginning of the Carter administration, however, inflation had

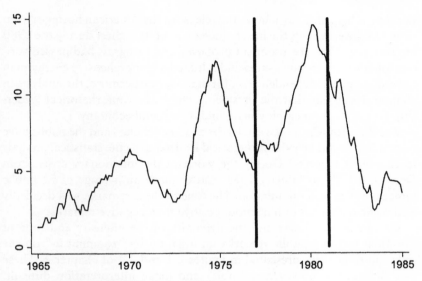

Figure 4.1 Inflation during the Stagflation Era

eased to around 5 percent. From Carter's inauguration through late 1978, inflation resumed its rise due to excess demand, a wage-price spiral, and high energy prices (Peretz 1983). However, another large oil shock began on December 25, 1978, when the Iranian Revolution against the Shah of Iran resulted in cessation of Iranian oil exports. Panic in the oil markets led to sharply increased prices that filtered into the economy. In 1980 due to the Iran/Iraq War, Iran's oil production again fell significantly, and Iraq's crude oil production fell by 2.7 million barrels per day. The combination of these events resulted in crude oil prices more than doubling from $14 in 1978 to $35 per barrel in 1981 (United States Energy Information Administration 1997).

Through this period, the U.S. inflation rate increased sharply to peak in March 1980 at 14.6 percent. The economy also slipped, with economic growth initiating a decline in mid-1979 and moving into recession early in the 1980 election year. Additionally, beginning in mid-1979, unemployment rose from 5.7 percent to 7.5 percent by January 20, 1981. Rampant inflation together with these consequent changes in the economy presented a major challenge for the Carter administration.[3]

Of course, it is widely believed that President Carter did not live up to these challenges. Experts ranking the presidents do not place Carter high among others (Cohen and Nice 2003, 115–117). He was turned out of office in 1980 under a wide perception that he was a weak economic and foreign policy leader. Carter was perceived as weak on foreign policy because of his failure to achieve the release of the American hostages from Iran. On the economy, the misery index was at its highest during the 1980 election year.[4] Yet, the president proposed and Congress had passed various inflation control measures and initiated a comprehensive energy plan for reducing U.S. dependence on foreign oil. Furthermore, the analysis in chapter 3 suggests that the president exhibited strong rhetorical leadership on inflation, unemployment, and the general economy.

Was President Carter a weak leader as some scholars and the public have concluded, or did he exhibit rhetorical leadership as the statistical analysis in chapter 3 suggests? During the worst of the inflationary crisis, from December 1978 to January 1981, Carter made an average of 92 public remarks per month on inflation. The tone of these remarks was decidedly optimistic with a net of nine more positive than negative remarks.

We can better understand the dynamics of the intensity and tone of President Carter's public remarks on inflation by "zooming in" on the inflation time series presented in figures 2.1 and 2.2 of chapter 2. These raw time series, however, are noisy and make interpretation difficult. Therefore, lowess smoothing was applied to facilitate interpretation.[5] Figure 4.2 contains a graph of the smoothed intensity time series over the period covered by the graph in figure 4.1. Again, the outer heavy vertical markers identify the start and end points of the Carter administration. The inner heavy vertical marker identifies the peak of the inflation rate graphed in figure 4.1.

Consider first the intensity of presidential rhetoric on inflation. Figure 4.2 shows that the intensity of presidential rhetoric responded to the severity of the inflation problem. As the inflation rate increased, presidential rhetoric on inflation rose steadily from the late 1960s through around 1980. The intensity of presidential rhetoric also followed the sharp peaks in inflation over this period. The intensity of President Carter's rhetoric on inflation increased sharply as the inflation rate increased. There were two peaks in intensity during the Carter administration, the first coming after the December 1978 oil shock and the second coming after the peak in the inflation rate in March 1980.

Now look at the tone graph in figure 4.3. It shows that, consistent with the statistical results in table 3.3a, Presidents Nixon and Carter were more optimistic on inflation than other presidents. For both presidents, the peak in optimism of presidential rhetoric occurred before the highest inflation rates. In particular, Carter was highly optimistic as inflation increased sharply between his inauguration and 1979. He remained significantly more optimistic than all other presidents through the December 1978 oil shock when his optimism peaked. Following this, Carter's optimism on inflation dropped off but remained higher on average than

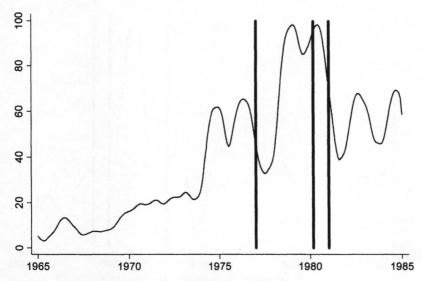

Figure 4.2  Lowess Smoothed Inflation Rhetoric Intensity

Nixon's. Even after inflation peaked at 14.6 percent in March of the 1980 election year, Carter never became a pessimist on the issue of inflation.

What specifically did President Carter say during the inflationary crisis of the late 1970s? In his State of the Union message on January 23, 1979, he alluded to inflation fourteen times. In spite of recently higher prices and the oil shock, Carter struck a decidedly positive tone. Here are some excerpts from that speech:

> Tonight, there is every sign that the state of our Union is sound. Our economy offers greater prosperity for more of our people than ever before. Real per capita income and real business profits have risen substantially in the last 2 years. Farm exports are setting an all-time record each year, and farm income last year, net farm income, was up more than 25 percent. . . . In our economy, it is a myth that we must choose endlessly between inflation and recession. Together, we build the foundation for a strong economy, with lower inflation, without contriving either a recession with its high unemployment or unworkable, mandatory government controls. . . . Together, we've already begun to build the foundation for confidence in our economic system. During the last 2 years, in bringing our economy out of the deepest recession since the 1930's, we've created 7,100,000 new jobs. The unemployment rate has gone down 25 percent. And now we must redouble our fight against the persistent inflation that has wracked our country for more than a decade. That's our most important domestic issue, and we must do it

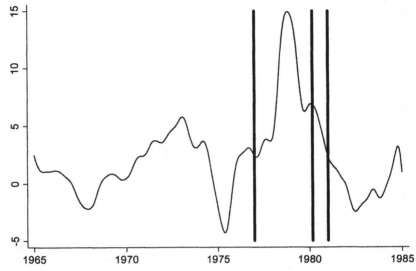

Figure 4.3 Lowess Smoothed Inflation Rhetoric Tone

together. . . . We know that inflation is a burden for all Americans, but it's a disaster for the poor, the sick, and the old. . . . Three months ago, I outlined to the Nation a balanced anti-inflation program that couples responsible government restraint with responsible wage and price restraint. . . . This budget is a clear message that, with the help of you and the American people, I am determined, as President, to bring inflation under control. . . . I call on Congress to take other anti-inflation action. . . . American workers who enlist in the fight against inflation deserve not just our gratitude, but they deserve the protection of the real wage insurance proposal that I have already made to the Congress. . . . A strong economy and an effective government will restore confidence in America.

President Carter's 1979 State of the Union message acknowledged inflation as the most important problem facing the nation and pointed to specific plans to combat the problem. His speech seemingly attempted to produce a sense of unity among Americans in the fight against inflation.

Throughout 1979, President Carter made speeches, held news conferences and town meetings, and made various other public remarks that focused on inflation. Here are some representative comments from these events.

- Message to the Congress Transmitting the Annual Economic Report of the President, January 25, 1979—"My administration's major domestic priority is to reduce the rate of inflation, while maintaining economic growth. . . . Last October I announced an anti-inflation program which can aid significantly in the effort to reduce inflation. . . . The elements of my anti-inflation program are mutually supportive and designed to mount a sustainable attack on our long-run inflation problem. . . . My anti-inflation program will support the health of our economy in 1979."

- Speech before the Georgia General Assembly, February 20, 1979—"And as President I pledge to you that I am determined to bring inflation under control. . . . We've set forth now an anti-inflation program that recognizes the basic causes of inflation and attacks this problem on a broad front."

- Remarks and a Question and Answer Session at a Town Meeting, March 24, 1979—"The point is I'm doing all I can as head of our Government to control inflation. . . . But I am absolutely determined and I am absolutely convinced that if we work together we can bring inflation under control."

- Energy Address to the Nation, April 5, 1979—"Our Nation's energy problem is very serious—and it's getting worse. . . . As Government controls end, prices will go up on oil which has already been discovered, and unless we tax the oil companies, they will reap huge and undeserved windfall profits. We must, therefore, impose a windfall profits tax on the oil companies to capture part of this money for the American people. . . . The actions and plans that I have announced tonight will move us away from imported oil and toward a future of real energy security. These actions will give us a better life."

- Remarks to the Iowa State Association of Counties, May 4, 1979—"But the knowledge that we can deal with these special problems, using proven, sometimes ancient principles which our ancestors would understand very well, gives me confidence that we can control the enormous, overall problems of energy and inflation."

- Remarks and a Question and Answer Session by Satellite to an Annual Convention in Las Vegas, Nevada, May 23, 1979—"It's going to get better in the near future, but we cannot abandon a permanent commitment to control inflation because we have a temporary disappointment for a few months after it was initiated."

- Remarks at a News Conference, May 29, 1979—"All of these factors working together will have a long-range, beneficial effect in controlling inflation. . . . So, we have a good, sound, anti-inflation program."

- Labor Day Statement by the President, August 30, 1979—"The most serious challenge is inflation which erodes the paychecks of all working Americans. Working together, we can forge a long-term partnership that will reduce inflation and keep it down."

- White House Statement on Actions by the Board of Governors of the Federal Reserve System, October 6, 1979—"The administration believes that the actions decided upon today by the Federal Reserve Board will help reduce inflationary expectations, contribute to a stronger U.S. dollar abroad, and curb unhealthy speculations in commodity markets."
- Remarks on Announcing Candidacy for President in 1980, December 2, 1979—"With calm, strong, and effective leadership, with a prosperous and expanding economy, with inflation and energy shortages behind us, with people believing again, we can set our course for the kind of future about which we have all dreamed."

Inflation was increasing steadily over the entire period of these remarks and reached a high of 14.6 percent in March 1980. Amid perceptions of poor economic conditions, President Carter's public approval rating dipped to a low of 29 percent in mid-1979 and averaged only 37 percent for the entire year. Rising energy prices and inflation were crisis conditions for the U.S. economy and the administration.

Another (related) crisis, however, soon pushed these conditions out of the attention frame of the American people. On November 4, 1979, Iranian militants stormed the United States Embassy in Tehran and took sixty-six Americans hostage. This act triggered the most profound foreign policy crisis of the Carter presidency. Moreover it was an ordeal lasting through the 1980 election year. Additionally, on December 21, 1979, Soviet troops moved into Afghanistan initiating an invasion that led to Soviet occupation of that country for the next ten years.

Foreign policy crises displaced inflation as the top agenda item for most Americans. Thus, President Carter's annual State of the Union message on January 23, 1980, did not deal primarily with the economy. Rather, it dealt mainly with recent foreign policy events. Nevertheless, the president did attend to the pressing issue of inflation near the end of his speech. Here are some of those remarks:

> The crises in Iran and Afghanistan have dramatized a very important lesson: Our excessive dependence on foreign oil is a clear and present danger to our Nation's security. . . . At long last, we must have a clear, comprehensive energy policy for the United States. As you well know, I have been working with the Congress in a concentrated and persistent way over the past 3 years to meet this need. We have made progress together. . . . The American people are making progress in energy conservation. Last year we reduced overall petroleum consumption by 8 percent and gasoline consumption by 5 percent below what it was the year before. Now we must do more. . . . With these energy and economic policies, we will make America even stronger at home in this

decade—just as our foreign and defense policies will make us stronger and safer throughout the world. . . . We move into the 1980's with confidence and hope and a bright vision of the America we want.

Shortly after the president's 1980 State of the Union message, inflation began a decline that continued until 1983. Inflation, however, remained above 12 percent throughout the 1980 election year. During the election year, the president continued the fight with new policies intended to address the problem and with continuing optimism. Following are excerpts from President Carter's election year remarks on inflation:

- Remarks at the President's News Conference on a New Anti-Inflation Program, March 14, 1980—"Just a few hours ago I described the basic elements of this program, to intensify America's battle against inflation. . . . Toward the end of this year the inflation rate will begin to drop, I think drop substantially. . . . The final point I'd like to make before I take your questions is that our Nation is strong and vital. We are similar to a superb athlete who has simply gotten out of shape. The American economy has an underlying strength and resiliency. With discipline and restraint and with a willingness to accept, perhaps, some aching muscles at first, our economy can perform again like a champion."

- Remarks to the National Conference of State Legislatures, March 28, 1980—"We expect substantial reductions, in the near future, we hope, in interest rates and inflation rates—certainly, I hope, by the end of this year. I would like to see it done before the first week in November if possible. [*laughter.*] And I think next year we intend to see additional help."

- Remarks and a Question and Answer Session with Editors and Broadcasters of Harte-Hanks Communications, April 23, 1980— "I believe that we will see, during this summer, substantial reductions in the inflation rate, and we are already seeing fairly good trends downward in the interest rates."

- Remarks at a Carter/Mondale Campaign Rally, May 29, 1980— "We have moved strongly on a broad-based front since the second week in March with an anti-inflation program, which is very successful, to cut interest rates and inflation. . . . My prediction to you—and you watch what I say and see if I'm accurate—is that during the summer months and toward the end of this year, we'll have a sharp reduction in the inflation rate."

- Remarks to the National Association for the Advancement of Colored People, July 4, 1980—"I've taken the dangerous and the difficult steps to control inflation and to cut down interest rates, and these measures are working. . . . The inflation rate is coming down also very rapidly, and I predict to you that later on in the summer you'll see the inflation rate reach fairly low levels."

- Remarks to the World Bank Group and International Monetary Fund at the Annual Meetings of the Boards of Governors, September 30, 1980—"We've adopted a strong anti-inflation program of fiscal and monetary restraint. . . . The program will reduce inflation."

Throughout the 1980 election year the inflation rate steadily declined, and continued to decline until September 1983, when it bottomed at 2.75 percent. Unfortunately for President Carter, inflation did not come down fast enough to produce the perception that his economic plans were working. His reelection failure in 1980 is widely perceived as a failure of presidential leadership. Of course, Carter proposed and implemented specific policies to fight inflation. He advocated those policies vigorously through economic rhetoric. The optimistic tone of his remarks suggests a personal style that emphasized positive rhetorical leadership. Ultimately, however, he was unable to inspire public confidence and establish a favorable tone for the economy.

## PRESIDENT REAGAN AND THE 1982–83 RECESSION

President Reagan served during the worst recessionary period since the Great Depression. The graphs in figures 4.4 and 4.5 illustrate the severity of the recession. These graphs plot U.S. economic growth and unemployment rates between 1975 and 1995. The heavy vertical lines represent the start and end of the Reagan administration.

The financial press often defines a recession as having occurred when there are two or more consecutive quarters of negative economic growth. The National Bureau of Economic Research (NBER) definition, however, is more flexible, calling a recession "a significant decline in economic activity, spread across the economy, lasting more than a few months." (Business Cycle Dating Committee 2003). Using the two consecutive quarters criterion, figure 4.4 shows that the nation had also experienced a recession during the 1980 election year. The NBER concurred with this conclusion (Business Cycle Dating Committee 2003). However, economic growth had turned positive by the last quarter of 1980, and the economy grew marginally over the next year.

Less than a month after assuming office, President Reagan formally proposed the Economic Recovery Tax Act of 1981. The purpose of this legislation was to stimulate the economy and reduce the size of government. The president signed the legislation on August 13, 1981. The legis-

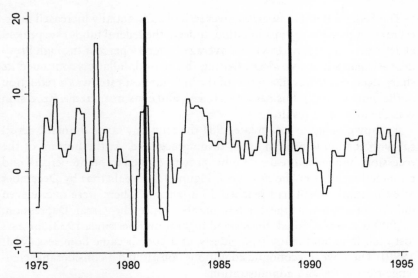

Figure 4.4  Economic Growth between 1975 and 1995

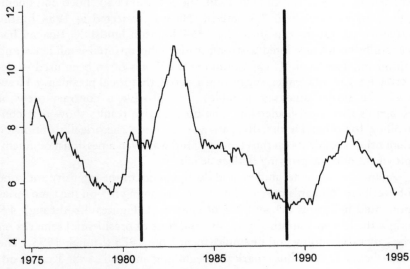

Figure 4.5  Unemployment between 1975 and 1995

lation implemented massive personal and corporate tax cuts and reductions in government spending. The program was based on "trickle down" economics: tax cuts were directed more toward upper-income groups, who were supposed to invest in business and jobs to stimulate higher economic growth.[6]

The Federal Reserve Board, however, had substantially increased interest rates in the fight against inflation. Indeed, the federal funds rate peaked at 19.1 percent in June 1981 and averaged over 14 percent through President Reagan's first two years. During this period, inflation continued its sharp decline. However, a result of the high interest rates was a reduction of the money supply, business investment, and consumer credit. Recession was the inevitable result.

As shown in figure 4.4, in late 1981 the economy saw a dramatic reversal with economic growth again turning negative. At the bottom of the recession, annualized real economic growth dipped to –6.56 percent and remained weak over the next year. Figure 4.5 reveals that by December 1982 unemployment had reached 10.8 percent. There were over eleven million unemployed, the highest number since the Great Depression; 17,000 businesses failed, the second highest number since 1933; farmers lost their land; and many sick, elderly, and poor became homeless (Wolf 1999). These weak economic conditions constituted a considerable challenge for the Reagan administration.

Of course, it is widely believed that President Reagan lived up to these challenges. By election time in 1984, the recession had ended and unemployment was down to 7.3 percent. He was reelected in 1984 by the largest electoral margin since the 1964 Johnson landslide. Reagan has generally been considered a strong leader who inspired confidence and optimism. The label "Great Communicator" has often been used to describe Reagan as a leader, suggesting a strong rhetorical presidency. However, the earlier analyses in tables 3.3a provide a contrary view of Reagan's rhetorical leadership. The quantitative results show that controlling for other factors, Reagan was no more rhetorically optimistic than other presidents on the economy, and was even a pessimist on unemployment and the growing budget deficit.

Again, we can better understand the dynamics of the intensity and tone of President Reagan's public remarks by "zooming in" on the time series presented in figures 2.1 and 2.2 of chapter 2. Figures 4.6 through 4.9 graph the lowess smoothed intensity and tone of presidential remarks on the general economy and unemployment from 1975 through 1995.[7] The outer heavy vertical lines mark the beginning and end of the Reagan administration. The center heavy vertical line marks the peak of the recession, defined here as the point of highest unemployment.

Consider first President Reagan's rhetoric as he was trying to pass the Economic Recovery Tax Act of 1981. Figures 4.6 and 4.7 reveal that during this early period the president actually talked less about the economy and unemployment. Figures 4.8 and 4.9 show that Reagan's rhetoric was no more or less optimistic during these seven months than at the time of his inauguration. Thus, the president neither "talked down" nor

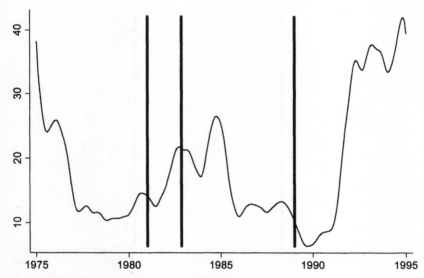

Figure 4.6  Lowess Smoothed Economy Rhetoric Intensity

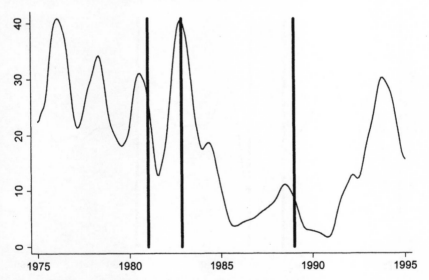

Figure 4.7  Lowess Smoothed Unemployment Rhetoric Intensity

"talked up" the economy during the period when he was attempting to pass significant economic legislation.

Starting in late 1981, however, it became clear that the United States was experiencing another recession. After this time, the data show that Reagan talked a lot more about the general economy and unemployment. Figure 4.7 shows that the intensity of the president's rhetoric on unemployment

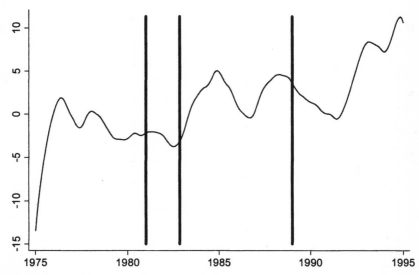

Figure 4.8  Lowess Smoothed Economy Rhetoric Tone

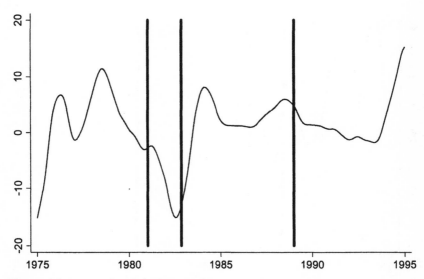

Figure 4.9  Lowess Smoothed Unemployment Rhetoric Tone

increased sharply to peak during the month of the highest unemployment and then sharply declined as unemployment declined. Figure 4.6 shows that rhetoric on the general economy reached an intermediate peak this same month, but did not peak globally until the 1984 election year. Reagan talked a lot about the economy in general terms during the 1984 election year, but deemphasized specific problems such as unemployment and inflation. After the 1984 election there was significantly less presidential rhetoric on the economy and unemployment.

What was the tone of President Reagan's remarks over this period? Figures 4.8 and 4.9 reveal that Reagan was not an optimist, but a pessimist during the 1982–83 recession, particularly on unemployment. On the general economy, presidential rhetoric remained significantly negative between the election and the worst of the recession. It was only after unemployment turned down that presidential rhetoric turned more positive. The optimism of Reagan's remarks on the general economy peaked in the 1984 election year, suggesting a response to electoral incentives.

President Reagan's rhetoric on unemployment was very pessimistic during the recession. Indeed, a look back at figure 2.2 shows that Reagan was more pessimistic about unemployment than any other president. Following the downturn in unemployment in December 1983, the president's public remarks became increasingly positive. Presidential optimism on unemployment peaked in the 1984 election year, again suggesting a response to electoral incentives. Thus, the empirical evidence shows that Reagan mirrored the downs and ups of the economy and political incentives. As the economy declined, the president was a pessimist; as the economy improved, the president became an optimist. The president was also optimistic during the 1984 election.

What specifically did President Reagan say about the economy through this period? On January 26, 1982, in his State of the Union message, President Reagan alluded to the economy seven times. His remarks on the economy were not lengthy, but were decidedly positive, even in the face of the oncoming recession. Here are some excerpts from that speech:

> Late in 1981 we sank into the present recession, largely because continued high interest rates hurt the auto industry and construction. And there was a drop in productivity, and the already high unemployment increased. This time, however, things are different. We have an economic program in place, completely different from the artificial quick fixes of the past. It calls for a reduction of the rate of increase in government spending, and already that rate has been cut nearly in half. . . . Already interest rates are down to 15 3/4 percent, but they must still go lower. Inflation is down from 12.4 percent to 8.9, and for the month of December it was running at an annualized rate of 5.2 percent. If we had not acted as we did, things would be far worse for all Americans than they are today. . . . A year ago, Americans' faith in their governmental process was steadily declining. Six out of 10 Americans were saying they were pessimistic about their future. A new kind of defeatism was heard. Some said our domestic problems were uncontrollable, that we had to learn to live with this seemingly endless cycle of high inflation and high unemployment. . . . The economy will face difficult moments

in the months ahead. But the program for economic recovery that is in place will pull the economy out of its slump and put us on the road to prosperity and stable growth by the latter half of this year. And that is why I can report to you tonight that in the near future the state of the Union and the economy will be better—much better—if we summon the strength to continue on the course that we've charted.

Contrary to the president's predictions, economic growth remained negative for all of 1982, and unemployment did not return to pre-recession levels until October 1984, a month before the election. As conditions worsened, the tone of Reagan's public remarks grew more cautious. The president consistently cast blame on prior administrations and policies for the nation's economic woes. His rhetoric was often a mix of realism about the poor state of the economy, combined with a hope that administration policies would effectively address the problems. Following are excerpts from various speeches, news conferences, and public appearances that illustrate the tone of Reagan's remarks during the 1982 recession:

- Remarks on United States Agricultural Policy to Representatives of Agricultural Publications and Organizations, March 22, 1982—"Our recovery program was passed too late to avert the present painful slump brought about by past pump-priming and those 21 1/2 percent interest rates. There's no quick fix for the economy or for our farmers. . . . Some farmers will not make it through this difficult period of readjustment. But I think the vast majority will. And they're going to discover a better environment to conduct their business and realize a meaningful profit."
- Remarks at the Legislative Conference of the National Association of Realtors, March 29, 1982—"This administration holds no patent on recession. We didn't invent sky-high interest rates and inflation or the tragedy of unemployment. Those problems were in place long before we took office. . . . Our program has already begun to work. . . . These economic gains are early harbingers of recovery, signs that have strong implications for future prosperity."
- Remarks at a Question and Answer Session with Students at St. Peter's Catholic Elementary School in Geneva, Illinois, April 15, 1982—"Question. Mr. President, when do you think there will be more jobs for people? The President. More jobs for people? The answer to that has to be making it possible for the economy to expand, and by that I mean with this great unemployment, we're down now to where many industries are only working at a fraction of their capacity to produce. And this has been, I think, because the

government over the years has been taking an increasing amount out of the earnings of the people and the gross national product."

- Remarks at the Opening Ceremonies for the Knoxville International Energy Exposition (World's Fair) in Tennessee, May 1, 1982— "Now, we still have a long way to go before our economy is back in shape. And this recession is causing great pain to too many of our people. But there was a thing called the misery index that was created in the 1976 Presidential campaign. . . . Well, in the 1980 campaign, they didn't mention the misery index, because it had risen to 20.8 percent. I'm happy to tell you the misery index is now currently 9.8 percent."

- Remarks and a Question and Answer Session in Los Angeles at a Meeting with Editors and Broadcasters from Western States, July 1, 1982—"Historically, whenever the economy hit a slowdown or recession in the past, the hounds of big government started their ritualistic baying, and there were demands for all sorts of pump-priming, make-work programs, public-service jobs, increased spending, and bigger deficits. You remember how we were always told with those deficits not to worry about the debt; we were told that we owe to ourselves. Well, during our present economic troubles we've managed not only to stifle the calls for government spending and expansion or intervention, but we've actually attacked the root causes of the recession by reducing taxes, dramatically slowing the rate of growth in Federal spending, and cutting and streamlining hundreds of Federal regulations, and getting a firm hand on inflation."

- Remarks at a News Conference, July 28, 1982—"Back-to-back decades of red ink spending have brought our economy to its knees. Long years of runaway inflation, interest rates, and high taxes had robbed people of their earnings and weakened every family's ability to pay its bills and save for the future. The American people understand that we need fundamental reform—reform that goes beyond promises and gives them real protection for their earnings. They want this government to draw the line and to pass without delay a constitutional amendment making balanced budgets the law of the land."

- Address to the Nation on Federal Tax and Budget Reconciliation Legislation, August 16, 1982—"There's an old saying we've all heard a thousand times about the weather and how everyone talks about it but no one does anything about it. Well, many of you must be feeling that way about the present state of our economy. Certainly there's a lot of talk about it, but I want you to know we're doing something about it. . . . I'm sure you've heard that 'we're proposing the largest single tax increase in history.' The truth is we're proposing nothing of the kind. And then there's the one that 'our economic recovery program has failed, so I've abandoned it and turned to increasing taxes instead of trying to reduce Federal spending.' Well, don't you believe that one either."

- Address to the Nation on the Economy, October 13, 1982—"In recent days all of us have been swamped by a sea of economic statistics—some good, some bad, and some just plain confusing. . . . The value of the dollar is up around the world. Interest rates are down by 40 percent. The stock and bond markets surge upward. Inflation is down 59 percent. Buying power is going up. Some economic indicators are down; others are up. But the dark cloud of unemployment hangs over the lives of 11 million of our friends, neighbors, and family. . . . Now, I don't pretend for a moment that, in 21 months, we've been able to undo all the damage to our economy that has built up over more than 20 years. . . . We've still got a long way to go before we restore our prosperity. But what I can report to you tonight, my fellow Americans, is that at long last your government has a program in place that faces our problems and has already started solving them. . . . We can do it, my fellow Americans, by staying the course."

- Remarks and a Question and Answer Session during a United States Chamber of Commerce Teleconference on Job Training Programs, November 19, 1982—"While we've made solid progress against the disease that crippled our economy—the runaway inflation, taxes, and interest rates—unemployment remains far too high. It is unacceptable. . . . We can take action to lower structural unemployment and to promote more savings and investment—the keys to stronger growth, more jobs, and a higher standard of living. . . . Now, one such initiative, the Job Training Partnership Act, is the subject of this meeting today."

Throughout 1982, President Reagan's remarks offered a mixed message. He consistently acknowledged the poor economic conditions, but he also shifted blame to earlier administrations and policies. His early rhetoric was often rooted in classic "free market" and "anti-tax" ideologies for which he was so famous. However, as economic conditions worsened, Reagan offered new economic prescriptions such as the 1982 tax increase (see table 3.1), a balanced budget amendment, and the Job Training Partnership Act. He also consistently expressed confidence that his administration's policies would be effective. His message on the future economic outlook was positive. His typical remarks on unemployment, however, were guarded.

By the end of 1982, economic growth had turned positive and inflation was below 4 percent. However, unemployment was at its worst level since the Great Depression and was continuing upward. In spite of renewed economic growth and reduced inflation, American economic confidence was very low.[8] Between the start of the recession and December 1983, President Reagan's job approval rating averaged only 44 percent and fell as low as 37 percent by January 1983. These were the conditions surrounding Reagan's 1983 State of the Union message. This message was devoted almost entirely to the economy.

> As we gather here tonight, the state of our Union is strong, but our economy is troubled. For too many of our fellow citizens—farmers, steel and auto workers, lumbermen, black teenagers, working mothers—this is a painful period. We must all do everything in our power to bring their ordeal to an end. . . . We have a long way to go, but thanks to the courage, patience, and strength of our people, America is on the mend. . . . The problems we inherited were far worse than most inside and out of government had expected; the recession was deeper than most inside and out of government had predicted. Curing those problems has taken more time and a higher toll than any of us wanted. Unemployment is far too high. . . . This recovery will bring with it a revival of economic confidence and spending for consumer items and capital goods—the stimulus we need to restart our stalled economic engines. . . . The inflationary expectations that led to a 21 1/2 percent interest prime rate and soaring mortgage rates 2 years ago are now reduced by almost half. . . . So, interest rates have tumbled, paving the way for recovery in vital industries like housing and autos. The early evidence of that recovery has started coming in. . . . No domestic challenge is more crucial than providing stable, permanent jobs for all Americans who want to work. The recovery program will provide jobs for most, but others will need special help and training for new skills. Shortly, I will submit to the Congress the Employment Act of 1983, designed to get at the special problems of the long-term unemployed, as well as young people trying to enter the job market. . . . We who are in government must take the lead in restoring the economy.

One month after the 1983 State of the Union message, unemployment began to improve. However, the unemployment rate required another fifteen months to return to pre-recession levels. During this period as the economy improved, President Reagan's public comments mirrored the increasingly positive news about the economy and unemployment. He touted the success of his policies and applauded the new economic expansion. He also frequently cautioned that unemployment is a lagging indicator that is unlikely to improve as rapidly as the rest of the economy. Here are some excerpts from his remarks over this period:

- Remarks and a Question and Answer Session with Reporters on Domestic and Foreign Policy Issues, February 4, 1983—"Today, millions of Americans can take heart. Unemployment has finally started down. This dip in unemployment, coming just after the word of higher retail sales, higher auto sales, is one more sign that America is on the mend."
- Remarks at the National Conference on the Dislocated Worker in Pittsburgh, Pennsylvania, April 6, 1983—"The leading economic indicators, and you probably know, are positive, and I can tell you, so am I. January's surge was the largest in 33 years. The indicators are up for February as well. The double-digit inflation of 1980 has been knocked down to 0.4 percent in the last 6 months, the lowest 6-month rate in nearly 22 years. And the prime interest rate, which was 21.5 percent when we took office, is down to 10.5 percent today, and we're not finished with it yet. Housing starts and permits are at the highest level since September of 1979. Unemployment, while still painfully high, has decreased to 10.3 percent from a 10.8 percent peak in December."
- Remarks at a Fund-Raising Dinner Honoring Former Representative John M. Ashbrook in Ashland, Ohio, May 9, 1983—"Now, all of us hope, of course, that the unemployment situation will ease much more quickly than current predictions suggest. But if past recessions were the rule, unemployment will remain a lagging indicator in an otherwise brightening economy, so the unemployed will be among the last to feel the benefits of the recovery."
- Radio Address to the Nation on Economic and Fair Housing Issues, July 9, 1983—"In recent weeks, even the gloomiest critics have had trouble denying that things are getting better for you and your families. The number of people working is up 1.1 million from last December. Unemployment remains too high, but it's coming down— 9.8 percent in June, as announced yesterday. We're seeing strong economic growth, and we're seeing it while inflation is at its lowest level in a decade—3 1/2 percent over the last year. This sharply lower inflation and the first decent tax cut since the 1960's are allowing families to keep more of their own earnings to spend or save. Contrary to propaganda blasts you hear, America is heading in a better direction today than before."
- Remarks at a Fund-Raising Dinner of the Republican National Hispanic Assembly, September 14, 1983—"The cumulative effect of all our economic efforts is now being felt. That's why they don't call it

Reaganomics anymore. [*laughter*] As they say down at Cape Canaveral, we have liftoff. Our economy is lifting off, and it's because of the policies that we've been passing over the past 2 1/2 years."

- Remarks at the Biennial Convention of the National Federation of Republican Women in Louisville, Kentucky, October 7, 1983—"But you know that the best clue that our program is working is our critics don't call it Reaganomics anymore. [*laughter*] Unemployment, which, tragically, is often the last indicator to turn around in a recovery, is on a downward path."

- Radio Address to the Nation on the American Family, December 3, 1983—"If we strengthen families, we'll help reduce poverty and the whole range of other social problems. We can begin by reducing the economic burdens of inflation and taxes, and we're doing this. Since 1980 inflation has been chopped by three-fourths. Taxes have been cut for every family that earns a living, and we've increased the tax credit for child care. Yesterday we learned that our growing economy reduced unemployment to 8.2 percent last month. The payroll employment figure went up by 370,000 jobs."

President Reagan's remarks on the economy continued along this trajectory during the 1984 election year. As economic conditions continued to improve, he highlighted favorable economic statistics in comparison to those of earlier administrations and times. He also increasingly touted the success of his administration's policies in overcoming economic problems.

The preceding evidence again suggests that President Reagan's remarks followed the path of the economy. During the worst of the recession, the president's remarks were pessimistic, especially on unemployment. The president frequently cast blame on others and previous policies for the poor state of the economy. Throughout the crisis, his remarks were cautiously laced with optimism about the ultimate success of his policies and the future. As the economy improved through 1983–84, his caution disappeared and remarks became ever more positive along all economic dimensions. By the time of the 1984 election, Reagan was perceived by many to be a strong economic leader. The favorable momentum of the economy fed the increased public perceptions of strong economic leadership, ultimately resulting in reelection in November 1984.

## PRESIDENT CLINTON AND THE DEFICIT

President Clinton's personal style was decidedly optimistic with respect to the economy. Indeed, the graphs and statistical analyses in chapter 2 show that he was far more intense and optimistic than all other presidents.

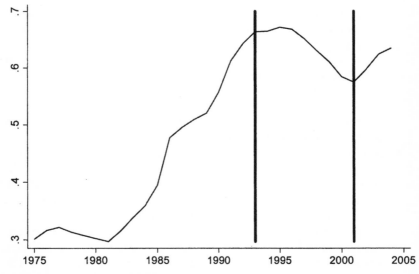

Figure 4.10 Debt-GDP Ratio between 1975 and 2005

Of course, he also served during the longest economic expansion in modern U.S. history, so there was reason to be optimistic.

At the start of the Clinton administration, however, there was reason for concern about the economy. There had been another recession in 1991. At the start of the Clinton administration, the recession had technically been over for more than a year. However, the employment situation had again lagged significantly behind the economic recovery. Unemployment peaked at 7.8 percent in July 1992 and remained near this level at election time in November.

Another cause for concern was that the government faced a serious fiscal crisis. To provide a sense of the dynamics of the problem, figures 4.10 and 4.11 show the federal debt to GDP ratio and federal deficit between 1975 and 2005. The federal debt as a percentage of GDP was 66.4 percent when President Clinton entered office, the highest level since the 1950s, when government was paying down the large debt for World War II. The annual federal deficit that was adding to the federal debt was at its highest level since World War II. Interest payments on the growing federal debt were consuming a large proportion of the federal budget, crowding out important programs. Financing the growing deficits placed the federal government in direct competition with private investors for money, thereby raising interest rates and putting a damper on U.S. economic growth.

During the 1992 election, presidential candidate H. Ross Perot was partially responsible for increasing the visibility of the federal government's

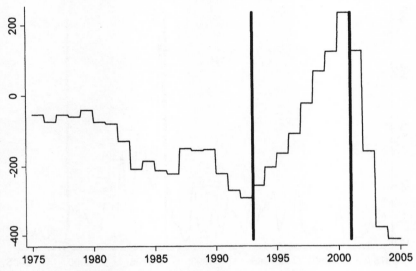

Figure 4.11  Federal Surplus/Deficit from 1975 through 2005

financial problems. Running as an independent Reform Party candidate, he frequently focused "infomercials" on the federal debt. These spot-ads included Perot's colorful graphs and interesting humor. He was the first third-party candidate to participate in the presidential debates, where he also raised this issue. Perot polled 19 percent of the popular vote in the 1992 election, which suggested much dissatisfaction with politics as usual.

While Perot raised the visibility of the federal debt and deficits, the public remained far more concerned about the general economy and unemployment. At the time President Clinton took office in January 1993, the Gallup Most Important Problem Survey showed that 83 percent of respondents viewed some dimension of the economy as the most important problem facing the nation. Fully 37 percent of respondents viewed the economy generally as most important, 27 percent viewed unemployment as most important, with only around 9 percent viewing the federal deficit as such. Clearly, the public viewed economic performance as critical, but few linked the federal deficit to the economy.

President Clinton did not make the federal deficit a major campaign theme in the 1992 election. Nevertheless, he focused heavily on the deficit soon after his inauguration. Again, we can gain a sense of the dynamics of the president's rhetoric by "zooming in" on the longer time series of chapter 2. Figures 4.12 and 4.13 contain lowess smoothed plots of the intensity and tone of the president's rhetoric on the deficit from 1975 through 2005. The heavy vertical lines mark the beginning and end of the Clinton administration.[9]

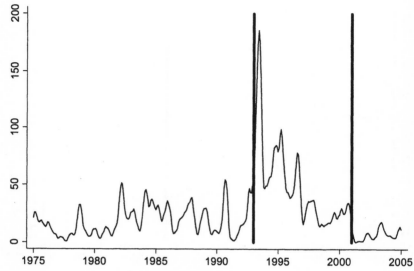

Figure 4.12 Lowess Smoothed Deficit Rhetoric Intensity

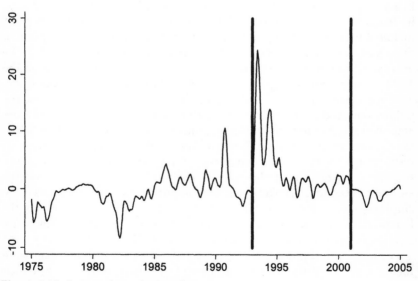

Figure 4.13 Lowess Smoothed Deficit Rhetoric Tone

President Clinton made tackling the federal deficit a major policy priority immediately after assuming office. Figure 4.12 shows a very sharp increase in the intensity of presidential rhetoric on the deficit beginning in February 1993. The sharp peak up front in Clinton's term is the seven-month period when he was campaigning successfully for passage of economic stimulus/deficit control legislation. Moreover, the graph shows that the deficit was an important focus of presidential rhetoric during Clinton's entire first term. Over this period, he made an average of seventy-seven remarks per month on the federal deficit. He spoke more frequently about the deficit than any president before or after. He also spoke more frequently about the deficit than any other economic issue during his administration.

President Clinton also stands in stark contrast with other presidents because of the optimistic tone of his remarks on the deficit. Figure 4.13 shows that soon after the inauguration, the president became highly positive about addressing the deficit problem. Again, the sharp peak up front in Clinton's term is the period when he was campaigning for economic stimulus/deficit control legislation. The data show that between May and August 1993, when the legislation was passed, the president made on average of thirty more optimistic than pessimistic comments on the deficit per month. The president continued to be optimistic about the deficit through his first term. No other president had exhibited such optimism about a problem that had persisted since the early 1970s.

So what specifically did President Clinton say about the economy and federal deficit over this period? In his inaugural address of January 20, 1993, President Clinton emphasized the challenges ahead in making America more prosperous, while at the same time making government more accountable for its financial and economic obligations. Here are some excerpts from that speech:

> Raised in unrivaled prosperity, we inherit an economy that is still the world's strongest but is weakened by business failures, stagnant wages, increasing inequality, and deep divisions among our own people. . . . We know we have to face hard truths and take strong steps, but we have not done so; instead, we have drifted. And that drifting has eroded our resources, fractured our economy, and shaken our confidence. Though our challenges are fearsome, so are our strengths. . . . We must do what no generation has had to do before. We must invest more in our own people, in their jobs, and in their future, and at the same time cut our massive debt. And we must do so in a world in which we must compete for every opportunity. It will not be easy. It will require sacrifice, but it can be done and done fairly, not choosing sacrifice for its own sake but for our own sake. We must provide for our Nation the

way a family provides for its children. . . . We must do what America does best: offer more opportunity to all and demand more responsibility from all. It is time to break the bad habit of expecting something for nothing from our Government or from each other. Let us all take more responsibility not only for ourselves and our families but for our communities and our country.

One day after his inaugural address, President Clinton released a message to the leadership in Congress through his director of communications. The message was that pursuant to the Balanced Budget and Emergency Deficit Control Act of 1985, he had made a technical adjustment that prevented across-the-board reductions in accounts such as national defense that could "undermine the credibility of economic and budget estimates." The previous Bush administration had in three successive years adjusted such accounts to make the federal deficit appear less serious. The message also stated, "President Clinton will soon put before Congress a real economic program aimed at reducing the deficit and providing long-term economic growth." While these quick actions were not broadly publicized, they do highlight the immediate priority the new president placed on the economy and deficit reduction.

President Clinton made stimulating the economy and deficit reduction the primary domestic policy initiative in 1993. A little less than a month after the inauguration, the president put forth his plan for economic stimulus through deficit reduction.

- Address Before a Joint Session of Congress on Administration Goals (State of the Union), February 17, 1993—"Our Nation needs a new direction. Tonight I present to you a comprehensive plan to set our Nation on that new course. . . . I well remember 12 years ago President Reagan stood at this very podium and told you and the American people that if our national debt were stacked in thousand-dollar bills, the stack would reach 67 miles into space. Well, today that stack would reach 267 miles. . . . We have to cut the deficit because the more we spend paying off the debt, the less tax dollars we have to invest in jobs and education and the future of this country. And the more money we take out of the pool of available savings, the harder it is for people in the private sector to borrow money at affordable interest rates for a college loan for their children, for a home mortgage, or to start a new business."

Following his February 17th speech to Congress announcing the legislative proposals, the president continued his public campaign for an economic stimulus and deficit reduction package. He spoke at town meetings, news conferences, radio addresses, live television talk shows, and other events, rarely missing a chance to plug his plan. Here are some representative remarks by President Clinton during this period:

- Remarks on the Economic Program in St. Louis, Missouri, February 18, 1993—"Today as we speak, a lot of big corporate executives are endorsing this plan, even though their income tax bills will go up, their companies' bills will go up, because they want a healthy, strong, well-educated, vibrant America with an investment climate that's good, with stable interest rates, with a declining deficit, with a health care issue addressed, and with a country that can grow into the 21st century."

- Exchange with Reporters Prior to a Meeting with the Congressional Black Caucus, March 8, 1993—"Let me just make the economic argument. Our deficit reduction package—and Senator after Senator said today, you know, that this is the most credible budget I've seen in 15 or 17 or however many years—it is producing the desired results: low interest rates, stock market back up and doing well."

- Remarks on Signing Enabling Legislation for the National Commission to Ensure a Strong Competitive Airline Industry, and an Exchange with Reporters, April 7, 1993—"Investment and deficit reduction are long-term ingredients for making the recovery durable, and we've gone a long way toward doing that over the long run."

- Nomination for an Assistant Secretary of the Treasury, May 14, 1993—"Look at the progress. Just 3 months ago, I submitted to Congress a balanced economic plan that asked everyone to work together to invest a little more in deficit reduction today, so that we can all enjoy better jobs and higher incomes tomorrow. It says we can do what no generation has ever been called upon to do before, that we can reduce our deficit sharply and still increase investment wisely in jobs and education and new technology, because we must do both to be a competitive America, to create more jobs and economic growth."

- Remarks at City Hall in Philadelphia, May 28, 1993—"We said yes to a brighter future to America, yes to lower deficits, yes to more jobs, yes to higher incomes, yes to a future in which we have a real chance to compete and win. Things are going in the right direction. Stay with us. Fight with us. Help to lift this country up, and believe in its future. And we can do it."

- The President's News Conference, June 17, 1993—"We began to see a substantial drop in long-term interest rates after the election when Secretary of the Treasury Bentsen announced that we were going to have a serious deficit reduction plan that would include entitlement cuts, other budget cuts, tax increases on the wealthy, and an energy tax."

- The President's Radio Address, June 19, 1993—"Most importantly, if we pass this plan, there will be a big payoff down the road for Americans who work hard and play by the rules. A lower deficit and a healthier economy means more jobs, lower interest rates, more opportunity, and more rewards for your hard work. That's why I'm fighting for this change."

- Remarks to the American and Korean Chambers of Commerce in Seoul, July 11, 1993—"The positives are that, because of the progress of the deficit reduction package, we've got long-term interest rates down now to a 20-year low, tens of billions of dollars being generated back into the economy through refinancing of homes and business loans, about a million new jobs coming into this economy in the first 6 months of this year as compared with about a million in the previous 3 years."

In spite of the president's optimistic remarks about the benefits of deficit reduction, the negotiations over the economic stimulus and deficit reduction packages were fierce (Quirk and Hinchliffe 1996). In trying to marshal the necessary votes to pass the legislation, President Clinton often went public to apply pressure on Congress and specific members involved in the negotiations. When those efforts seemed ineffective, he made a major televised address to the nation on August 3, 1993.

This week, Congress will cast a crucial vote on my plan for economic recovery. In a comprehensive economic plan, there are always places for give and take, but from the first day to this day, I have stood firm on certain ideas and ideals that are at the heart of this plan. Tonight I can report to you that every one of those principles is contained in the final version of the plan: first, the largest deficit reduction in history, nearly $500 billion, with more spending cuts than tax increases. Rather than the games and gimmicks of the past, this plan has 200 specific spending cuts, and it reduces Government spending by more than $250 billion. . . . Why must we take extraordinary action now? Well, this chart shows you why. America faces a choice. We can continue on the path of higher deficits and lower growth, or we can make a fundamental change to improve our Nation's economy by adopting my economic plan. Now, it won't be easy, and it won't be quick. But it is necessary. Without deficit reduction, we can't have sustained economic growth. . . . At this exceptional moment of promise, why are so many in Washington so reluctant to take action? Why is it so hard for so many in this city to break the bad habits of the past and take the steps we all know we have to take? . . . I need your help. I need for you to tell the people's representatives to get on with the people's business. Tell them to change the direction of the economy and do it now, so that we can start growing again, producing jobs again, and moving our country forward again.

On August 10, 1993, President Clinton signed the Omnibus Budget Reconciliation Act that implemented his plans for the economy and deficit reduction. The legislation passed in the House of Representatives by only two votes, and Vice-President Al Gore cast the deciding vote in the Senate.

It is unclear whether President Clinton's "going public" strategy affected the legislative outcome. The president's efforts, however, made Americans significantly more aware of the pressing nature of the federal deficit. Evidence from the Gallup Most Important Problem Survey demonstrates the effectiveness of the president's remarks in raising public concern. In August 1992 before Clinton was elected, the proportion of Americans viewing the deficit as the most important problem facing the nation was 4 percent. By August 1993 when the legislation was passed, this proportion had risen to 15 percent. As Clinton continued to talk about the problem during the 1996 election, the proportion had increased to 26 percent.

The preceding evidence suggests that President Clinton's public remarks on the economy during his first term were driven by perceptions of a crisis in federal government finances. Immediately upon entering office, he sensed a problem with federal finances that threatened the economy. He had campaigned in 1992 on the promise of promoting a sound U.S. economy. Therefore, he put forth plans both to stimulate the economy and address the fiscal crisis. He worked hard to convince Americans and Congress of the urgency of the crisis, but he did so in a positive way. As he campaigned for the economic stimulus and deficit reduction package, the underlying message was continually positive. The president claimed that deficit reduction would bring a bright future for the long-term health of the U.S. economy.

Ultimately, President Clinton was perceived as a strong rhetorical leader who exercised effective economic leadership. As shown in figure 4.11, the large federal deficit had turned into a near balanced budget by 1997. Between 1998 and 2001, the federal debt was reduced by $559 billion, the largest proportional four-year reduction in American history. With lower interest rates, the economy expanded for a record 112 months, with average quarterly economic growth of around 3.65 percent. During this period, the economy produced twenty-two million new jobs, and the unemployment rate steadily declined to 3.9 percent at the end of his administration.

## President George W. Bush and Taxation

During the 2000 election campaign, presidential candidate George W. Bush advocated a large tax cut. The proposed reduction was $1.6 trillion over ten years, roughly three times that proposed by Democratic candidate Al Gore. The projected budget surplus that had developed during the Clinton administration was $2.17 trillion over ten years (Congressional Budget Office 2000). Both candidates recognized the need to direct some of that money toward lower taxes. The two proposals, however, differed sharply in magnitude, as well as in how the surplus was to be allocated (Iyengar 2000). Candidate Gore wanted smaller, targeted tax cuts for middle- and lower-income groups, and to shore up the Social Security and the healthcare systems (Gore 2000). In contrast, candidate Bush wanted a larger reduction in overall tax rates, as well as abolition of the estate tax and the marriage penalty (Bush 2000).

Candidate Bush's tax proposal was probably crafted to shore up support by the Republican base during the 2000 election. When he assumed office in January 2001, however, there was little economic justification for a large tax cut. The most recent economic reports showed the economy was in its 112th month of economic expansion with the unemployment rate at 3.9 percent, inflation at 3.4 percent, and a $237 billion federal budget surplus. With unemployment so low and the economy sizzling, a large tax cut could be inflationary. Indeed, the Federal Reserve Board had increased the interest rate six times between June 1999 and May 2000 to head off inflation. When Chairman of the Federal Reserve Board Alan Greenspan testified before Congress on January 25, 2001, about the outlook for the federal budget, he urged a gradual approach to cutting taxes and reducing the budget surplus (Greenspan 2001).

There were some hints, however, that the economy might be slowing. In November 2000, a drop occurred in the University of Michigan's Index of Consumer Sentiment. This may have been due to the intense public focus on the Florida election debacle. It may also have been related to stock market declines earlier in 2000. Due to the stock market decline, the total financial assets of households had decreased by 5 percent, or $1.7 trillion, from the end of 1999 to the end of 2000 (Weller 2001). Still, there were only hints that the longest economic expansion of the modern era might soon be ending.

On January 24 after the inauguration, a reporter asked the president how he could convince congressional Democrats to go along with the large proposed tax cut. He responded "I look forward to explaining to any Member that's concerned about tax relief and why, why I proposed it. And I think the evidence is going to become more and more clear that the economy is—it's not as hopeful as we'd like, which I hope will strengthen my case" (Remarks Prior to a Meeting with Bipartisan Congressional Leaders and an Exchange with Reporters, January 24, 2001).

Later on February 2, the president spoke to Republicans at a congressional retreat. He said,

> It is so important for us to understand some facts. One, the economy is slowing down. And it's important for us to combine good monetary policy with good fiscal policy. . . . I come from the school of thought that by cutting marginal rates for everybody who pays taxes is a good way to help ease the pain of what *may be* an economic slowdown. I'm going to make that case over and over and over again until we get a bill through. (Remarks at the Republican Congressional Retreat in Williamsburg, Virginia, February 2, 2001)

The economy actually did experience a slowdown in 2001. On November 26, 2001, the National Bureau of Economic Research's (NBER) Business Cycle Dating Committee stated that a peak in business activity had occurred in March 2001.[10] A peak marks the end of an economic expansion and the beginning of a recession. The committee later concluded that a trough in business activity had occurred in November 2001.[11] A trough marks the end of a recession and the beginning of an economic expansion. Using this criterion, the NBER initially concluded that a recession had occurred that lasted about eight months. Subsequently, the NBER revised its statistics for economic growth to reveal that there were not actually two consecutive periods of economic downturn over this period. However, even after revising the economic statistics, the NBER did not declassify the period from calling it a recession.

According to the NBER, there have been ten recessions since World War II. Of these, the 2001 recession was the mildest on record. In an NBER working paper, Yale Economist William D. Nordhaus (2002) classified 2001 as a Category I recession, which constitutes a "pause in economic activity," rather than an economic downturn, recession, or depression. To illustrate the dynamics of the 2001 recession relative to other recessions, figures 4.14 and 4.15 graph economic growth and unemployment from 1950 through 2005. The heavy vertical lines mark the beginning and end of the first term of the George W. Bush administration.

Figure 4.14 shows that the period of negative economic growth in 2001 was miniscule compared with prior U.S. recessions. The revised NBER statistics show that the actual decline in economic growth in 2001 occurred in the January and July quarters, and the cumulative decline in economic growth for the January through July quarters was only 0.8 percent.

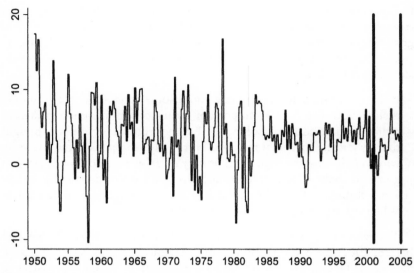

Figure 4.14  Economic Growth from 1990 through 2005

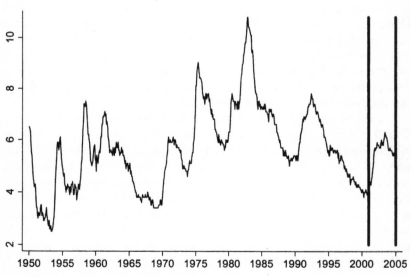

Figure 4.15  Unemployment from 1990 through 2005

Figure 4.15 shows that the increase in unemployment was also mild compared with earlier recessions. By the end of 2001, the unemployment rate had increased to 5.7 percent to finally peak in June 2003 at 6.3 percent. Thus, relative to other recessions the economic statistics did not show that the U.S. economy was in a crisis condition.

Yet, true to his words to congressional Republicans, President George W. Bush used an economic rationale to push for and obtain three tax cuts in three years. As he was campaigning for the tax cuts, the president repeatedly pounded home the message that the U.S. economy was doing poorly and that the cuts were needed to stimulate economic growth and jobs. The 2001 and 2003 tax cuts were the largest and third largest in U.S. history. By the end of his term, the cumulative reduction in expected tax collections due to the legislation was about $2 trillion over ten years, substantially more than the campaign promise.[12]

We can again trace the changing intensity and tone of the president's remarks by "zooming in" on the graphs presented in figures 2.1 and 2.2 of chapter 2. Figures 4.16 and 4.17 plot the lowess smoothed intensity of President George W. Bush's rhetoric on the general economy and unemployment during his first term.[13] Again, the outer heavy vertical lines mark the start and end of the first George W. Bush administration. The inner heavy vertical line marks the month of highest unemployment.

Figure 4.16 shows that the intensity of presidential remarks on unemployment declined very sharply the month President George W. Bush assumed office. He also spoke little about unemployment between 2001 and the 2004 election, *even as unemployment rose*. However, during the 2004 election from August through the end of October, the intensity of presidential remarks increased sharply. Interestingly, once the election was over Bush again said little or nothing about unemployment.

Figure 4.17 shows that between January 2001 and February 2004, President Bush talked about the general economy with about the same intensity as had President Clinton. However, beginning in March 2004 as the election heated up, the intensity of presidential remarks on the general economy also increased very sharply. Indeed, the intensity of Bush's remarks during the 2004 election season significantly exceeded the intense earlier rhetoric of Clinton. Interestingly, Bush's rhetoric on the economy again dropped off sharply in November after the 2004 election. The election year changes for both the unemployment and economy time series suggest that Bush responded strongly to reelection incentives.

While the intensity of President Bush's remarks on the general economy was at times comparable to that of President Clinton, the tone of his remarks was starkly different. Figure 4.18 shows that between January 2001 and June 2003, Bush was far less optimistic on unemployment than

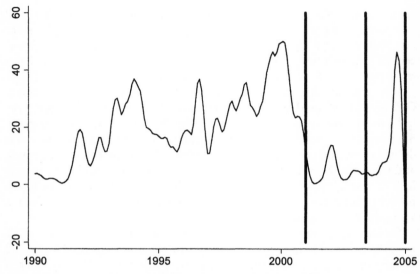

Figure 4.16  Lowess Smoothed Unemployment Rhetoric Intensity

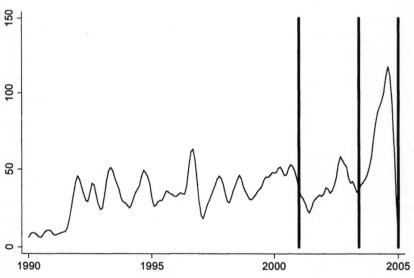

Figure 4.17  Lowess Smoothed Economy Rhetoric Intensity

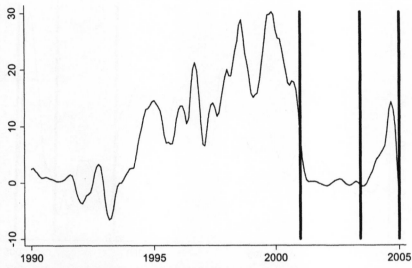

Figure 4.18 Lowess Smoothed Unemployment Rhetoric Tone

was Clinton. Indeed, he was far less optimistic on this issue than most other presidents. Bush's remarks turned significantly more optimistic, however, between August and the end of October 2004. He touted his tax legislation as responsible for declining unemployment. However, he said little in the way of positive remarks about unemployment after the 2004 election had ended.

Similarly, figure 4.19 shows that President Bush was far more negative than any other president on the general economy when he was pushing for tax cuts (see also figure 2.2 in chapter 2). The president repeatedly "talked down" the economy during this period. In late 2003, however, the president turned more positive on the economy. Indeed, beginning in March 2004 the relative optimism of Bush's remarks on the general economy grew significantly beyond that of Clinton to exceed all other presidents. The reason for these changes cannot be ascertained with certainty, but the overall dynamics suggest that Bush was responsive both to institutional prerogatives and political incentives. He "talked down" the economy during the period when he was seeking tax cut legislation. Then he later "talked up" the economy, perhaps in response to reelection incentives flowing from the impending 2004 presidential election.

What specifically did President Bush say over this period? He framed the need for a tax cut in urgent terms on February 27 in his 2001 State of the Union message. Here is an excerpt from that speech:

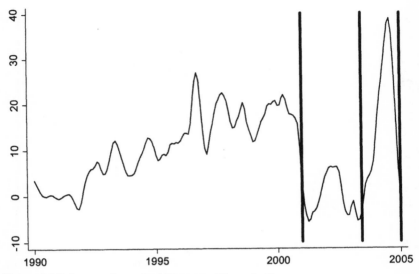

Figure 4.19  Lowess Smoothed Economy Rhetoric Tone

Tax relief is right, and tax relief is urgent. The long economic expansion that began almost 10 years ago is faltering. Lower interest rates will eventually help, but we cannot assume they will do the job all by themselves. Forty years ago, and then 20 years ago, two Presidents, one Democrat, one Republican, John F. Kennedy and Ronald Reagan, advocated tax cuts to, in President Kennedy's words, "get this country moving again." They knew then what we must do now. To create economic growth and opportunity, we must put money back into the hands of the people who buy goods and create jobs. We must act quickly. The Chairman of the Federal Reserve has testified before Congress that tax cuts often come too late to stimulate economic recovery. So I want to work with you to give our economy an important jump-start by making tax relief retroactive. We must act now because it is the right thing to do.

This speech marked the beginning of a presidential campaign to secure the largest tax cut in U.S. history. During the course of the campaign, the president repeatedly stressed the urgency of tax relief in terms of an ongoing economic downturn. Over the next three months, President Bush appeared in various public settings to make remarks that alluded to an economy in poor condition. Here are some representative remarks from this period:

- Remarks in Sioux Falls, South Dakota, March 9, 2001—"This is a plan that is good for the entrepreneur and small-business people. It makes sense to be that way. And by the way, there is a need to make this happen quickly. We got a issue with our economy. It's beginning to sputter. It's beginning to get a little shaky. And one way to make sure that we provide a second wind to the economy is to give people their own money back. That's called economic recovery."

- Remarks Prior to Discussions with Prime Minister Ariel Sharon of Israel and an Exchange with Reporters, March 20, 2001—"Question. Mr. President, yesterday you said that you were very confident about the U.S. economy. Today you said that it's slowing down. Which is it? Are you trying to have it both ways?" President Bush "I was talking about the long-term health of our economy is going to be very strong. . . . We've got some problems, some short-term problems, and if Congress were to act quickly on my tax stimulus package, it would make our recovery quicker."

- Exchange with Reporters in Kansas City, Missouri, March 26, 2001—"Question. Do you agree with your spokesman's formulation, that we're in the middle of a downturn? The President. It has slowed down, and we better do something about it. And that's one of the reasons I'm here in Kansas City, to talk about tax relief as part of an economic stimulus package."

- Remarks in New Orleans, Louisiana, April 25, 2001—"But thanks to the hard work and the phone calls and e-mails of hundreds of Americans from across the country, we have begun to define the parameters. Out of the House came a $1.6 trillion plan, and now the Senate—somewhat reluctant, but nevertheless—they passed a $1.2 trillion plan. Because of you all, because of the voices of America, tax relief is on the way. . . . we have a little slowdown in our economy, and tax relief will help. It's a part of how we recover the steam necessary to get our economy chugging again."

- Statement on House of Representatives Action on the Budget, May 9, 2001—"Today's bipartisan budget vote in the House is a victory for fairness and the American people. I commend Republicans and Democrats for joining together to pass a budget framework that will return money to the taxpayers and provide reasonable spending increases. The economy continues to show troubling signs, and we must take decisive steps, like this vote today, to ensure sound fiscal policy."

- Remarks at a Republican National Committee Gala, May 22, 2001—"I can remember during the campaign, and perhaps you all do as well, about the collective yawn from members in the Fourth Estate about tax relief. People used to say, 'Well, he's just saying that because it might make good politics.' No, Dick Cheney and I talked about tax relief because we thought it was right for the country. This Nation can afford tax relief, and we can't afford not to have it, with our economy slowing down."

- Remarks at a Military Reenlistment Ceremony, May 23, 2001— "The economy needs a shot in the arm, so I call on the House and the Senate to reach an agreement on the final tax relief package this week. The sooner the Congress completes its work, the sooner the American people will have their own money in their own pockets to save and invest as they see fit. Our economy cannot afford any further delays."

The president signed the Economic Growth and Tax Relief Reconciliation Act on June 7, 2001. The legislation reduced taxes by roughly $1.3 trillion over the next ten years. It reduced the estate tax, cut the top four income tax rates, shifted the tax burden away from upper-income groups, and carved out a new 10 percent tax bracket from part of the existing 15 percent bracket. The president had achieved the largest tax cut in U.S. history, thereby keeping a campaign promise to his partisan base.

Three months after the president signed tax relief legislation, a shock occurred that held the potential to do serious damage to the U.S. economy. The September 11th terrorist attacks affected economic confidence,[14] and also had effects on specific industries such as the hospitality, travel, and airline industries. Presidential rhetoric following the attacks emphasized their heinous nature as well as their potential damage to the U.S. economy. Initially, the president expressed confidence in the nation's economic resilience. He later continued to "talk down" the economy, however, to make the case for additional tax relief. Here is a sample of President Bush's remarks from shortly after the attacks through March 9, 2002, when a second tax bill was signed:

- Remarks on Arrival at the White House and an Exchange with Reporters, September 16, 2001—"I understand that there are some businesses that hurt as a result of this crisis. . . . People will be amazed at how quickly we rebuild New York, how quickly people come together to really wipe away the rubble and show the world that we're still the strongest Nation in the world. But I have great faith in the resiliency of the economy."
- Remarks Following a Meeting with Congressional Leaders and an Exchange with Reporters, September 19, 2001—"Question. Sorry to ask another one, but did you mean to say just now that we are in a recession? The President. No, I said—well, I said—let me put it this way—tough economic times. There's no question it's tough times. And Ron, I don't have all the numbers, but let me just say this: I can pick up all the statistics, but make no mistake about it, this has affected our economy in a big way."

- The President's Radio Address, September 22, 2001—"The terrorists who attacked the United States on September 11th targeted our economy, as well as our people. They brought down a symbol of American prosperity, but they could not touch its source. Our country's wealth is not contained in glass and steel. It is found in the skill and hard work and entrepreneurship of our people, and those are as strong today as they were 2 weeks ago. Our economy has had a shock. . . . Yet, for all these challenges, the American economy is fundamentally strong."

- Remarks to Department of Labor Employees, October 4, 2001—"And they've also changed a lot of lives, these evil actions. It's clear, as a result of today's new unemployment claims, that the attack of September the 11th sent a shock wave throughout our economy. And we need to do something about it. And I'm going to lead the Congress in a way that provides the help and stimulus necessary for there to be economic growth." (Note: Unemployment had changed from 4.9 percent in August to 5.0 percent in September prior to the president's remarks on this date.)

- Remarks to Business, Trade, and Agricultural Leaders, October 26, 2001—"Now, there's another front on the war, as well, and that's our economy. And there's no question the terrorists want to cast a shadow of fear on the businesses of America. . . . But it's clear that our economy has been shocked. . . . We believe the best way to stimulate and restore confidence to the economy is not through additional spending, but through tax relief."

- Remarks to the Farm Journal Forum, November 28, 2001—"Yet the terrorist attack of September the 11th, no question, dealt our economy a serious blow. So while we fight our enemies and states that harbor terrorism and while we defend our homeland and our airways, we must take further action to strengthen our economy."

- The President's Radio Address, January 5, 2002—"I made my proposals to create new jobs and help dislocated workers on October the 4th, 3 months and 943,000 lost jobs ago. The House of Representatives accepted my proposals, but the Senate Democratic leadership would not even schedule a vote. Some in the Senate seem to think we can afford to do nothing, that the economy will get better on its own, sooner or later."

- Address before a Joint Session of the Congress on the State of the Union, January 29, 2002—"To achieve these great national objectives—to win the war, protect the homeland, and revitalize our economy—our budget will run a deficit that will be small and short term, so long as Congress restrains spending and acts in a fiscally responsible manner. . . . The way out of this recession, the way to create jobs, is to grow the economy by encouraging investment in factories and equipment and by speeding up tax relief so people have more money to spend."

The president signed the Job Creation and Worker Assistance Act on March 9, 2002. The legislation provided an extension of benefits for unemployed workers. By this time, unemployment was hovering around 5.7 percent and some workers were near exhausting their benefits. The legislation also provided tax relief for businesses and increased the depreciation allowance on new investment.

About a year later, when the economy was obviously no longer in recession, the president initiated yet another effort to achieve a large tax cut. He laid out his recommendations for additional tax relief totaling $550 billion over ten years in the January 28, 2003, State of the Union Message:

> Our first goal is clear: We must have an economy that grows fast enough to employ every man and woman who seeks a job. After recession, terrorist attacks, corporate scandals, and stock market declines, our economy is recovering. Yet, it's not growing fast enough or strongly enough. With unemployment rising, our Nation needs more small businesses to open, more companies to invest and expand, more employers to put up the sign that says, "Help Wanted." Jobs are created when the economy grows. The economy grows when Americans have more money to spend and invest, and the best and fairest way to make sure Americans have that money is not to tax it away in the first place. . . . We should also strengthen the economy by treating investors equally in our tax laws. It's fair to tax a company's profits. It is not fair to again tax the shareholder on the same profits. To boost investor confidence and to help the nearly 10 million seniors who receive dividend income, I ask you to end the unfair double taxation of dividends. Lower taxes and greater investment will help this economy expand.

Over the next several months, the president campaigned for the third largest tax cut in U.S. history. Again, he repeatedly "talked down" the economy while pursuing the proposed measure. Here are excerpts from President Bush's remarks on the economy between February and May, 2003:

- Remarks in a Discussion with Small-Business Owners in Jacksonville, Florida, February 13, 2003—"Now, if the economy is still not as strong as it should be and if Congress has already recognized that tax rate reduction helps economic growth, my message to the United States Congress is: Speed up the growth. . . . This economy needs immediate help. . . . We're recovering from three shocks to the system, and we need a little further wind at the back of this economy."

- Remarks to the National Governors Association Conference, February 24, 2003—"My attitude is, since the economy is not as good as we like it to be, we ought to accelerate the tax relief which they've already planned. That will put about $70 billion immediately into our economy, since I intend to ask for this plan to be made retroactive to January 1st of this year."
- Remarks Following Discussions with Business Leaders, April 15, 2003—"The Nation needs quick action by our Congress on a pro-growth economic package. We need tax relief totaling at least $550 billion to make sure our economy grows. . . . The proposals I announced 3 months ago were designed to address specific weaknesses slowing down our economy and keeping companies from hiring new workers. . . . With the economy as it is, the American people need that relief right away."
- Remarks to Employees of United Defense Industries in Santa Clara, California, May 2, 2003—"Well, listen, our economy needs a shot in the arm now, not 3, 5, or 7 years from now. . . . When I get back to Washington, DC, I want to see a bill on my desk that recognizes, well, that may be a little fast. How about in a couple of weeks after I get back to Washington? [*laughter*] I urge the United States Congress to look at the unemployment numbers that came out today and pass a tax relief plan that will matter, a tax relief plan robust enough so that the people of this country who are looking for work can find a job." (Note: Unemployment increased from 5.8 percent in March to 6 percent in April at the time of the president's remarks.)
- The President's Radio Address, May 10, 2003—"This week with a vote in the House of Representatives, Congress took a positive step towards passage of my jobs-and-growth proposal. The plan I submitted would create more than a million jobs by the end of next year through immediate tax relief for American families and businesses. Since I sent my plan to Congress in January, the need for action on the economy has become even more urgent."

President Bush signed the Job and Growth Tax Relief and Reconciliation Act on May 28, 2003. The legislation provided an additional $350 billion in tax cuts for the nominal purpose of creating more jobs and stimulating economic growth. The legislation again cut income tax rates to shift the tax burden increasingly away from upper-income groups. It also reduced the capital gains tax rate and eliminated double taxation of investment dividends. As Bush stated on signing the legislation, "This law reflects a commonsense economic principle: The best way to have more jobs is to help the people who create new jobs." Thus, the third largest tax cut in U.S. history was again driven by supply side economic principles.

As shown by figures 4.16 through 4.19, President Bush became increasingly intense and optimistic in talking about the economy after he was no longer pursuing tax relief, and as the 2004 election got underway. Here is an excerpt from his 2004 State of the Union message that is representative of this period:

> We have come through recession and terrorist attack and corporate scandals and the uncertainties of war. And because you acted to stimulate our economy with tax relief, this economy is strong and growing stronger. You have doubled the child tax credit from 500 to $1,000, reduced the marriage penalty, begun to phase out the death tax, reduced taxes on capital gains and stock dividends, cut taxes on small businesses, and you have lowered taxes for every American who pays income taxes. Americans took those dollars and put them to work, driving this economy forward. The pace of economic growth in the third quarter of 2003 was the fastest in nearly 20 years; new home construction, the highest in almost 20 years; homeownership rates, the highest ever. Manufacturing activity is increasing. Inflation is low. Interest rates are low. Exports are growing. Productivity is high, and jobs are on the rise. These numbers confirm that the American people are using their money far better than Government would have, and you were right to return it."

These remarks accurately reflect the tone of President Bush's rhetoric on the economy up to the election. Over this period, the president consistently touted his administration's accomplishments in providing tax relief and a more positive outlook for the economy.

Yet, there is also an irony associated with the president's remarks during the 2004 election season. Consider the following comment made just a few weeks before the 2004 election:

- Remarks in a Discussion in Rochester, Minnesota, Oct 20, 2004— "When you get through all the political noise, the facts are clear. Our economy is growing at rates as fast as any in nearly 20 years. . . . The national unemployment rate is 5.4 percent, which is lower than the average rate of the 1970s, the 1980s, and the 1990s."

The president repeated remarks similar to these numerous times in the run-up to the 2004 election. However, the economic growth and unemployment numbers at the time the president was pushing for tax cut legislation were comparable to and also lower than those that existed over the past 20 years and during the 1970s, 1980s, and 1990s.

Prior to the first tax bill, in the first quarter of 2001, economic growth was slow, but unemployment was only 4.4 percent. Prior to the second tax bill, in the first quarter of 2002, the rate of economic growth was 3.4 percent and the unemployment rate was 5.7 percent. Prior to the third tax bill, in the second quarter of 2003, the rate of economic growth was 4.1 percent and the unemployment rate was around 6.0 percent. Over the twenty years prior to the third tax bill, however, the rate of economic growth averaged 3.3 percent. Between 1970 and 2000 the average unemployment rate was 6.4 percent. Thus, the president interpreted the severity of economic conditions to suit his political purposes.

This and earlier evidence suggest that President Bush used economic rhetoric opportunistically. In early 2001, the president told the press and congressional Republicans that he would "talk down" the economy until he had achieved his legislative goals.[15] True to his word, Bush spoke more pessimistically about the nation's economy than any other past president to make the case for two of the three largest tax cuts in U.S. history. He spoke very optimistically about the economy, however, while he was seeking reelection. Indeed, he was more optimistic during this period than any other past president even though economic conditions had not changed all that much.[16] After the 2004 election, the president's optimistic rhetoric fell off significantly. This suggests that Bush's personal style was distinctly different from that of earlier presidents.[17]

## CONCLUSION

We theorized in the previous chapter that the changing intensity and tone of presidential rhetoric on the economy is a function of personal style, institutional prerogatives relating to the economy, and political incentives. We also theorized that differences in personal style might affect presidential responses to institutional prerogatives and Political incentives. The statistical analyses confirmed the theory. The case studies in this chapter, however, refine our understanding of how personal style has differed across presidencies and affected presidential responses to institutional prerogatives and political incentives. Let us now summarize the major themes of this chapter.

First, the case studies show how different presidents have responded to adverse economic conditions. President Carter faced the worst non-war inflationary conditions of the twentieth century. As inflation worsened between 1977 and 1980, he grew more intense and optimistic on inflation than any other president. Indeed, he was never pessimistic on inflation even as it peaked at 14.6 percent in March of 1980. Thus, Carter responded to adverse economic conditions with a positive personal style.

President Reagan was also highly responsive to adverse economic conditions, but in the opposite direction. As economic growth turned negative in late 1981 and unemployment grew to 10.8 percent by December 1982, Reagan became increasingly intense and pessimistic about the economy and unemployment. Indeed, he was more pessimistic about unemployment than any other president. It was only after unemployment started to decline in January 1983 that he became a cheerleader for the economy. President Reagan was not the "eternal optimist" that some have suggested (Associated Press 2004; Will 2004). Rather, he was a "fair weather" optimist who merely responded rhetorically to changing economic conditions. Thus, we could label Reagan's personal style as acquiescent.

President Clinton entered office at the end of a mild recession. Unemployment was declining, but still a problem. Clinton, however, also faced a budget crisis with a federal debt higher than at any time since World War II and large federal deficits. Public opinion did not place deficit reduction high on the list of government priorities when Clinton assumed office. Nevertheless, he pressed for deficit reduction to restore fiscal responsibility and stimulate the economy. During the period when he was pressing for deficit reduction, the president was very intense and optimistic about the economic future. More generally, the analyses show that Clinton was the most optimistic president of the modern era along all economic dimensions.

President George W. Bush was also responsive to adverse economic conditions, but we might also say that he was "hyper-responsive." Not knowing with certainty that the nation was entering a recession,[18] and as unemployment grew slightly, the president became more intense and pessimistic about the economy than any past president. Bush continued to be intensely pessimistic about the economy even as economic growth improved and unemployment declined. Indeed, Bush was "hyper-responsive" to economic conditions that did not differ much from the typical economy of the 1970s through 1990s.

Thus, under adverse economic conditions some presidents attempt to exercise confident leadership. Other presidents respond to adverse conditions with rhetoric that simply mirrors the economy. Still others use adverse economic conditions strategically for political purposes. Which personal style is best is a topic for later chapters. The results presented here, however, do show that personal style matters to the flow of economic rhetoric.

Second, the case studies show that presidents have differed in how they pursued important economic legislation. Following the stagflation era and a mild recession in 1980, President Reagan sought and achieved the largest tax cut in U.S. history up to that time. During the period between proposing and signing the legislation, he was no more intense or optimistic about the U.S. economy than he was when inaugurated. Thus, Reagan's leadership style while pursuing important economic legislation was rhetorically passive.

Presidents Clinton and George W. Bush also pushed for an economic stimulus package following a mild recession. The plan for Clinton's stimulus package was to gain control of the federal deficit, thereby lowering interest rates to stimulate investment, consumption, and economic growth. During his seven-month campaign to achieve a deficit reduction package, he was consistently intense and upbeat about the implications for the economy if the measure were enacted. Clinton's leadership style while pursuing important economic legislation emphasized the positive.

President George W. Bush sought to stimulate the economy through multiple tax cuts intended to put more money directly into people's pockets. During an almost three-year campaign, he was persistently downbeat about the state of the U.S. economy. He continuously stressed the urgency of action and the ill consequences of not implementing his plans. Thus, Bush's leadership style while pursuing important economic legislation emphasized the negative.

Obviously, presidents differ in how they pursue important economic legislation. Which strategy is more appropriate is again a question for later chapters. It is abundantly clear, however, from the evidence that personal style mediates presidential responsiveness to institutional prerogatives.

Finally, the case studies also demonstrate how different presidents have responded to election year incentives. The statistical analysis in the previous chapter showed a strong relationship between election year incentives and the intensity and tone of presidential remarks on the economy. Along all economic dimensions, presidents tend to become more intense during election years. They also tend to be optimists on the general economy and unemployment. The results in this chapter confirm this effect, but also suggest variations across presidencies in the degree of presidential responsiveness to election year incentives.

For example, the graphs for President Carter show no response in either the intensity or tone of inflation rhetoric during the 1980 election. The earlier evidence suggests that President Reagan *may* have responded to reelection incentives when talking about unemployment and the general economy. The evidence is unequivocal, however, that President

George W. Bush turned exceedingly intense and positive on both the economy and unemployment during the 2004 election season. Additionally, he immediately became passive on both dimensions when the election was over. Given the timing and magnitude of responses for Bush, there is little doubt that he was far more responsive to election incentives than earlier presidents.

The evidence in chapters 3 and 4 has shown how and why presidents talk about the economy. In doing so, it has attempted to explain variations in the intensity and tone of the presidents' economic rhetoric. However, does any of this matter for economic and political outcomes? We turn to answer these questions in the next two chapters.

# Do Presidents Affect Public Approval of Their Job Performance through Economic Rhetoric?

> A president, especially, may believe that he personifies the
> government since he was chosen, after all, as the sole
> representative of the entire country. A loss of popularity,
> therefore, can be interpreted as a blow against the American
> system. As a result, his sense of urgency to better his ratings
> increases, and so does his reliance on the techniques of the
> permanent campaign. . . . He falls back on the calculations
> that served him so well in the first place. The citizenry is
> viewed as a mass of fluid voters who can be appeased by
> appearances, occasional drama, and clever rhetoric.
> Campaigning never ends. What was once a forced march
> for votes becomes unceasing forays for public approval.
>
> (Blumenthal 1982, 24)

ALL PRESIDENTS seek the public's approval of their job performance. High public approval is a resource that presidents can use to affect policy (Bond, Fleisher, and Wood 2003; Brace and Hinckley 1992, 1980, 1989, 1997; Neustadt 1960; Ostrom and Simon 1985; Rivers and Rose 1985). It also consistently translates into a larger probability of reelection for presidents and their parties (Brody and Sigelman 1983; Erikson and Wlezien 2004; Holbrook 2004; Lewis-Beck and Rice 1992; Lewis-Beck and Tien 2004; Sigelman 1979). Over the long term, public approval also promotes the perception of a successful presidency, which may enhance a president's historical standing.

Consistent with this goal, presidents and their staffs strongly believe they can shape public opinion (Edwards 2003, chap. 1). As a result, modern presidents have increasingly used a sophisticated communications apparatus to help shape public opinion and bolster their approval ratings (Grossman and Kumar 1981; Maltese 1992). The White House attempts to "spin" the news to place the president in the most favorable light. Presidents engage in a perpetual campaign of public rhetoric to shape public opinion on policies and on their ongoing job performance (Edwards 1983; Kernell 1997; Tulis 1987).

From 1949 to present, the average of Americans approving of the president's job performance has been around 56 percent.[1] This average, however, masks substantial variation across presidencies and through time. President Kennedy had the highest average public approval at 71 percent, while President Truman rated the lowest at 37 percent. President Eisenhower's early public approval was around 74 percent, but this fluctuated with economic conditions and was around 60 percent when he left office. President Kennedy started his presidency with public approval of around 83 percent, but this had fallen to 56 percent the month before he was assassinated. Presidents Johnson, Nixon, and Carter started their presidencies with public approval of 78, 65, and 75 percent respectively, but left office with approval of only 44, 24, and 34 percent. Similarly, President George H. W. Bush had a single approval rating of 89 percent at the start of the Persian Gulf War, but this had fallen to only 34 percent the month before the 1992 election. President George W. Bush had the highest single-poll approval rating of 90 percent shortly after the September 11th attacks, but his approval had dropped to only 31 percent by May 2006.

This pattern of declining public approval through time has been characteristic of all modern presidents except two: Presidents Reagan and Clinton. Reagan entered office with public approval around 55 percent. His approval fluctuated considerably with the assassination attempt, the 1982–83 recession, and the Iran-Contra affair. However, he left office with public approval significantly higher at 63 percent. Clinton's initial approval rating was 58 percent. His approval dropped initially during his first term but increased steadily to stabilize at around 60 percent for the remainder of his presidency. He left office with a much higher 67 percent public approval rating. Interestingly, Reagan and Clinton were noted for their strong rhetorical skills, effective communications staff, and good rapport with the public.

Can modern presidents affect their own public approval ratings through economic rhetoric? This chapter addresses this question. It also looks, more specifically, at whether presidents' economic rhetoric can alter the public's assessment of how well they handle the economy. The foregoing anecdotal evidence suggests that some presidents have successfully manipulated public opinion. The remainder of this chapter develops systematic evidence for answering these questions.

## Presidency Scholarship and the President's Public Approval

Scholars of the presidency have often been concerned with whether presidents can affect their own approval ratings through various means. For example, a literature exists on the ability of presidents to alter public approval ratings through strategically timed military interventions, sanctions, travel, and other activities. Indeed, past research shows that the probability of military intervention is higher when the nation is experiencing a weak economy (DeRouen 1995; Fordham 1998; James and Oneal 1991; Ostrom and Job 1986). However, there is little evidence from the literature that presidents deliberately use these tools to bolster their public approval or reelection prospects. Indeed, researchers have found that presidential uses of force are more likely when public approval is high than when it is low (James and Oneal 1991; Ostrom and Job 1986), and rarely occurs just prior to an election. Moreover, public support for American presidents routinely increases in the short term after uses of force, but this support is often ephemeral and wanes if a conflict becomes long-term (Brody and Page 1975; Cotton 1987; Kernell 1978; MacKuen 1983; Mueller 1973). Therefore, past research suggests that presidents face mixed incentives for using military force to bolster public approval.

A more direct approach for presidents wanting to affect public approval is through persuasion and rhetoric. Most presidency scholars studying this effect have focused on single presidential speeches. For example, Ragsdale (1984, 1987) finds that presidents often succeed in altering their approval ratings through major speeches. Her analysis suggests that each major speech lifts presidential approval by about three percentage points, but the effect is short-lived, often lasting only one or two months. Similarly, Brace and Hinckley (1992) find that major speeches during a president's first term boost presidential approval by about six percentage points, but have no impact during the president's second term. Various work by Simon and Ostrom also suggests that presidential speeches produce higher public approval, but only when accompanied by an approval-enhancing event. Generally, they conclude that political and economic environments are the main determinants of presidential approval (Ostrom and Simon 1985, 1988, 1989; Simon and Ostrom 1985, 1988, 1989).

Other studies cast significant doubt on presidents' ability to manipulate public approval ratings through speeches (Brody and Shapiro 1989; Edwards 1983; Kernell 1997; Mondak 1993; Rosen 1973; Sigelman 1980b; Sigelman and Sigelman 1981; Thomas and Sigelman 1985). Variously, these studies found small effects, no effects, and even negative effects of presidential speeches on public opinion.

In the most recent and comprehensive analysis, Edwards (2003) examines presidential approval immediately before and after major speeches from Presidents Reagan through George W. Bush. Based on this pre-test/post-test research design, he concludes that presidents are not regularly able to affect their public approval through speeches. Additionally, when presidents do garner public support through speeches, the effects tend to be brief. Thus, the current understanding among presidency scholars is that presidents are not very successful in manipulating their own approval ratings.

A major limitation of *all* past work is the empirical focus on major speeches. Many studies have examined polls immediately before and after major presidential speeches to look for change in public approval. Yet, it is doubtful that White House public relations strategies are so simplistic. Presidents maintain an extensive apparatus for transmitting a continuous stream of messages. Certainly, major speeches are one tool of presidential communication. However, they also transmit their messages through other means. Non-major speeches, radio addresses, group appearances, news conferences, town hall meetings, policy briefings, news releases, and so forth should also be important to transmitting a president's message. Moreover, modern presidents engage in a perpetual campaign to get their messages across, and major speeches are only part of that campaign. As presidents engage in the perpetual campaign, they generate a continuous stream of stimuli intended to produce a sustained message.

The focus of past research on people's responses *immediately after* major presidential speeches is also problematic. Presidential messages may not produce an immediate response. Rather, delay may occur and responses may be distributed over time. Message recipients often require time to receive and absorb the president's sustained message through the news and other outlets. Citizens are limited in their cognitive abilities and may require multiple stimuli to hear and understand fully the president's message (Berelson, Lazarsfeld, and McPhee 1954; Campbell et al. 1960; Stimson 1999; Zaller 1992). As a sustained presidential message develops, the response may occur immediately, or be delayed. The response may not be fully realized in a single time period, but be distributed more subtly over several time periods. Therefore, if we are to evaluate effectively the impact of presidential rhetoric on public approval, it is important to consider a sustained presidential message from diverse outlets, and the possibility that the response to the president's message may be dynamic.

## POLITICAL BEHAVIOR SCHOLARSHIP AND THE PRESIDENT'S PUBLIC APPROVAL

Another body of research on the public's approval of presidents' job performance flows from scholars studying mass political behavior. These scholars have typically explained presidential approval as a function of four concepts: inertia, a president's base level of support, political drama, and the economy. They have routinely ignored, however, presidents themselves as important in affecting presidential approval. This seems strange, given that the president is the central actor in the presidential approval story.

Inertia is important for explaining presidential approval, because approval tends to persist through time. That is, survey respondents' political evaluations in a current survey tend to depend on responses in past surveys. Moreover, within the mass public only a small percentage of the electorate is amenable to change, and so change in presidential approval often occurs gradually rather than in sudden shifts. Political behavior researchers typically implement the concept of inertia using a lagged dependent variable. That is, a president's prior public approval is used as an explanatory variable for the current public approval. Generally, the strongest predictor in political behavior models of presidential approval has been this variable.

Presidents' base level of support is important in explaining shifts in presidential approval across administrations. Researchers generally characterize each president as having a different level of base support that should be relevant to that individual's approval. Base support effects have been measured as dummy variables for each presidency. Others have included an indicator variable for the first time period of each presidency. This second approach assumes that the lagged dependent variable for inertia captures continuing changes in the level of base support for each president. It also takes into account that the inertia variable for new presidents is not captured by the lagged dependent variable, since the prior time period belongs to the prior president.

Political drama is important because international events and other occurrences can significantly alter public support for the president. For example, the Reagan assassination attempt resulted in roughly a 12 percent increase in the presidential approval rating. Conversely, the Iran-Contra scandal produced roughly a 15 percent decline in presidential approval. Such events usually result in relatively short-term changes that decay rapidly once they are no longer salient. However, this is not always the case. The September 11 terrorist attacks resulted in an increase in public approval for President George W. Bush lasting for at least two years.

Finally, the economy is important because most past statistical evidence shows that citizens hold presidents accountable for the economy through public opinion and elections. From the early days of political behavior research on the determinants of presidential approval, the core theoretical concern has been how and why the economy affects the public's approval of the president's job performance. Following Mueller's (1970) classic study, a virtual cottage industry developed around this topic.

Early work concluded that objective indicators of economic performance were important to the public's assessment of presidents. When the economy does poorly, the president receives much of the blame; when it does well the president receives much of the credit. Mueller's (1970) correlational analysis found a strong relationship between unemployment and presidential approval. Hibbs' (1974) reanalysis of Mueller's data, however, found no statistically significant relationship between unemployment and presidential approval after accounting for autocorrelation. Kernell (1978) found that unemployment is not a key determinant of presidential popularity, but Kenski (1977) concluded that inflation is important. The consensus that emerged from this early work was muddled on how objective economic conditions affect the president's popularity. Most work concluded that inflation is probably more important than unemployment, but that unemployment could also be important (Monroe 1978, 1979).

MacKuen (1983) improved research in this area by highlighting the importance of political drama to changes in presidential approval. The theory behind the political drama perspective is that people tend to "rally around the flag" during international crises, but may abandon the president during periods of scandal. MacKuen identified a lengthy list of dramatic events that produced short-term changes in presidents' approval. Using dynamic statistical methods, he compared the effects of these dramatic events to effects due to economic variables. He found that political drama has about as much impact on presidential approval as economic variables.

Another refinement of the economic models of presidential approval concerned whether the public is retrospective or prospective in forming attitudes about a president. Following the lead of Key (1968), early scholars concluded that it is current or past economic performance that affects public evaluations of a president. The public was deemed psychologically retrospective in such evaluations. That is, in forming their attitudes about the president people look to how the economy is or has been doing, rather than how it will be doing in the future.

Challenging this perspective, Chappell and Keech (1985) found that voters are sophisticated when allocating political support based on economic performance. Their empirical results showed that a model where citizens look to the future when evaluating the presidents' job performance works as well or better than models based purely on objective economic indicators or retrospective judgments.

Building on this perspective, MacKuen, Erikson, and Stimson (1992) concluded that "controlling for business expectations, no other measure of economic sentiment directly affects approval. Economic conditions affect presidential popularity only to the extent that economic conditions alter expectations of the economic future" (603). They showed that the effects of unemployment and inflation on presidential approval disappear once citizens' expectations about the future state of the economy (prospective evaluations) are included in the statistical analysis. In a subsequent study, Erikson, MacKuen, and Stimson (2002) found that prospective evaluations of the economy also moderated both objective economic indicators and retrospective evaluations in explaining presidents' job approval. Both studies were a serious challenge to conventional wisdom that citizens are retrospective of the economy when forming attitudes on the president.

Various scholars have questioned MacKuen, Erikson, and Stimson's (1992) work, suggesting that it is implausible that the electorate is actually this rational or insulated. For example, Norpoth (1996) found that economic expectations do not explain presidential approval once appropriate political interventions are included. He also concluded that economic expectations merely encapsulate information about the current state of the economy and that retrospective evaluations are more important to evaluations of the president.

Others suggested that MacKuen, Erikson, and Stimson's statistical analysis was flawed because it failed to consider the stationarity properties of the approval time series.[2] Indeed, there has been considerable debate over whether the presidential approval time series is stationary (Alvarez and Katz 1996; Beck 1993; Box-Steffensmeier and Smith 1998; DeBoef and Granato 1997; Ostrom and Smith 1993; Smith 1993; Williams 1993). Clark and Stewart (1994) attempted to strike a middle ground by estimating an error-correction model that treats presidential approval as non-stationary, but in a long-term equilibrium relationship with economic evaluations.[3] Using this approach, they found that presidential approval responds to both retrospective and prospective economic evaluations.

Of course, all of these analyses assumed that the relationship between economic evaluations and a president's job approval is stable through time. Questioning this assumption, Wood (2000) explicitly modeled presidential approval as a time-varying parameter process. His analysis showed that prospective evaluations of economic performance do not predict presidential approval consistently over time. He also showed that the impact of inflation on presidential approval has varied over time, with much less impact since the 1980s. Evidence of time-varying parameters can indicate an omitted variable problem in a statistical model. That is, past models may be missing one or more important variables that mediate the relationship between economic evaluations and presidential approval.

Aside from this statistical evidence, there are also substantive reasons to believe that past political behavior models of presidential approval omit important variables. For example, Edwards, Mitchell, and Welch (1995) showed that issue salience is important in determining how the economy and international relations affect presidential approval. As issues become more salient through time, their impact on presidential approval increases; as they become less salient, their impact becomes smaller. Thus, as people report hearing more news about economic conditions, their economic evaluations should change when assessing a president's job performance.

Similarly, Hetherington (1996) showed that the economic news people hear is important to their economic evaluations, which in turn affects presidential approval. Indeed, the news can significantly alter people's perceptions of objective economic conditions, and there can be a large disparity between objective conditions and citizen perceptions. For example, as President Reagan was campaigning for reelection in 1984, the unemployment rate was 7.3 percent, barely lower than when he took office. The media spin, however, was that the economy was improving. Reagan's public approval rating was 62 percent the month of the 1984 election, and he was easily reelected. In contrast, the electorate turned President George H. W. Bush out of office in 1992 when the unemployment rate was 7.4 percent and the economy was improving after the 1990–91 recession. His public approval rating was only 34 percent the month before the 1992 election. A possible explanation for this disparity is that the economic news that people were hearing significantly altered their perceptions of the economy. Thus, the news that people report hearing about the economy should be an important variable to consider when modeling public approval of a president's job performance.

Perhaps the most serious limitation of political behavior research on presidential approval is that it has generally ignored the role of presidents in affecting people's evaluations of them. Political behavior scholars have virtually always included an indicator variable in their models to capture different levels of presidential base support. Implicit in this limited approach to representing the presidency, however, is the assumption that presidents cannot themselves alter the dynamics of their own public approval. According to this perspective, presidents are passive actors with no impact. Presidential speeches and the continuous stream of messages are irrelevant to altering the public's perceptions of the economy or presidential leadership.[4]

Again, this approach seems strange given that the central character in the presidential approval story is the presidency itself. Moreover, it would seem odd that news emanating from and about the presidency would not affect what people think about the presidency. The White House transmits a continuous stream of messages intended to shape public opinion and media coverage. The media consistently covers presidential messages, and may have independent effects. News about the president is omnipresent

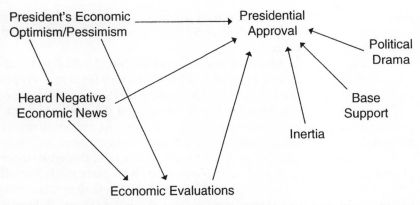

Figure 5.1 Potential Paths of Influence of Presidential Rhetoric on Presidential Approval

and a topic of daily attention for most Americans. To ignore this component in explaining presidential approval is to omit a potentially important influence.

## A Theory of Presidential Influence on Public Approval

Like past research, the analysis in this chapter posits that public approval of a president's job performance is a function of inertia, the president's base level of support, political drama, and economic evaluations. However, unlike past research, it theorizes that other variables should enter into the explanatory system. The news that people report hearing about the economy should be important to people's economic evaluations, as well as to their evaluation of a president's job performance. A president should influence public approval *indirectly* by affecting people's perceptions of the economic news and their evaluations of the economy. A president should also affect public approval *directly* by establishing a perception of strong economic leadership. The measure of presidential rhetoric described in this chapter enables capturing these direct and indirect effects. It also focuses on a sustained message rather than single speeches.

Figure 5.1 contains a path diagram of the theory and potential avenues of presidential influence on public approval. First, consider the link at the top left of the diagram. It suggests that presidential rhetoric on the economy can affect public approval *directly*. Druckman and Holmes (2004) provide experimental and survey evidence that presidents can directly impact their own approval by altering public images. Here the hypothesis is that presidents affect public approval by projecting an image of strong economic leadership, independent of the economic news people hear and their economic evaluations.

Producing an image of strong economic leadership should directly affect whether people view a president's job performance favorably. People look to presidents for leadership, and leadership on the economy is especially important. The economy is highly salient, and there is a public expectation that presidents be strong economic leaders. As a result, virtually all presidents put forth an economic program. As they pursue their economic programs, presidents and their staffs understand the importance of projecting an image of leadership (Grossman and Kumar 1981; Kernell 1997; Kumar 1997; Maltese 1992). They uniformly believe that communicating with the public is important to their legislative success (Edwards 2003, 15–19). Therefore, they attempt to lead not only through policy but also with words.

Of course, the analysis in chapter 4 showed that the style of presidential leadership of the economy has differed widely across presidencies. For example, President Clinton took seriously the mantra "It's the economy, stupid!" He was highly optimistic in the tone of public remarks during 1993 when attempting to achieve a balanced budget and economic stimulus package. He was also very optimistic about the economy after the package was passed, becoming an economic cheerleader for the remainder of his administration. In contrast, President George W. Bush was highly pessimistic about the economy while attempting to pass three major tax cuts between 2001 and 2003. He continually referred to weak U.S. economic performance in a public setting and the need for large tax cuts to stimulate jobs and economic growth. Indeed, he only turned optimistic about the economy during the 2004 presidential election, perhaps in recognition of the importance of the economy to public evaluations of his leadership.

Expressing confidence and optimism about the current and future economy should produce a sense of strong leadership resulting in higher public approval. People generally like hearing positive news and tend to view favorably the bearer of such news. In contrast, expressing pessimism and uncertainty about the current and future state of the economy should be associated with weak leadership and result in lower public approval. Therefore, the relative optimism/pessimism of presidential remarks on the economy should directly affect public approval, independent of the economic news and citizen evaluations of the economy.

Second, consider the indirect links on the left side of figure 5.1. Presidential rhetoric should affect public approval indirectly through presidential effects on people's perceptions of the economic news and citizens' evaluations of the economy. Almost forty years of public opinion research has produced an understanding that evaluations of the economy are important to presidential approval. When evaluating the economy citizens take cues and receive information from a variety of sources, including personal experience, the experiences of others, economic news, and elite economic actors. Presidential rhetoric, manifest through a stream of speeches and other public comments that are widely reported in the news, is one of those sources of cues and information.

As presidents become more positive/negative with respect to the economy, we should expect the economic news that people report hearing to be more favorable/unfavorable. Presidents help establish a tone for economic perceptions. If the president "talks up" or "talks down" the economy, then this should affect people's perception of the economic news. In turn, we should expect the economic news that people report hearing to affect the president's job approval. People evaluate a president's job performance at least partially on how well they think the economy is doing. Hopeful news about the economy is more likely to produce favorable political evaluations of a president. Dismal news should produce poor political evaluations.

We should also expect the economic news to affect people's general evaluations of the economy, which may in turn affect presidential approval. Good or bad economic news should lead to more or less positive evaluations of the current and past state of the economy. It should also affect people's evaluations of the future state of the economy. Of course, a significant body of past research suggests that both retrospective and prospective economic evaluations are important predictors of a president's job approval rating.

Key to the theory is that presidential rhetoric on the economy should affect both the economic news that people report hearing and their economic evaluations. Why should presidential rhetoric matter to these variables? The receptor of a president's message, the public, is highly attentive to the economy. Since 1946 the Gallup poll has asked a random sample of respondents about every three months, "What do you think is the most important problem in this country today?" On average since World War II, around 44 percent of respondents have listed some dimension of the economy as the most important problem facing the nation.

People get most of their information about the economy from the news. News outlets provide frequent coverage and commentary on reports of economic growth, unemployment, inflation, the deficit, and other economic conditions. Presidents' plans for the economy are also widely publicized, along with administration comments on economic reports. The news media also reports on presidents' campaigns to address economic problems legislatively, as well as their demeanor with respect to the economy. Often coverage of the economy occurs simultaneously with coverage of presidents' remarks about the economy.

Additionally, the transmitter of the message (the president) is a highly visible and authoritative economic actor. The press is hungry for news about the presidency. As a result, hardly a newscast or newspaper passes without some coverage of the presidency. Presidents use this to their advantage to help establish particular images. Presidents and their staffs control the timing and release of information, and try hard to "spin" the news to their advantage.

The message from a president also commands greater public attention because it is authoritative. The Employment Act of 1946 (PL 79–304), as amended by the Humphrey-Hawkins Act of 1978 (PL 95–523), formally institutionalized the role of the president as the nation's economic leader. Presidents are required to make an annual Economic Report to Congress detailing the current and future state of the economy, as well as their administration's plans and recommendations for promoting economic goals. Presidents usually campaign for their economic plans and often comment on U.S. economic performance. Thus, presidents are assumed by virtue of their role and supporting expertise to be more knowledgeable on the economy than most other actors.

Finally, presidents have the advantage of being able to send a sustained message. Modern presidents are on a perpetual campaign where content is at the discretion of the administration. Through a continuous stream of speeches and other public comments, presidents establish a *tone* for federal involvement in the economy, which in turn affects the economic news and sentiment for business and consumers. While a single presidential speech may produce little or no shift in public opinion, a sustained message offers an opportunity to produce lasting impressions of the economic climate and presidential leadership. Thus, it is through the *indirect* and *sustained* effect of presidential rhetoric working on the news and economic evaluations that the president should primarily affect public approval.

## MEASUREMENT AND RESEARCH DESIGN

How do presidential rhetoric, people's perceptions of the economic news, their economic evaluations, and public approval of presidents' job performance relate to one another? If presidential rhetoric does affect public approval, does it work directly and/or indirectly through economic news and economic evaluations as described in figure 5.1? Are the arrows in figure 5.1 single-headed, as drawn, or are some of them actually double-headed? We turn now toward answering these questions statistically.

## Measurement

The statistical analysis used two different measures of presidential approval: the general Gallup measure used in most past research and a measure of the president's economic approval. The general Gallup measure contained responses to the survey question, "Do you approve or disapprove of the way [president's name] is handling his job as president?" The Gallup survey organization has asked this question at least monthly since 1978, sometimes multiple times in the same month.

The economic approval question was, "Do you approve or disapprove of the way [president's name] is handling the economy?" This question was first asked by a survey organization in April 1981. Since then it has been used periodically by multiple survey organizations, but on a less frequent basis than the general Gallup approval measure. Therefore, the data from multiple survey organizations were combined to construct a monthly measure of economic approval.[5] Even using data from multiple survey organizations there were a few missing months. Also, in some months the question was asked multiple times.

These potential complications were addressed using the procedure and software WCALC developed by Stimson (1991). The software produced a recursively created smoothed monthly time series for both measures, running from the start of the Reagan administration through the end of George W. Bush's first term.

The series started at the Reagan administration for both technical and research design reasons. Technically, no data exist on economic approval prior to early 1981. Gallup approval data were available for a much longer period, but the monthly Survey of Consumers started in 1978. This means that only part of the Carter presidency could be included in the Gallup approval analysis. Thus, it was deemed appropriate to omit the partial Carter presidency to obtain comparability among analyses.

A more important reason to restrict the period of analysis to these years is that it enables a better test of whether presidents can affect their own approval. Presidents Reagan and Clinton were widely known for their strong communications skills. Reagan especially employed an extensive staff of political consultants to project a positive image for the presidency. As noted by Blumenthal (1982, 329), "The president who spent his entire adult life as a media performer, understands as Jimmy Carter never did the use of the media as an instrument of policy." If presidential rhetoric made no difference for this later subset of presidencies, then it probably never made a difference. Therefore, the choice of this period for analysis provides a critical test of whether presidents' economic rhetoric ever makes a difference.

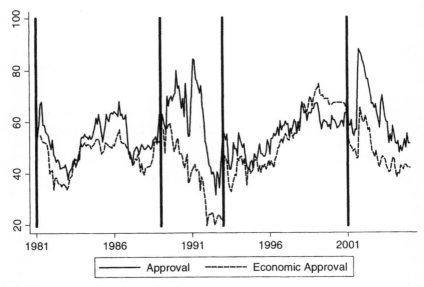

Figure 5.2 Presidential Approvals

Figure 5.2 provides a graph of the two approval time series along with heavy vertical markers indicating the start of each presidential administration.[6] Note that both the approval and economic approval time series were subject to sharp fluctuations due to changing presidential administrations and political drama. Therefore, indicator variables for each presidency were included in the analysis for the start of each presidency to reflect each president's base level of support. An events series was also included to represent changes due to crisis, scandal, and other interventions.[7]

The economic news that people report hearing was measured using monthly data from the University of Michigan's Survey of Consumers. The Survey of Consumers routinely asks the question, "During the last few months, have you heard of any favorable or unfavorable changes in business conditions?" There is also a follow-up question: "What news did you hear?" The possible responses on the follow-up question cover a number of topics, including unemployment, consumer demand, inflation, interest rates, energy problems, the stock market, the trade deficit, and government policy. Rather than focusing on each topic separately, the responses for each category were summed across the multiple topics. Thus, the measure of economic news was the monthly percentage of respondents reporting that they had heard negative economic news on any topic. Figure 5.3 contains a graph of the negative economic news time series along with markers for the start of each presidential administration.

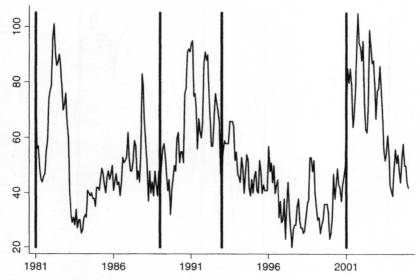

Figure 5.3 Heard Negative Economic News

Objective indicators of economic performance were *not* included in the analysis. Past research on presidential approval has concluded that it is citizen evaluations of the economy that are important, rather than objective economic indicators (Chappell and Keech 1985; Erikson, MacKuen, and Stimson 2002; MacKuen, Erikson, and Stimson 1992). Therefore, we impose this constraint based on past empirical research. It should also be noted, however, that the core relationships reported in this chapter do not change with the inclusion of objective economic indicators.[8]

Moreover, the measure for economic news made their inclusion unnecessary for our purposes. The economic news variable is a strong control for a broad range of information perceived by citizens about the economy, including the release of economic reports on unemployment, inflation, economic growth, and stock market performance. Indeed, it is a better measure for our purposes than including the actual reports. This measure gauges what people actually *perceive* about these conditions,[9] rather than relying on reports spottily covered by the media for a public that is only "boundedly rational." Thus, the economic news that people report hearing provides a more direct measure of the factors affecting people's economic and political evaluations.

Economic evaluations were measured using the University of Michigan's Index of Consumer Sentiment (ICS). The ICS is constructed from five questions about current and expected personal finance and business conditions.[10] It combines both retrospective and prospective evaluations

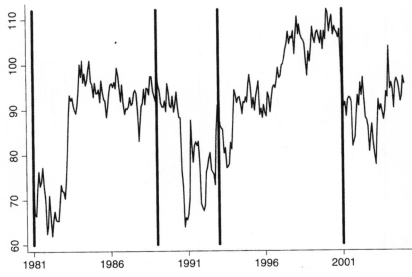

Figure 5.4 Economic Evaluations

of the economy into a single measure. This measure was chosen over the specific questions comprising the ICS to enable parsimony. Past research suggests that both retrospective and prospective evaluations may be important to presidential approval, but it is divided over which is more important.[11] Therefore, the combination measure was deemed appropriate. Figure 5.4 contains a graph of economic evaluations along with markers for the start of each presidential administration.

Of course, the key research concept for the theory depicted in figure 5.1 is that reflecting the relative optimism of presidential rhetoric on the economy. The analyses of this chapter use a composite of the measures developed in chapter 2 and depicted in figures 2.1 through 2.2. Specifically, presidential optimism is measured as the sum of presidential optimism on the general economy, unemployment, inflation, and federal deficit. This results in an index of presidential optimism that captures the president's overall optimism along the most important dimensions of the economy. The overall presidential optimism measure is in the graph of figure 5.5, again with markers for the start of each presidential administration.

*Statistical Method*

Vector autoregression (VAR) methods were used to evaluate the direction of relationships and track the temporal dynamics among the variables in the system (Freeman, Williams, and Lin 1989; Sims 1980). The VAR-X variant was used to enable inclusion of the exogenous measures for each presidency and political drama.[12]

VAR methods were chosen for estimating the relationships in figure 5.1 for several reasons. First, there is a strong possibility of two-way causal relations between variables. The direction of causality is a major concern since presidential optimism may both cause and be caused by the other three variables in the system. Similarly, there may be other double-headed arrows in figure 5.1. It would be undesirable to attribute causal effects to the president when the effect actually runs the other way. VAR methods enable ascertaining the direction of causal relations between variables.[13]

Second, the VAR approach enables strong controls for inertia. The core research concepts in figure 5.1 are all subject to inertia. Past research has treated presidential approval as inertial by including a lagged dependent variable. Presidential optimism may also be inertial such that past presidential optimism causes current presidential optimism. The past may also predict the present for the economic news and economic evaluations variables. When using VAR, each dependent variable is regressed on multiple lagged values of itself, as well as multiple lagged values of the other variables in the system.[14]

Including multiple lags of each variable typically makes estimation of individual regression coefficients imprecise.[15] For this reason, VAR analysts generally ignore the regression coefficients and use different tools for interpretation. Granger (1969) tests are performed that evaluate joint hypothesis tests for blocks of coefficients associated with each variable. Granger tests are one of the VAR tools for assessing the direction of causality.[16] A statistically significant block of coefficients implies a causal relationship from the independent variable to the corresponding dependent variable.[17] However, as proven by Lutkepohl, "the lack of a Granger-causal relationship from one group of variables to the remaining variables cannot necessarily be interpreted as a lack of a cause and effect relationship" (1993, 41–42).

Another tool for determining the direction of causal relations is performing dynamic simulations based on the estimated system. The dynamic simulations take into account dynamic feedback between variables. They also contain far more information than the Granger tests. Using this approach, one can observe the direction, magnitude, and time path of each relationship. This approach augments Granger tests by enabling a more accurate description of relationships, and enables observing feedback that can occur between variables. Simulations are accomplished by shocking each variable mathematically to produce an implied response in the other variables in the system.[18] This approach is called the moving average response approach. In this study, confidence intervals for the moving average responses are computed using Monte Carlo integration and

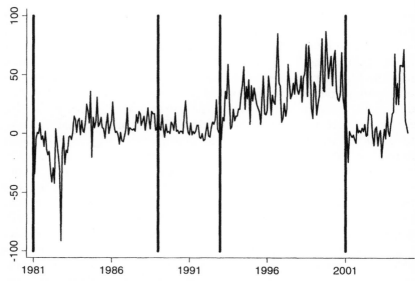

Figure 5.5 Presidential Economic Optimism

the fractile method recommended by Sims and Zha (1999). Results of the simulations are reported in matrices of graphs to enable the simultaneous viewing of all relationships.[19]

## STATISTICAL RESULTS

Again, two separate analyses were conducted to evaluate the effects of presidential optimism on presidential approval. One analysis used the standard Gallup approval measure, and the other used a measure of presidents' economic approval. The results from the two analyses are similar and reinforcing, and so they are discussed together.

The Granger tests are reported in tables 5.1 and 5.2. The arrows in the tables indicate a Granger causal relationship from the left-side variable to the right-side variable. The moving average responses are reported in figures 5.6 and 5.7. The graphs along the diagonals of these figures contain the variables being shocked in the simulations (as indicated by the left-side labels). The responses to the shocks appear in rows horizontally (as indicated by the top labels). The magnitudes of the simulated shocks along the diagonals of figures 5.6 and 5.7 are one standard error of the regression. The dashed lines around the responses mark the fractile confidence intervals.

TABLE 5.1
Granger Tests for Presidential Optimism, the News, Economic Evaluations, and
Presidents' Approval

| Independent Variable | | Dependent Variable | p-value |
| --- | --- | --- | --- |
| Presidents' Economic Optimism | → | Presidents' Economic Optimism | 0.00 |
| Heard Negative Economic News | | | 0.17 |
| Economic Evaluations | → | | 0.05 |
| Presidents' Approval | | | 0.48 |
| Presidents' Economic Optimism | | Heard Negative Economic News | 0.81 |
| Heard Negative Economic News | → | | 0.00 |
| Economic Evaluations | → | | 0.00 |
| Presidents' Approval | | | 0.21 |
| Presidents' Economic Optimism | | Economic Evaluations | 0.13 |
| Heard Negative Economic News | | | 0.12 |
| Economic Evaluations | → | | 0.00 |
| Presidents' Approval | → | | 0.02 |
| Presidents' Economic Optimism | | Presidents' Approval | 0.17 |
| Heard Negative Economic News | | | 0.33 |
| Economic Evaluations | | | 0.21 |
| Presidents' Approval | → | | 0.00 |

Note: The arrows indicate Granger causality from the block of coefficients for the independent
variable to the dependent variable based on 0.10 significance levels.

### Evaluating Reverse Causality

In evaluating the effect of presidential rhetoric on presidential approval,
it is important to consider the possibility that presidential rhetoric also
responds to the other variables in the system. Thus, we consider first the
relative responsiveness of presidential rhetoric to the other variables. The
first panel of tables 5.1 and 5.2 provides a consistent picture showing that
presidential optimism responds to people's economic evaluations. Table
5.2 also suggests that presidential optimism responds to a president's economic approval. This suggests that presidents may act strategically to adjust their economic rhetoric to affect public approval.

Granger tests are limited in that they do not show the sign or magnitude
of statistical relationships. Additionally, they do not take account of dynamic feedback between variables. Therefore, the moving average responses depicted in figures 5.6 and 5.7 provide a more descriptive and
accurate picture of the reverse causal dynamics. These graphs are consistent in showing that presidential optimism responds both to negative economic news and economic evaluations. Presidential rhetoric, however,
does not definitively respond to public approval for either analysis.

TABLE 5.2
Granger Tests for Presidential Optimism, the News, Economic Evaluations, and
Presidents' Economic Approval

| Independent Variable | | Dependent Variable | p-value |
|---|---|---|---|
| Presidents' Economic Optimism | → | Presidents' Economic Optimism | 0.00 |
| Heard Negative Economic News | | | 0.15 |
| Economic Evaluations | → | | 0.05 |
| Presidents' Economic Approval | | | 0.20 |
| Presidents' Economic Optimism | | Heard Negative Economic News | 0.27 |
| Heard Negative Economic News | → | | 0.00 |
| Economic Evaluations | → | | 0.00 |
| Presidents' Economic Approval | | | 0.27 |
| Presidents' Economic Optimism | → | Economic Evaluations | 0.08 |
| Heard Negative Economic News | | | 0.13 |
| Economic Evaluations | → | | 0.00 |
| Presidents' Economic Approval | → | | 0.02 |
| Presidents' Economic Optimism | | Presidents' Economic Approval | 0.34 |
| Heard Negative Economic News | | | 0.26 |
| Economic Evaluations | → | | 0.03 |
| Presidents' Economic Approval | → | | 0.00 |

Note: The arrows indicate Granger causality from the block of coefficients for the independent
variable to the dependent variable based on 0.10 significance levels.

Specifically, a one standard error increase in the negative economic
news that people report hearing (shown at the intersection of row 2 and
column 2 of figures 5.6 and 5.7) results in a maximum of roughly 2.5
fewer net optimistic remarks by the president each month (shown at the
intersection of row 2 and column 1). The total decline in optimistic remarks due to the shock is distributed over time as shown by the rise in
the response and subsequent decay starting the fourth month after the
shock. Thus, presidents become more pessimistic in their economic remarks as people's perceptions of the economic news become more pessimistic, and vice versa.

Similarly, a one standard error increase in people's economic evaluations (row 3, column 3) produces a maximum net increase of about two
optimistic remarks by the president each month (row 3, column 1). Again,
the effect rises and then declines after about the fourth month. Thus, presidents become more pessimistic in their economic remarks as people's evaluations of the economy become more pessimistic, and vice versa.

These findings show that there are actually double-headed arrows in
figure 5.1 between presidential optimism and the economic news, and

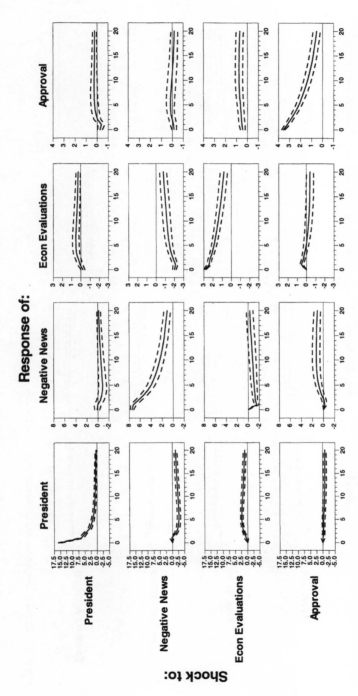

Figure 5.6 Impulse Responses for Approval System

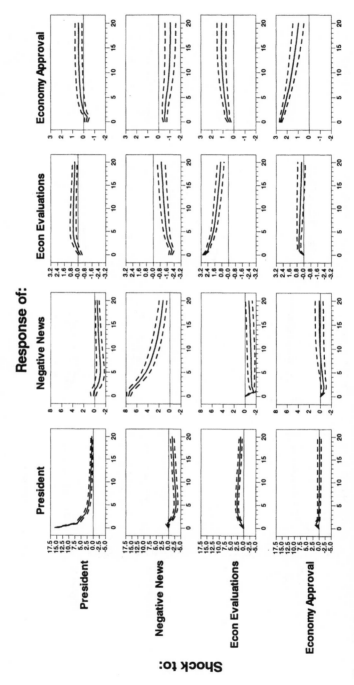

Figure 5.7 Impulse Responses for Economic Approval System

presidential optimism and economic evaluations. It is also worth noting the other reverse causal relationships that exist in figure 5.1. There is a reverse causal relationship between people's economic evaluations and their reporting that they have heard negative economic news. The Granger tests in the second panel of tables 5.1 and 5.2 show that economic evaluations cause negative economic news. Figures 5.6 and 5.7 demonstrate the sign, magnitude, and dynamic of these effects. They show that a one standard error rise in economic evaluations (row 3, column 3) produces about a 1.75 percent maximum decline in the number of people reporting negative economic news (row 3, column 2) for both systems. Again, the effect is distributed over time to produce a much larger total effect. Thus, people's reports of the economic news are colored by their preconceptions about the economy.

The Granger tests in third panel of tables 5.1 and 5.2 also show that people's economic evaluations respond to their approval of the president's job performance. In other words, people are more confident about the economy when they approve of the president's leadership. This result is confirmed in figures 5.6 and 5.7, which show that a one standard error increase in the president's approval (row 4, column 4) produces about a half-unit increase in people's economic evaluations (row 4, column 3). The effect is distributed more over time for the economic approval system. Both responses are small given that people's economic evaluations range on a scale from a low of 62 to a maximum of 112.[20]

Finally, there is a reverse causal relationship between the president's Gallup approval and the news that people report hearing about the economy. The Granger test in the second panel of table 5.1 with $p$-value 0.09 shows that presidential approval Granger causes the economic news that people report hearing. Similarly, figure 5.6 shows a statistically significant increase in such negative news after an increase in presidential approval. The intuitive reason for this change is unclear, but it might be due to a media thrust for bad news when there is a strong presidency.

### Evaluating the Direct and Indirect Effects of Presidential Optimism on Public Approval

Controlling for these reverse causal relationships, does presidential optimism affect presidential approval either directly or indirectly? The analysis of the direct effects of presidential optimism on presidential approval is contained in the fourth panel of tables 5.1 and 5.2 and figures 5.6 and 5.7 at row 1, column 4. The Granger tests cast doubt on whether presidents can directly affect their own approval ratings through optimistic rhetoric. The test for Gallup approval in table 5.1 is suggestive, but has a $p$-value of only 0.17. The test for economic approval in table 5.2 is also non-significant with a $p$-value of 0.34.

Figures 5.6 and 5.7 confirm that any direct effect of presidential optimism on presidential approval must be weak. Specifically, a one standard error increase in presidential optimism (row 1, column 1 of figure 5.6) produces only about a 0.25 percent increase in the president's Gallup approval several months after the shock (row 1, column 4). While statistically significant, the response decays gradually toward zero over ensuing months. The same increase in presidential optimism produces no significant change in presidents' economic approval. Consistent with past presidency research, the evidence suggests that presidential rhetoric has only a marginal direct effect on public approval.

Are there indirect effects of presidential optimism on presidential approval? The evidence shows that there are strong indirect effects operating through multiple paths. The third panel of tables 5.1 and 5.2 suggests a Granger causal relation between presidential optimism and people's economic evaluations. However, again these tests ignore feedback among variables, and so the moving average responses in figures 5.6 and 5.7 contain a more descriptive and accurate picture.

They show that a one standard error increase in presidential optimism produces an initial decline of about 1 percent in the number of people reporting that they heard negative economic news (row 1, column 2). The same shock produces an initial increase of about a half unit in people's economic evaluations (row 1, column 3). The total effect from these shocks is calculated by summing the effects under the curves. Using the numbers in the graph over the next year, this implies a decline of about 8 percent in the number of people reporting that they heard negative economic news and about a four-unit increase in people's economic evaluations.

Additionally, the reverse feedback effects (rows 2 and 3, column 1) imply that less negative economic news and higher economic evaluations cause presidents to be more optimistic about the economy. Higher economic evaluations also produce greater presidential optimism through reverse feedback effects through the news (row 3, column2), which in turn affects presidential optimism (row 2, column 1). These indirect paths further accelerate the effect of presidential optimism on the economic news that people report hearing and their economic evaluations.

Less negative economic news also affects people's economic evaluations (row 2, column 3). This also has an impact on presidents' economic approval rating (figure 5.7, row 2, column 4). Higher economic evaluations due to presidential optimism also substantially affect presidents' approval ratings (row 3, column 4). Thus, the indirect effects of presidential optimism on presidential approval operate through multiple paths and are potentially much larger than the direct effects in the first row.

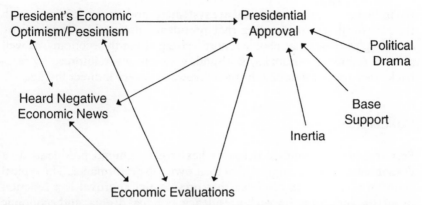

Figure 5.8 Statistical Results for the Effect of Presidents' Economic Rhetoric on Presidential Approvals

What is the potential magnitude of these effects? Ignoring reverse feedback, the total impact of presidential optimism on the news and economic evaluations calculated over a year is about the same as a one standard error shock to each of these variables. Using this information, we can take the indirect effects as roughly equivalent to the total effects shown for approval in response to these variables (figures 5.6 and 5.7, rows 2 and 3, column 4).

The indirect effects through the news produce no significant change in presidents' Gallup approval. However, they change the president's economic approval by about 0.5 percent initially, with a total effect of about 6 percent distributed over a year. The indirect effects through economic evaluations produce a change in the president's Gallup approval of about 0.5 percent initially to peak at about 0.9 percent and ultimately decay toward zero. The implied total effect on Gallup approval distributed over a year is about 9.9 percent. The same shock produces a larger change in presidents' economic approval of initially 0.4 percent to peak subsequently at over 1 percent and then decay toward zero. The implied total effect of economic evaluations on economic approval distributed over a year is about 11.9 percent. Of course, these estimates are rough due to the confidence boundaries. They suggest, however, that the indirect effect of presidential optimism on the president's public approval may be substantial.

We can also summarize the results of the statistical analysis using a revised path diagram as shown in figure 5.8, which now contains both single- and double-headed arrows. The path diagram says that presidents have historically affected their own approval ratings both directly and indirectly. The direct path is a bit tentative, functioning only marginally for the presidents' Gallup approval ratings. The indirect paths of presidential influence on public approval are systematic and strong, however, with the statistical results showing that presidents alter public approval by changing the news that people report hearing about the economy, as well as their economic sentiment. Both indirect paths are reinforced by feedback since there are double-headed arrows for every indirect linkage.

## Conclusion

Past research on political behavior has largely ignored presidents as a determinant of public approval of their own job performance. The typical claim of this research has been that presidential approval is a function of inertia, indicators for each presidency, political drama, and economic evaluations. Yet omitting presidents from explanations of presidential approval seems anomalous, given that presidents are central to the concept under investigation.

Past research by presidency scholars has mainly been concerned with whether major presidential speeches affect public opinion. It has generally found that the effect of presidential speeches on public approval is small, short-term, and conditional. Yet modern presidents do not depend solely on major speeches to get their messages across. They and their staff run a sophisticated communications operation to conduct a sustained campaign transmitted through a variety of instruments and outlets. Therefore, it should be the sustained message, rather than single speeches, that is important to presidential effects on public opinion.

The analysis in this chapter differs from past research by considering presidents as transmitting a sustained message through multiple instruments to influence public opinion both directly and indirectly. Virtually all past research has agreed that the economy is important to people's assessments of presidents' job performance. Therefore, the theory posited here holds that presidential optimism about the economy should directly affect public approval by altering people's assessments of presidential leadership. A positive leadership style should produce a more favorable image that translates *directly* into higher public approval. Presidential optimism should also affect presidential approval *indirectly* by coloring the economic news that people report hearing and their evaluations of how well the economy is performing.

The theory was evaluated using time-series methods that account for reverse feedback, inertia, and dynamic relationships. The statistical analysis showed that presidents do affect their own public approval. The direct effects of presidential optimism on public approval are small. However, the indirect effects of presidential optimism on public approval are substantial through multiple paths. The president affects the news that people report hearing about the economy, which in turn affects presidents' economic approval. Presidential effects on the economic news alter people's economic evaluations, which in turn affect presidents' approval. Presidents also affect people's economic evaluations directly, which in turn affects president approval. These indirect effects are reinforced through reverse feedback effects that further increase the impact of presidential optimism on presidents' approval. The consistent picture that emerges from the analysis is that presidents are adaptive to and influential of people's assessments of the economy. This in turn affects the public's approval of the president's job performance.

The results in this chapter challenge current understandings of how and why people arrive at their assessments of the economy and of presidents. Presidents are relevant to public assessments of their own job performance. They are influential through multiple paths not previously considered. The results presented here also shed light on the importance of the perpetual campaign for presidential leadership. Some scholars have concluded that the perpetual campaign is ineffective. The analysis reported here, however, suggests that it is important but requires time to produce results through indirect paths. Moreover, the effects are more gradual and distributed over time than can be captured by examining single speeches.

Presidential rhetoric on the economy matters to public opinion. Does it also matter with respect to economic behavior and performance? We turn to a discussion and analysis of this question in the next chapter.

# Does Presidential Rhetoric on the Economy Affect Economic Behavior and Performance?

> Question from Reporter. Do you believe that President-elect Bush's comments about the economy, slowing economy, and the Vice President's comments about that the economy is possibly heading towards recession is actually a self-fulfilling prophecy and perhaps potentially dangerous talk?
>
> President Clinton. Well, I don't want to get into characterizing that. I think it's not wise for me to do that, and not appropriate. I can only tell you what I've tried to do for 8 years. What I've tried to do for 8 years is to level with the American people based on the evidence and to be conservative in my estimates when it came to the tax cuts I advocated and the spending I advocated.
>
> (Remarks on the 2001 Economic Report and an Exchange with Reporters, January 12, 2001)

THE TONE OF PRESIDENTIAL RHETORIC on the economy changed dramatically across the Clinton and two Bush administrations. In 1991 and 1992 as the United States was coming out of a recession, the senior President Bush was somewhat pessimistic in his public remarks on the economy, making an average of four negative comments each month. When President Clinton assumed office in January 1993, the tone of presidential rhetoric on the economy turned decidedly more positive. During the first six months of the Clinton administration, while the economy was still sluggish, the president struck an optimistic tone an average of fifty times per month. Over the entire Clinton administration the president made an average forty-two positive statements about the economy each month. This pattern was sharply reversed, however, when the junior President Bush assumed a more pessimistic stance. Between February and September 2001, George W. Bush made an average of eleven pessimistic comments on the economy each month. During September, the month of the terrorist attacks, the president alluded to potentially poor U.S. macroeconomic performance seventeen times. Following the attacks, he briefly turned more positive, but the evidence in chapters 3 and 4 shows that he was substantially more pessimistic than other presidents up to the 2004 election season.

Interestingly, the graphs in chapter 4 also show that these variations in presidential rhetoric corresponded roughly with variations in U.S. macroeconomic performance. The last two years of the senior Bush administration saw an average unemployment rate of 7.2 percent, with economic growth of only 2 percent. The Clinton administration averaged about 5.2 percent unemployment, with economic growth at 3.7 percent. Early in George W. Bush's administration, economic growth slowed, and unemployment increased from 3.9 percent to over 6 percent two years later. Given these facts, one is tempted to conclude that there might be a relationship between presidential rhetoric and U.S. economic performance.

Of course, this type of "seat of the pants" analysis would be subject to multiple flaws. It fails to consider potential reverse causality between presidential rhetoric and U.S. economic performance. Presidential rhetoric may be a response to economic performance, rather than a cause. Such an analysis also fails to consider the inertial nature of economic variables and the considerable lags that can occur between stimuli and subsequent responses. There may have been factors in the first Bush administration that produced a better economy during the Clinton administration, or factors in the Clinton administration that were responsible for poor U.S. economic performance during the second Bush administration. Additionally, a bivariate analysis such as this also fails to consider other variables that may mediate the relationship between presidential rhetoric and U.S. macroeconomic performance. In other words, other variables such as economic shocks, economic news, or citizen evaluations of the economy can be important determinants of macroeconomic performance.

While it would be a mistake to draw strong conclusions from the anecdotal evidence above, it does point to the important research questions of this chapter. Did President Clinton's "cheerleading" of the economy between 1993 and 2001 somehow enhance U.S. economic performance? Did President George W. Bush's "talking down" of the economy between 2001 and 2004 somehow impede U.S. economic performance? More generally, does presidential optimism on the economy affect economic behavior and performance? If the president's economic rhetoric does matter, what are the mechanisms of the effects? Which particular economic actors are affected by presidential rhetoric? Are the mechanisms direct or indirect?

This chapter explores all of these questions using the same statistical approach as was used in chapter 5. Specifically, VAR analysis is applied to examine relationships among presidential optimism, economic news, economic evaluations, interest rates, economic performance, and the economic behavior of consumers and businesses. Before we examine these relationships, however, we must first posit a theory of why presidential rhetoric should matter to economic behavior and performance.

## A THEORY OF PRESIDENTIAL RHETORIC AND THE ECONOMY

The link between presidential rhetoric and the economy involves how presidents' words affect the economic confidence of a myriad of economic actors throughout the U.S. system.

### Uncertainty and Economic Behavior

The micro-foundations of U.S. economic performance are rooted in the behavior of millions of economic actors making billions of market transactions daily throughout the U.S. economy. As individuals make choices about how to use their money, aggregate economic outcomes result. Fully two-thirds of all U.S. economic activity is due to choices by individual consumers through their personal consumption expenditures.[1] The remaining economic activity is heavily affected by personal consumption expenditures. However, decisions by other economic actors such as businesses and investors can also be important.

If economic actors turn cautious, the result can be declining national income, unemployment, and generally poor business conditions. If they throw caution to the wind, the result can be hyper-growth and inflation.[2] Ideally, economic actors will spend, borrow, invest, and save at a pace consistent with maintaining a strong economy. Whichever result occurs in aggregate, it is important to keep in mind that macroeconomic outcomes always result from the behavior of a myriad of individual economic actors.

In making decisions about how to use their money, economic actors evaluate their current and expected financial situation. Current finances are a constraint on current spending, and they may affect the actor's future income stream. Expectations about the future are also important. Indeed, two Nobel laureates have recognized the importance of expectations in explaining economic behavior. Modigliani's life cycle theory (1954) and Friedman's permanent income hypothesis (1957) emphasized the role of expectations in explaining current spending and saving decisions. The main thrust of both theories was the assumption that rational economic actors would attempt to maximize utility by allocating their lifetime stream of income into an optimal pattern of lifetime consumption.

Later advances in economic theory emphasized the role that uncertainty plays in how expectations affect economic decisions. The early work had emphasized the expected income stream, but uncertainty implied the importance of the variance in expectations about the income stream. Once uncertainty about future income was incorporated into theoretical models of economic behavior, this factor was demonstrated empirically to have an impact on current consumption and saving decisions. For example, Kimball (1990) showed that consumers accumulate precautionary savings as a hedge against uncertainty. A growing body of more recent empirical research has also confirmed the importance of uncertainty to decisions on spending and borrowing (Caballero 1991; Carroll 1994, 1997; Carroll and Samwick 1997, 1998).

Expectations about the economy factor into these decisions by altering the psychology of economic behavior. Economic actors attempt to calculate their current and future economic situation when allocating current income. Their degree of certainty in these calculations, however, is variable. As uncertainty about current and future income increases, they become less willing to assume risk. For example, during uncertain times individuals may become risk-averse in choosing not to spend, but rather to pay down debt or save for an impending "rainy day." As their certainty increases, they become more willing to assume risk, and the same individuals may be willing to finance current spending or investment by taking on debt or reducing savings.[3]

Of course, the processes used by most economic actors for deciding whether and how much to spend, borrow, invest, and save are often more fragmented than coherent and may display internal inconsistencies (Souleles 2001). Their ability to interpret economic events is limited by their beliefs, environment, education, intellect, exposure to information, and available time. These limitations mean that economic actors typically use shortcuts when deciding how to allocate their income. To be sure, many economic actors sometimes make bad decisions with adverse consequences. Nevertheless, they strive to achieve a coherent interpretation of the economic factors that directly affect their lives. They do the best that they can, by relying on a wide range of cues and information from their environment.

Even if individual actors are only "boundedly" rational when allocating income (Simon 1947), there is considerable evidence that *in aggregate*, attitudes strongly determine future macroeconomic outcomes. The research cited here provides a strong intellectual link between consumer attitudes and consumer behavior. Furthermore, economic forecasters are so convinced of the importance of economic expectations that a measure is incorporated into virtually all macroeconomic forecasting models. Consumer confidence is part of the Index of Leading Economic Indicators published monthly by the Department of Commerce. Survey results on consumer confidence are routinely reported by the popular press and in the economic news. The success of this approach to forecasting the economy is confirmed by the many other organizations that monitor consumer confidence at the national, state, and local levels in the United States, and across the twenty-six other countries that conduct analogous surveys (Curtin 2000). Indeed, there is also empirical evidence that the University of Michigan Survey Research Center's Survey of Consumers outperforms professional economists when forecasting some economic indicators (Thomas 1999). Thus, while individual economic actors are only "boundedly" rational, the aggregation of information across individuals can provide a strong indicator of future macroeconomic trends.[4]

## Determinants of Economic Uncertainty

Economic actors take cues and receive information about their current and future economic status from a variety of sources, including personal experience, the experiences of others, economic reports, the media, and elite economic actors.

At a personal level, each economic actor has a distinct set of attitudes and experiences. Past behavior may be a strong determinant of current behavior so that an individual willing to assume risk in the past should be more willing to do so in the present. Attitudes toward uncertainty and risk are also rooted in personal experience. Each economic actor has particular income capabilities, economic history, and personal surroundings. Education, social status, profession, and income should also be important. Economic actors also observe others in their proximate environment. As they see others in economic difficulty or prosperity, the signals from these contacts should alter the psychology of their behavior. These individual-specific effects probably average out when considering impacts on the entire economy. They may also produce inertia, however, if there is some dominant tendency among individuals.

At a more general level, economic uncertainty can flow from stimuli emanating from a broader context. For example, the economic news that people hear should affect their level of certainty about the economic future. As discussed in the introductory chapter, the economy and its various dimensions are among the most salient policy issues for most Americans. People's future income, jobs, and economic well-being depend on U.S. economic performance. Therefore, they are intensely interested in the economy and its various dimensions. The media widely report the economic news, and they produce frequent commentary about the health of economy. These factors mean that people are subjected rather continuously to a stream of information on economic performance, unemployment, inflation, interest rates, the deficit, and other economic indicators.

As shown in chapter 5, signals flowing from the economic news alter people's economic evaluations and their approval of the president's job performance. People get most of their information about the economy from the news. The economic news provides an important backdrop for how people view the current and future health of the economy. As the economic news becomes more negative, economic actors become more negative and uncertain in their evaluations of the economy. Conversely, positive economic news produces greater certainty and stronger evaluations of the economy. When we aggregate those who are affected by the economic news, the impacts on the larger economy can be substantial.

As shown in chapter 5, presidential optimism is important to people's perceptions of the economic news and their evaluations of the economy. As the president speaks more favorably about the economy, people perceive the economic news to be more positive and form stronger economic evaluations. Why should this be so? Again, presidents are the most visible and important economic actors in the U.S. system. People look to presidents for economic leadership. Presidents are assumed by virtue of their role and supporting expertise to have more information about the economy. Because presidents want to be reelected and seek favorable approval, they have a strong incentive to attend to the economy in their public remarks. Presidential rhetoric on the economy is highly publicized through White House press releases and public relations efforts. The media widely report presidential remarks whether they flow from the various economic reports or speeches. While citizens may not be familiar with the details of presidential remarks, they do usually comprehend the broad contours, and the relative optimism that the president expresses about the economy. Thus, through speeches and other public comments the president establishes a *tone* for federal involvement in the economy that in turn affects the news and economic evaluations by business and consumers.

Past economic research shows that as economic actors become more positive and certain about their future income stream, they become less cautious in their economic behavior (Caballero 1991; Carroll 1994, 1997; Carroll and Samwick 1997, 1998; Kimball 1990). In other words, when economic actors hear positive news and evaluate the economy more positively, they should become more prone toward assuming risk. Practically, this translates into more spending, borrowing, and investing, but less saving.

Of course, U.S. economic performance is a function of the individual behaviors of a myriad of economic actors. So in aggregate such changes in behavior should mean stronger economic performance than would otherwise occur. Through these mechanisms presidential optimism about the economy should affect U.S. economic performance *indirectly* by affecting people's perceptions of the economic news and their confidence in the future of the economy.

Presidential optimism may also affect U.S. economic performance *directly* by producing independent perceptions of strong presidential leadership. Controlling for presidential effects on the economic news and economic evaluations, people may be more prone toward taking economic risk because the president is perceived to be a good economic leader. People feel confident that the current administration will maintain a sound economy for the foreseeable future, and therefore feel more comfortable spending, borrowing, and investing.

For example, throughout his administration President Clinton repeatedly pounded home the theme that the U.S. economy was strong and robust. Perhaps as a result of the president's continuously optimistic emphasis on the economy, people felt more confident of the president's economic leadership. In turn, they were more inclined to spend, borrow, and invest with a degree of abandon. This may have contributed to what was the longest period of economic expansion of the modern era.

In contrast, during his first three years President George W. Bush repeatedly stressed the theme that the economy was in trouble. As suggested in chapter 4, he was probably motivated by partisan ambitions to reduce taxes for conservative supporters. A side-effect of the president's "talking down" of the economy, however, was to produce a lack of confidence in the president's economic leadership. The president's economic pessimism heightened the degree of uncertainty about the future of the economy, thereby altering the risks that economic actors were willing to take. One might argue that the resulting lack of confidence in presidential leadership was partially responsible for the tepid economic performance through this period.

## Summary and Graphical Representation

The theory described in the foregoing discussion implies various potential paths of how presidential rhetoric on the economy might affect economic behavior and performance. To be concrete, the path diagram in figure 6.1 summarizes the potential avenues of presidential influence on economic behavior and performance. Presidential rhetoric on the economy can affect economic behavior *indirectly* through mechanisms similar to those already demonstrated in chapter 5 for public approval. It may also affect economic behavior *directly* by altering people's confidence in the president's economic leadership and their relative caution when making economic decisions.

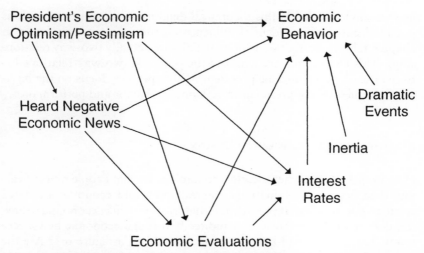

Figure 6.1 Potential Paths of Influence of Presidential Rhetoric on Economic Behavior and the Economy

Specifically, the links in figure 6.1 from the president passing through the news, economic evaluations, and interest rates to economic behavior suggest that presidential rhetoric on the economy can affect economic behavior *indirectly*. Presidential optimism affects the economic news that people report hearing. Presidential optimism affects people's economic evaluations directly, as well as indirectly through the economic news. Presidential optimism may also affect people's demand for money both directly and indirectly, which should be reflected through changing interest rates. All of these linkages may also affect the degree of risk that economic actors are willing to assume in their decisions to spend, borrow, and invest.

The link at the top of the diagram suggests that presidential rhetoric on the economy can also affect economic behavior *directly*. As presidents express optimism about the current and future of the economy, people become more confident in presidents' economic leadership. Perceptions of strong presidential leadership should enter into calculations by economic actors when making decisions to spend, borrow, and invest. As economic actors perceive the president as a strong economic leader, they are more willing to assume risk. Conversely, weak presidential leadership should produce more caution. In either case, presidential optimism about the economy should translate into altered economic behavior and performance.

Note also that figure 6.1 contains hypothetical single-headed arrows running from the president to various economic variables. We keep these arrows single-headed in this theoretical diagram to illustrate the various potential paths of presidential influence on the economy. We found in chapter 5, however, that some of these links are actually two-way relationships. This chapter further explores the potential two-way relations between the economy and the president, with a primary focus on the interconnectedness of the president to economic behavior and performance.

## MEASUREMENT AND RESEARCH DESIGN

How do presidential rhetoric, the economic news that people report hearing, their economic evaluations, interest rates, and economic behavior relate to one another? If presidential rhetoric does affect economic behavior, does it work directly and/or indirectly through economic news, economic evaluations, and interest rates as described in figure 6.1? Are the arrows shown in figure 6.1 really single-headed as drawn, or are some of them double-headed? We turn now toward answering these questions.

### Measurement

Our theory posits that spending, borrowing, and investing should depend on the degree of uncertainty that economic actors feel about the economy. The measures used to capture these effects were monthly time series running from January 1981 through January 2005 and obtained from the U.S. Federal Reserve Bank of St. Louis. The economic behavior concept in figure 6.1 was evaluated for two different kinds of economic actors: consumers and businesses.

First, a measure of personal consumption expenditure was used to capture the spending behavior of consumers. Personal consumption expenditures make up about two-thirds of all U.S. economic activity. Total personal consumption includes spending on items that are relatively inelastic in the face of economic uncertainty, as well as items that are highly elastic. For example, people seldom spend significantly less on food, energy, clothing, or healthcare as a function of increasing economic uncertainty. These items are necessities that people purchase under most circumstances. In contrast, as people become more uncertain about the economic future, they become reluctant to engage in discretionary spending. Items such as new housing, automobiles, appliances, luxury items, and other durable goods should more readily decline in the face of greater economic uncertainty. To increase the potential for a response in personal consumption to changing economic uncertainty, personal consumption was measured as real personal expenditures on durable goods as reported by the

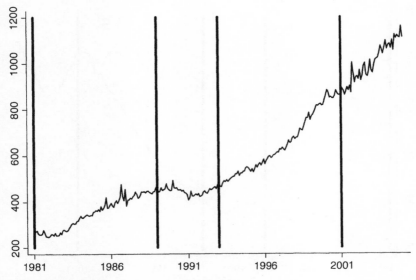

Figure 6.2  Personal Consumption of Durable Goods

U.S. Department of Commerce. Figure 6.2 graphs the personal consumption measure, along with indictors for each presidential administration.

Second, a separate analysis was done to evaluate the behavior of business actors. As with personal consumption, some business expenditures are required while others are discretionary. For example, expenditures for labor, maintenance, and materials are mandatory if a business is to continue operating. On the other hand, businesses may be reluctant to expand and purchase new equipment under conditions of uncertainty. Conversely, as economic uncertainty declines, we should see a greater willingness on the part of businesses and corporations to invest in new equipment and facilities. Thus, business investment was measured as real monthly investment in fixed capital. Again, this measure captures the willingness of businesses and corporations to make investments in equipment and facilities needed for an expanding economy. Figure 6.3 graphs this measure.[5]

The economic news variable in figure 6.1 was measured with monthly data from the University of Michigan's Survey of Consumers. This is the same measure as that used in chapter 5 and graphed in figure 5.3. The Survey of Consumers routinely asks the question, "During the last few months, have you heard of any favorable or unfavorable changes in business conditions?" This is followed up by the question, "What news did you hear?" The possible responses to the follow-up question include mul-

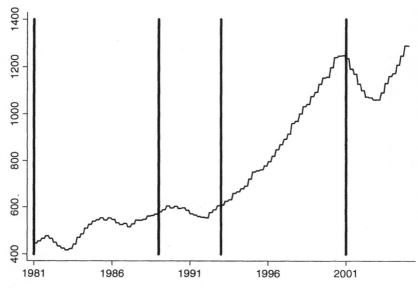

Figure 6.3  Business Investment in Fixed Capital

tiple dimensions of the economy, including unemployment, consumer demand, inflation, interest rates, energy problems, the stock market, the
trade deficit, and government policy. The measure of economic news was
the monthly percentage of respondents reporting that they had heard negative economic news of any kind.

As noted in the last chapter, the economic news variable is a strong
control for how consumers and businesses see the economy. However,
because the central concept under investigation in this chapter is economic behavior, the analysis also contains a summary measure of current
U.S. economic performance. Specifically, I included the monthly percent
change in the Conference Board's Composite Index of Coincident Indicators. This is an index of four time series chosen because they can be
shown to be consistently in step with the current economy.[6] The four
time series making up the Coincident Index are payroll employment,
personal income, industrial production, and manufacturing and trade
sales, the last three in 1996 dollars. According to the Conference Board
(2001, 13), the Coincident Index is a "broad series that measures aggregate economic activity; thus they define the business cycle." Figure 6.4
graphs this measure.

The economic evaluations concept in figure 6.1 was measured using the
University of Michigan's Index of Consumer Sentiment. Again, this is the
same measure as that used in chapter 5 and graphed in figure 5.4. It is

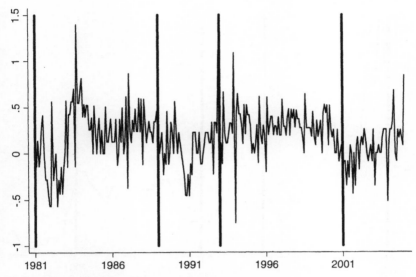

Figure 6.4  Coincident Index of Economic Indicators

also one of two measures routinely used by economic forecasters as an indicator of consumer confidence.[7] Survey results on consumer sentiment are routinely reported by the popular press and in the economic news. Therefore, there should be some relation between the economic news that people report hearing and their economic evaluations. This approach to forecasting economic behavior is also widely believed to be an indicator of future macroeconomic performance (Curtin 2000).

Interest rates should, as shown in figure 6.1, strongly affect economic behavior by both consumer and business actors. Of course, interest rates are an integral part of the market for money, and so relations may also run in multiple directions. The supply of money is under the partial control of the Federal Reserve System as it manipulates the federal funds rate through open market operations. The federal funds rate, however, only partially determines other interest rates in the system. The prime rate is more important than the federal funds rate to most credit operations. This is the interest rate that banks charge their best customers. Consumer credit is strongly tied to the prime rate, as is credit extended to businesses. As interest rates increase, economic actors should borrow, consume, and invest less; as they decrease, economic actors should borrow, consume, and invest more. Interest rates are measured as the prime interest rate, and are graphed in figure 6.5.

In the other direction, economic confidence and behavior should affect interest rates. A lack of confidence about the economic future should

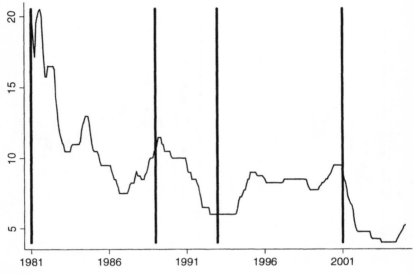

Figure 6.5 Prime Interest Rate

make consumers and businesses more reluctant to borrow, resulting in lower demand for money and downward pressure on interest rates. As consumers and businesses become more certain of a prosperous economic environment, they should be less reluctant to borrow, resulting in higher demand for money and upward pressure on interest rates. Thus, presidential optimism, the economic news, and economic evaluations should affect interest rates, which may in turn affect personal consumption and business investment expenditures.

Of course, the key research concept for the theory is that reflecting the relative optimism of presidential rhetoric about the economy. We are primarily interested in how presidential optimism affects the other variables in figure 6.1, and ultimately presidential impacts on economic behavior. Does presidential rhetoric affect the demand for money and interest rates? Does it affect consumer spending or business investment? To capture the presidential optimism concept, we use the same measure as in chapter 5. Again, this is a composite of the measures developed in chapter 2 taken as the sum of presidential optimisms on the general economy, unemployment, inflation, and federal deficit. This results in an index of presidential optimism that captures the president's overall optimism along the most important dimensions of the economy. The presidential optimism measure is graphed in figure 5.5.

Additionally, an events series similar to that presented in chapter 5 was included exogenously in the VAR analyses to capture changes due to dramatic events. Economic confidence is tied to confidence in institutions and the system generally. Crises such as September 11 produced sharp changes in most of the economic variables in figure 6.1 as greater uncertainty entered the system. Similarly, scandal, war, assassination attempts, and so forth tend to lower confidence in the system and the economy generally. This should impact most of the variables in figure 6.1. Therefore, it is important to control for these shocks to avoid confounding systematic effects with random events.[8]

## STATISTICAL RESULTS

As in chapter 5, vector autoregression (VAR) methods were used to evaluate the direction of relationships and track the temporal dynamics among the variables in the system (Freeman, Williams, and Lin 1989; Sims 1980). The VAR-X approach was employed to enable inclusion of the exogenous measure for political drama.[9] Again, two separate VAR analyses were done to evaluate the relations depicted in figure 6.1. One analysis focused on personal consumption expenditures for durable goods, while the other looked at business investment in fixed capital. The results of the two analyses are again similar and reinforcing, and so they are discussed together.

Granger tests are reported in tables 6.1 and 6.2. The arrows in the tables indicate a Granger causal relationship from the left-side variable to the right-side variable. The moving average responses are reported in figures 6.6 and 6.7. The graphs along the diagonals of figures 6.6 and 6.7 contain the variables being shocked in the simulations (as indicated by the left-side labels). The responses to the shocks appear in rows horizontally (as indicated by the top labels). The magnitudes of the simulated shocks along the diagonals of figures 6.6 and 6.7 are one standard error of the regression. The dashed lines around the responses mark fractile confidence intervals as recommended by Sims and Zha (1999).

### Evaluating Reverse Causality

In evaluating the effect of presidential rhetoric on economic behavior, it is important to control for possible responses by the president to the other variables in the system. Thus, we again consider first the relative responsiveness of presidential rhetoric to the other variables. The first panel of table 6.1 shows that presidential optimism responds to the economic news. Table 6.2 is also suggestive of this effect. The evidence in table 6.2 shows that presidential rhetoric responds to business investment. However, the Granger tests show no response in presidential rhetoric to personal consumption, economic evaluations, interest rates, or the economy.

TABLE 6.1
Granger Tests for Vector Autoregression on Personal Consumption System

| Independent Variable | | Dependent Variable | p-value |
|---|---|---|---|
| Presidents' Economic Optimism | → | Presidents' Economic Optimism | 0.00 |
| Heard Negative Economic News | → | | 0.04 |
| Economic Evaluations | | | 0.27 |
| Interest Rates | | | 0.43 |
| Personal Consumption | | | 0.47 |
| Coincident Indicators | | | 0.90 |
| | | | |
| Presidents' Economic Optimism | | Heard Negative Economic News | 0.26 |
| Heard Negative Economic News | → | | 0.00 |
| Economic Evaluations | → | | 0.00 |
| Interest Rates | | | 0.67 |
| Personal Consumption | | | 0.65 |
| Coincident Indicators | → | | 0.03 |
| | | | |
| Presidents' Economic Optimism | → | Economic Evaluations | 0.10 |
| Heard Negative Economic News | | | 0.25 |
| Economic Evaluations | → | | 0.00 |
| Interest Rates | | | 0.11 |
| Personal Consumption | | | 0.01 |
| Coincident Indicators | | | |
| | | | |
| Presidents' Economic Optimism | | Interest Rates | 0.28 |
| Heard Negative Economic News | → | | 0.09 |
| Economic Evaluations | → | | 0.04 |
| Interest Rates | → | | 0.00 |
| Personal Consumption | | | 0.94 |
| Coincident Indicators | → | | 0.05 |
| | | | |
| Presidents' Economic Optimism | | Coincident Indicators | 0.32 |
| Heard Negative Economic News | → | | 0.05 |
| Economic Evaluations | | | 0.54 |
| Interest Rates | → | | 0.00 |
| Personal Consumption | → | | 0.01 |
| Coincident Indicators | → | | 0.01 |
| | | | |
| Presidents' Economic Optimism | → | Personal Consumption | 0.06 |
| Heard Negative Economic News | | | 0.43 |
| Economic Evaluations | | | 0.81 |
| Interest Rates | | | 0.16 |
| Personal Consumption | → | | 0.00 |
| Coincident Indicators | | | 0.70 |

*Note*: The arrows indicate Granger causality from the block of coefficients for the independent variable to the dependent variable based on 0.10 significance levels.

TABLE 6.2
Granger Tests for Vector Autoregression on Investment System

| Independent Variable | | Dependent Variable | p-value |
|---|---|---|---|
| Presidents' Economic Optimism | → | Presidents' Economic Optimism | 0.00 |
| Heard Negative Economic News | | | 0.12 |
| Economic Evaluations | | | 0.25 |
| Interest Rates | | | 0.55 |
| Business Investment | → | | 0.04 |
| Coincident Indicators | | | 0.89 |
| Presidents' Economic Optimism | | Heard Negative Economic News | 0.49 |
| Heard Negative Economic News | → | | 0.00 |
| Economic Evaluations | → | | 0.00 |
| Interest Rates | | | 0.47 |
| Business Investment | → | | 0.05 |
| Coincident Indicators | → | | 0.06 |
| Presidents' Economic Optimism | | Economic Evaluations | 0.23 |
| Heard Negative Economic News | | | 0.27 |
| Economic Evaluations | → | | 0.00 |
| Interest Rates | → | | 0.10 |
| Business Investment | | | 0.66 |
| Coincident Indicators | → | | 0.00 |
| Presidents' Economic Optimism | | Interest Rates | 0.30 |
| Heard Negative Economic News | | | 0.17 |
| Economic Evaluations | → | | 0.05 |
| Interest Rates | → | | 0.00 |
| Business Investment | | | 0.82 |
| Coincident Indicators | | | 0.11 |
| Presidents' Economic Optimism | | Coincident Indicators | 0.15 |
| Heard Negative Economic News | → | | 0.07 |
| Economic Evaluations | | | 0.45 |
| Interest Rates | → | | 0.00 |
| Business Investment | → | | 0.01 |
| Coincident Indicators | → | | 0.01 |
| Presidents' Economic Optimism | → | Business Investment | 0.02 |
| Heard Negative Economic News | | | 0.14 |
| Economic Evaluations | → | | 0.07 |
| Interest Rates | | | 0.34 |
| Business Investment | → | | 0.00 |
| Coincident Indicators | | | 0.13 |

Note: The arrows indicate Granger causality from the block of coefficients for the independent variable to the dependent variable based on 0.10 significance levels.

**Response of:**

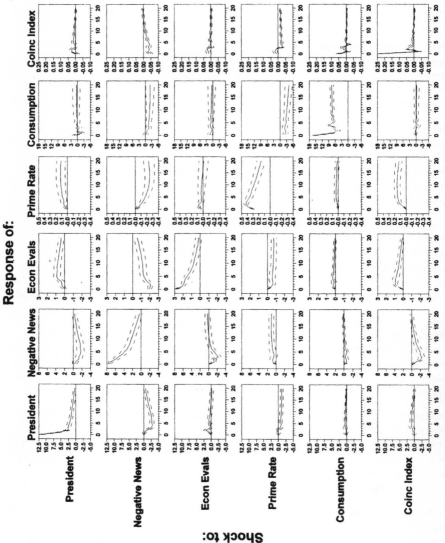

Figure 6.6 Impulse Responses for Personal Consumption System

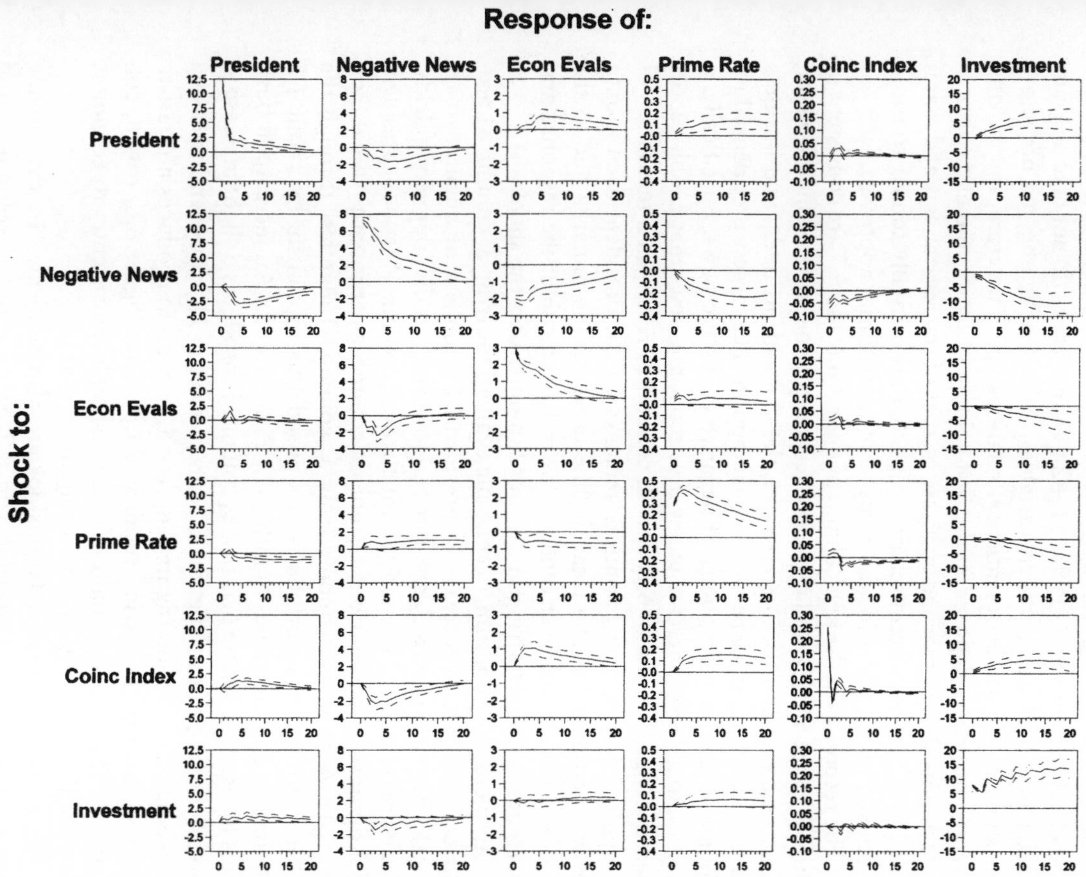

**Response of:**

Figure 6.7  Impulse Responses for Investment System

These tests are limited in several respects. As proven by Lutkepohl, "the lack of a Granger-causal relationship from one group of variables to the remaining variables cannot necessarily be interpreted as a lack of a cause and effect relationship" (1993, 41–42). Granger tests do not take account of dynamic feedback between variables. Additionally, they do not show the sign or magnitude of statistical relationships. Therefore, the moving average responses depicted in the first column of figures 6.6 and 6.7 provide a more descriptive and accurate picture of the reverse causal dynamics. These graphs contain relationships that are partially similar to those discussed in chapter 5 for the analysis of presidential approval.

The responses in the first column of figures 6.6 and 6.7 are consistent in showing that presidential optimism responds to negative economic news, economic evaluations, interest rates, the Coincident Index, and business investment, but not to personal consumption. The largest presidential response is due to perceptions of negative economic news. Specifically, a one standard error increase in negative economic news that people report hearing (figures 6.6 and 6.7, row 2, column 2) results in a maximum of roughly 2.5 fewer net optimistic remarks by the president each month (row 2, column 1). The total decline in optimistic remarks due to the shock is distributed over time as shown by the rise in the response and subsequent decay starting in the fourth month after the shock.

An increase in consumer economic evaluations (row 3, column 3) produces a short-term increase in presidential optimism of about two remarks per month (row 3, column 1). However, this dies out very quickly. An increase in the prime interest rate (row 4, column 4) reduces presidential optimism by about one optimistic comment per month (row 4, column 1). A stronger economy (row 5, column 5) manifest through the Coincident Index slightly increases presidential optimism by about 1.5 optimistic comments per month (row 5, column 1). An increase in business investment (figure 6.7, row 6, column 6) produces a slight increase in presidential optimism (figure 6.7, row 6, column 1). However, increasing personal consumption (figure 6.6, row 6, column 6) produces no statistically significant change in presidential optimism (figure 6.6, row 6, column 1). Thus, presidential optimism responds consistently to economic news and to a variety of other economic variables.

Other reverse causal relationships are also confirmed by the moving average responses. Figures 6.6 and 6.7 (rows 2 and 3, columns 2 and 3) confirm the result in chapter 5 that reports of hearing more negative economic news produce more negative economic evaluations. Conversely, more positive economic evaluations produce less perception of negative economic news. The magnitude of these reverse causal effects is roughly similar to that reported in chapter 5.

Figures 6.6 and 6.7 also show that the economic variables in our system respond interdependently in a manner consistent with common economic expectations. Increasing interest rates (row 4, column 4) produce an increase in negative economic news, and declines in economic evaluations, the Coincident Indicators and personal consumption and investment (row 4, columns 2 through 6). An increase in the Coincident Indexes (row 5, column 5) produces large declines in perceptions of negative economic news, and large increases in economic evaluations, the prime rate, personal consumption, and business investment (row 5, columns 2 through 6). Increasing personal consumption (figure 6.6, row 6, column 6) produces no statistically significant change in any other measure (figure 6.6, columns 2 through 6). Finally, increasing business investment (figure 6.7, row 6, column 6) produces a decline in negative economic news and slightly increasing interest rates, but no change in economic evaluations or the Coincident Index (row 6, columns 2 through 6). Thus, many of the single-headed arrows depicted in figure 6.1 are actually double-headed, as they were in chapter 5.

## Evaluating the Direct and Indirect Effects of Presidential Optimism on Economic Behavior

Controlling for these reverse causal relationships, does presidential optimism affect economic behavior either directly or indirectly as suggested in figure 6.1? The analysis of the direct effects of presidential optimism on economic behavior is contained in the sixth panel of tables 6.1 and 6.2 and in figures 6.6 and 6.7 at row 1, column 6. The Granger tests in both tables show a statistically significant effect of presidential optimism on both personal consumption ($p$-value = 0.02) and business investment ($p$-value = 0.06). The direction and magnitude of these direct effects, however, can be observed only by examining the moving average responses in figures 6.6 and 6.7.

Figure 6.6 suggests that any effect of presidential optimism on consumer behavior must be weak and short-term. The shock in presidential optimism (row 1, column 1) produces a moving average response that is statistically significant only in the first period (row 1, column 6). This implies that consumer memory of presidential remarks about the economy must be very fleeting when making personal consumption decisions.

Figure 6.7, however, *strongly* affirms the result in table 6.2 by showing a large direct and long-term effect of presidential optimism on business investment. A one standard error increase in presidential optimism (row 1, column 1) produces a statistically significant response in business investment extending for at least twenty months (row 1, column 6). The maximum increase in business investment for any single period is about

$6.75 billion. This is a small number relative to total business investment in 2004 of almost $1.3 trillion. However, the full response to the shock to presidential optimism is the sum of the responses under the curve. This totals $106 billion, a more impressive number. Thus, increased presidential optimism can have an important direct impact on business investment over an extended period.

Do consumers and businesses respond indirectly to presidential optimism working through the news and economic evaluations? The evidence shows that there are strong indirect effects through multiple paths. As in chapter 5, the Granger tests in table 6.1 suggest a Granger causal relation between presidential optimism and people's economic evaluations. Again these tests ignore feedback among variables, however, and so the moving average responses in figures 6.6 and 6.7 contain a more descriptive and accurate picture.

The first row of figures 6.6 and 6.7 shows that presidents' remarks about the economy affect the economic news that people report hearing and their economic evaluations. As in chapter 5, a one standard error increase in presidential optimism produces a maximum decline of about 2 percent in the number of people reporting that they heard negative economic news (row 1, column 2). The same shock produces a maximum increase of about one unit in people's economic evaluations (row 1, column 3). The total effect from both variables, is actually larger than that reported in chapter 5, after controlling for interest rates and economic behavior and performance. Again, the total effect from these shocks is calculated by summing the responses under the curves. This implies a decline of about 22 percent in the number of people reporting that they heard negative news about the economy, and about a 13-unit increase in people's economic evaluations. These are large effects.

The indirect effect of presidential optimism through these paths functions both through people's perceptions of the economic news and through economic evaluations. More negative economic news (row 2, column 2) results in less personal consumption and business investment (row 2, column 6). Stronger economic evaluations (row 3, column 3) produce slightly increased personal consumption (figure 6.6, row 3, column 6), and significantly higher business investment (figure 6.7, row 3, column 6). The reverse-feedback effects discussed earlier accentuate this indirect link since both the news and economic evaluations reinforce one another, as well as presidential tendencies toward speaking optimistically or pessimistically about the economy.

Figures 6.6 and 6.7 also show that increasing presidential optimism affects interest rates. A one standard error positive shock in presidential optimism (row 1, column 1) produces a maximum 0.13 percent increase in the prime interest rate (row 1, column 4). The total implied effect of a shock in presidential optimism on the prime rate is about 2 percent over the next twenty months. Given that the prime rate is determined by both the supply and demand for money through the U.S. system, there are at least two mechanisms whereby presidents might affect interest rates. First, presidential optimism might bias the decisions of the Federal Reserve Board toward decreasing the money supply to counteract the stimulative effect of presidential optimism on the economy. More likely though, a sense of strong economic leadership by presidents might produce greater demand for money. This in turn results in higher interest rates and consequent impacts on economic behavior.

A president's economic rhetoric affects interest rates. In turn, the change in interest rates affects all other variables in the system in a manner consistent with intuitive expectations. A one standard error shock in the prime rate (row 4, column 4) is around 0.40 percent, or, from the preceding analysis, about one third of such a change might be attributable to a shock in presidential optimism. An increase in the prime rate of this magnitude increases perceptions of negative economic news (row 4, column 2), and decreases economic evaluations (row 4, column 3). These changes in turn produce indirect effects on both personal consumption and business investment through the paths discussed previously.

Additionally, interest rates directly affect economic performance, personal consumption, and business investment (figures 6.6 and 6.7, row 4, columns 5 and 6). Calculating the effect across multiple months, a one standard error increase in the prime interest rate produces declining personal consumption across multiple months of about $57 billion. Similarly, the same shock produces declining business investment of about $32 billion. While these are not huge changes relative to total personal consumption on durable goods and business investment, they are indicative of how presidents can indirectly influence economic behavior by altering economic confidence and borrowing.

As in chapter 5, we can summarize the results of what may seem a complex statistical analysis using a revised path diagram. Figure 6.8 shows the linkages found empirically by the statistical analysis. Note that the only hypothesized linkage from the president to economic variables from figure 6.1 that is *not* double-headed is that from economic behavior to economic evaluations. This says that personal consumption and business investment decisions do not affect citizen evaluations of the economy. All of the other linkages suggest the strong interconnectedness of the U.S. economy, and of the president with that economy.

Moreover, if we consider both the direct and indirect effects of presidential optimism on economic variables through all paths, then it becomes obvious that presidential effects on economic behavior can be substantial. Presidents' words affect the economic confidence of actors throughout

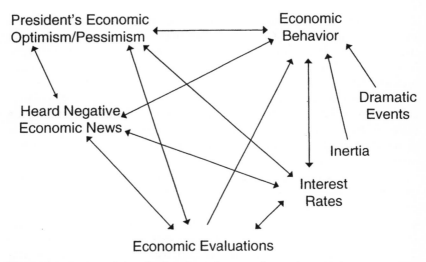

Figure 6.8 Statistical Results for the Influence of Presidential Rhetoric on Economic Behavior and the Economy

the U.S. system and their behavior. Of course, the micro-foundations of U.S. economic performance are rooted in the behavior of millions of economic actors making billions of market transactions daily. As individuals make choices about how to use their money, aggregate economic outcomes result. Therefore, presidential words can also have major impacts on U.S. economic performance through time.

CONCLUSIONS

The public imposes high expectations on presidents for maintaining a sound economy. In turn, chief executives have various tools for accomplishing these ends. A president can attempt to affect the money in consumers' pockets by altering the tax code or through federal spending decisions. The president can affect the cost of producer-consumer exchanges through regulatory policy. The president can also potentially affect interest rates and the money in consumers' pockets through nominations to the Federal Reserve Board. Yet, all of these tools are constrained by the need for cooperation from other institutions.

In affecting the economy through taxing or spending, presidents can make proposals, but the Congress must agree with the proposal for change to occur. Similarly, a president shares regulatory authority with both Congress and the bureaucracy. Monetary policy is the shared domain of the Federal Reserve, which is generally viewed as substantially independent of executive authority. These institutional features mean that there are impediments and delays for a president wanting to affect macroeconomic performance directly through these tools. Thus, while there are high expectations on the presidency, presidents' ability to accomplish economic ends is often limited by adverse institutional arrangements.

What has not been widely understood until now is that presidents have yet another tool that can affect economic behavior and performance, and which can be exercised in substantial independence of other political institutions: *economic rhetoric*. Past research on presidential rhetoric has discounted the importance of presidents' words. In this chapter, however, we have shown that presidents' words are a powerful instrument of economic leadership that can affect consumer and business perceptions of current and future economic conditions. Remarks that inspire confidence result in stronger economic confidence and perceptions that the economic news is good. Remarks that are pessimistic produce greater uncertainty and perceptions that the economic news is bad. Both effects produce tangible results for the U.S. economy by affecting the risks that consumers and businesses are willing to take. The analysis in this chapter shows definitively that optimistic presidential rhetoric makes a difference to consumer confidence, perceptions of the economic news, and interest rates. In turn, these effects produce stronger personal consumption and business investment.

The president's message, however, is only one of the signals affecting decisions by economic actors about how to allocate their income. Therefore, it is unlikely that presidential rhetoric affects economic behavior uniformly at the individual level. Individuals interpret their economic circumstances using their beliefs, ideology, information, education, and intellect. They do the best that they can by relying on cues and information from their environment. While presidential words are probably marginal to these processes, high visibility and ubiquitous media coverage mean that the tone of presidential remarks can affect a substantial number of economic actors. As the results reported in this chapter suggest, the aggregation of these effects across the entire economy can have meaningful effects on macroeconomic variables.

Of course, presidents always have multiple agendas that can produce conflicting incentives for using economic rhetoric. Some presidents may see economic optimism as a tool for promoting their own popularity. Others may want to satisfy various partisan goals that conflict with taking an optimistic stance on the economy. For example, a president driven by a partisan agenda of reducing taxes may find it expedient to "talk down" a robust economy in order to provide an economic justification for the policy.

In either case, the results reported here suggest that insincere rhetoric may be a dangerous game. This is because presidential rhetoric can have a substantial effect on macroeconomic outcomes. At times, the effect of presidential rhetoric may be even larger than suggested by the analysis. For example, the change in presidential optimism between the Clinton and second Bush administration was much larger than the movements evaluated in our simulations. Given the magnitude of the potential effects, presidents who seek reelection and approval may be better served by maintaining credible economic leadership.

Credible economic leadership requires chief executives to be an independent force, using rhetoric to establish a supportive tone for other economic actors. It also requires that the tone of presidential remarks be a reasonable assessment of current and future economic conditions. More generally, given the demonstrated power of a president's words, future presidents should jealously guard their credibility by using economic rhetoric wisely.

# CHAPTER 7

# Why Should We Care about Presidents' Economic Rhetoric?

WE LIVE IN THE ERA of the permanent campaign (Blumenthal 1982; Gergen 2000). "The line between campaigning and governing has all but disappeared, with campaigning increasingly dominant." (Ornstein and Mann 2000, vii). Modern presidents continually engage in public activities to affect their own approval, policy attitudes, and to facilitate governing. The permanent campaign has altered how individual presidents govern. It has also had an enduring influence on the institutions of the presidency (Tenpas 2000). The campaign style of governing is likely to continue for the foreseeable future (Jones 2000). Therefore, it is increasingly important to understand how presidents conduct the permanent campaign, and whether their activities have any consequences.

A major part of the permanent campaign involves the presidents' rhetoric on the economy. Unless there is a crisis, modern presidents talk more about the economy than any other single issue. Modern presidential styles are naturally rhetorical due to the requisites of achieving office. They also use institutional prerogatives to talk about the economy and campaign for policy proposals intended to affect the economy. Modern presidents are accountable for the economy, and they generally seek to convince others that their stewardship is good.

What are the causes and consequences of presidents' permanent campaign on the economy? This book has used empirical data and analysis to answer these questions.

## HOW AND WHY DO PRESIDENTS TALK ABOUT THE ECONOMY?

The analysis reported in this book shows that, historically, presidents have talked about the economy more and more through time. Why has this trend occurred? In part, it must be due to legal, political, and systemic changes. The legal requisites facing the modern presidency have increased from earlier eras. The Employment Act of 1946 (PL 79–304) charged the president with promoting "maximum employment, production, and purchasing power." The mandate for the president to promote a sound economy expanded with passage of the Humphrey-Hawkins Act of 1978

(PL 95–523). The reinforced mandate from the Humphrey-Hawkins Act placed responsibility for U.S. economic performance squarely on the shoulders of the president. Presidents have increasingly felt the burden of this institutional responsibility. Therefore, they have increasingly emphasized the economy in their public rhetoric.

Politically, citizens have held presidents accountable for the economy. When presidents fail the test of economic leadership, their approval suffers, as does the chance of reelection for them as well as their party. Presidents have recognized this linkage. The public relations apparatus that they maintain to build their presidential image and promote favorable perceptions has become increasingly sophisticated and active. An important way to give the appearance of presidential leadership is through public rhetoric. Therefore, modern presidents have increasingly talked about the economy.

Additionally, there have been systemic changes affecting who is likely to become president and what is required to maintain the public's approval. In earlier eras, party elites selected presidential candidates, and presidents relied on bargaining and compromise to govern. Since the 1970s, presidential primaries have been important, and media coverage of candidates has grown in intensity and significance. Due to changes in the environment for selecting presidential candidates, a more rhetorical style has emerged for the presidency. The rhetorical style required to achieve the presidency has increasingly carried over into governing. In an age of mass communication and entertainment media, the president is now both predisposed toward and expected to be inclined toward using public rhetoric (Blumenthal 1982; Gergen 2000; Ornstein and Mann 2000).

Riding on this trend of increasing economic rhetoric are significant variations across presidencies. The analysis showed that presidents are unique in their personal styles when using economic rhetoric. President Carter had an intensely positive personal style, even when there was significant inflation and economic adversity. In contrast, President Reagan had an acquiescent personal style, simply responding with consistent optimism and pessimism as the economy swung down and up. Indeed, at the bottom of the 1982–83 recession, Reagan was more pessimistic than any other president. President Clinton had the most intense and positive personal style of any president. His mantra "It's the economy, stupid!" came to life through his rhetoric on the deficit and all other dimensions of U.S. economic performance. President George W. Bush exhibited an opportunistic rhetorical style as he first became a pessimist when pursuing major tax cuts, and later became highly optimistic to make the case for reelection.

Beyond the historical trend and relatively fixed stylistic features characterizing each presidency, there are also predictable dynamics to the presidents' economic rhetoric within presidencies. Presidents seek to influence public attitudes about their economic leadership, and they do so with an eye toward public perceptions rather than actual economic outcomes. The analysis in chapter 3 showed that presidents do not consistently alter the intensity and tone of their economic rhetoric in response to reports of objective economic indicators. The analysis in chapters 5 and 6 showed that they do, however, alter the tone of their economic rhetoric when citizens alter their perceptions of the economic news and their evaluations of the state of the economy. In other words, presidents' economic rhetoric is sensitive to political signals emanating from the electorate, but not to actual economic indicators.

Hetherington's (1996) analysis showed that it is citizens' perceptions of the economy, rather than objective conditions, that matter most when they evaluate a president's job performance. Interestingly, this study shows a similar result for presidential rhetoric. Presidents adjust their economic rhetoric in response to citizen *perceptions* of the economy, not in response to objective economic conditions. This implies that presidents are very savvy about what moves the electorate. Presidents and their staffs feel the pulse of the public as they evaluate the economy. Presidential rhetoric adjusts accordingly to appear sympathetic or attentive to what concerns the public.

Consistent with this image of the presidency as perceptive about the electorate, other results in this study suggest that presidents talk about the economy and its various dimensions when it is politically beneficial. For example, the analysis in chapter 3 showed that presidents typically become more intense in their economic rhetoric when more people consider the economy to be the most important problem facing the nation. Moreover, presidents talk more about unemployment when people consider unemployment important. A similar set of results occurred for inflation and the deficit. The intensity of presidential rhetoric mirrors people's perceptions of the severity of specific economic conditions. Presidents obviously want to appear sympathetic and capable of leading when people are concerned about particular issues.

Controlling for presidential responses to public perceptions of specific economic conditions, the analysis in chapter 3 also showed that presidents talk more about the general economy when their public approval ratings are low. However, they talk less about specific dimensions of the economy. Perhaps presidents fear that discussion of specific dimensions of the economy will be too technical when trying to bolster lower approval ratings. Alternatively, they might view remarks about unemployment or inflation as emphasizing adverse conditions that tend to exist at the same time that their approval is low. Thus, they prefer sending a more general message with simple signals that people can readily understand and that emphasize the positive.

Interestingly, the analyses in both chapters 3 and 5 showed no consistent relationship between the public's approval of the president's job performance and the tone of presidential remarks on the economy. Some presidents talk positively about the economy when their approval ratings are high (e.g., Clinton). Others talk positively about the economy when their approval ratings are low (e.g., Carter). Still others are invariant in the tone of their remarks about the economy as their approval ratings change (e.g., George W. Bush). Thus, the nature of presidential responses to changing public approval of their job performance depends on presidents' personal styles, rather than on a uniform imperative across presidencies.

A very strong and consistent finding of this study is that presidents talk more, and more positively, about the economy during presidential election years. Of course, the economy is a perennial election year issue. By virtue of their incumbency, sitting presidents run on their record of economic leadership. Challengers generally deride incumbents' record of economic leadership to gain favor with voters. In turn, presidents respond to challenges by touting the effectiveness of administration policies and leadership. As presidents attempt to woo economic voters and stave off political opponents, they elevate the intensity of their economic remarks as well as become increasingly optimistic.

Beyond efforts to shape public opinion on their economic leadership, presidents also attempt to shape public opinion about their policy proposals. Thus, they talk more intensely about economic issues during efforts to pass important economic legislation. The analysis in chapter 3 showed that during the period between proposing major legislation and the time of passage by Congress, presidents make frequent public remarks about the economy and its various dimensions. Presidents "go public" to enlist the public's support with Congress during these legislative efforts (Kernell 1997).

Interestingly, however, the tone of presidential remarks while pushing significant economic legislation has differed markedly across presidents. For example, President Reagan was no more optimistic or pessimistic than usual when pushing for major tax cut legislation in 1981. In contrast, President Clinton was highly optimistic in his public remarks when pushing legislation to address the federal deficit and stimulate the economy in 1993. In further contrast, President George W. Bush was highly pessimistic while pushing for tax cut legislation between 2001 and 2003. Thus, the personal styles of presidents primarily determine *how* they make the case for economic legislation.

The overall image that emerges from the analysis in this book is that modern presidents are political creatures who seek personal or partisan benefit from economic rhetoric. Politics determines *how* and *why* presidents engage in the permanent campaign. Presidents talk about the economy to bolster their public approval, appear sensitive to the public, achieve policy ends, and secure reelection for themselves or their political party. For any student of American politics, this self-serving orientation of the presidency should not be surprising. The habits of a long political career are what drive most presidential behavior. Benefit-seeking is part of the hereditary code that characterizes most politicians, and only the best politicians become president in normal times.

## DOES PRESIDENTIAL RHETORIC ON THE ECONOMY MATTER?

We have explored the impact of presidential remarks about the economy on presidents' public approval and economic perceptions and behavior. Contrary to much past research, we found that presidential remarks *do* make a difference. There could be at least two reasons for this divergence from past findings.

First, past research has been exceedingly simplistic in considering how presidents might affect public opinion and attitudes. Indeed, one significant body of research on presidents' public approval has simply ignored the presidents themselves in models explaining presidential approval. These scholars have generally recognized the overarching importance of public perceptions of the economy to the public's assessment of presidents' job performance. They have uniformly failed, however, to make the connection between the president and public assessments of the economy or presidential approval.

We showed in chapter 5 that presidents *directly* affect their own approval ratings. As presidents talk more optimistically about the economy, their Gallup approval increases marginally. This suggests some benefit to presidents from positive economic leadership. However, a larger response to presidential rhetoric occurs through the *indirect* effect on the economic news that people report hearing and on their economic evaluations. As presidents become more optimistic about the economy, people report hearing less negative economic news. Additionally, they evaluate the economy more positively with more positive presidential rhetoric. These changes, in turn, produce indirect effects on public approval of a president's job performance. As should be obvious from these changes through multiple paths, presidents are important to the concept of presidential approval.

Another significant body of research has taken presidents seriously as having the potential to affect public opinion, but has also used simplistic causal models of how presidents might affect public opinion. The general conclusion from this research is that major presidential speeches have little or brief effects on either public approval or attitudes on policy. Most of this work has focused on whether single presidential speeches produce change in public opinion. Yet, it is doubtful that White House communication strategies place so much emphasis on single speeches. It is also doubtful that citizens perceive and translate single messages from the president into immediate responses.

The permanent campaign means that modern presidents engage in a sustained effort to shape public opinion. The sustained presidential message about the economy helps establish a context for assessing presidents and the economy. In this regard, presidents use a variety of tools including speeches, interviews, economic reports, press conferences, press releases, town meetings, and other forms of communication. Information from all of these sources flows into the news stream. People perceive the news and make judgments about presidents and the economy based on the flow of stimuli emanating from the presidency. A single presidential speech may have little or no impact since it is just one of many cues received by citizens. A sustained presidential message, however, can have a strong impact that spreads more slowly and evolves more dynamically over time.

This study has demonstrated that the presidents' public relations efforts with respect to the economy affect public attitudes dynamically through multiple causal paths. Presidential optimism about the economy affects people's perceptions of the economic news. This, in turn, affects their evaluations of the economy. Presidential optimism also affects people's economic evaluations directly. The economic news that people report hearing and their economic evaluations, in turn, affect their approval of a president's job performance and economic behavior. Thus, the sustained presidential message produces responses that develop over time through multiple paths not previously recognized or modeled by past research.

A second reason why the findings of this study may have differed from those of past research is that the study was designed to produce an optimal set of conditions for presidential influence on public opinion. The time frame for the empirical analysis was restricted to the period from the Reagan presidency through January 2005. Presidents Reagan and Clinton were especially strong in their rhetorical skills. During this period, the White House press operation became particularly sophisticated, and made strong efforts to alter public opinion on matters of importance to the president. Furthermore, choosing the economy as the issue for analysis was intended to offer the president maximum potential for impact on public opinion.

Zaller (1992) argued that moving public opinion is strongly conditional on whether a message is received by the public. For a message to be received, it must be well transmitted, and the potential receiver must be attentive and receptive. Past research has considered presidential rhetoric generally by focusing across a range of issues. This work, however, has focused intently on a single issue that has high public salience. Survey evidence discussed earlier shows that the economy is highly visible to many people most of the time. People are very attentive to economic issues because they can have personal effects. At the individual level, the economy determines "pocket book" outcomes such as jobs, prices, incomes, housing, poverty, etc. These are all matters that touch people's lives personally. Therefore, people should be very attentive and receptive to cues emanating from the presidency on the economy.

Presidents also transmit a strong message. Absent a crisis, presidents talk more about the economy than any other single issue. Modern presidents have engaged in an extended effort to shape public perceptions of their economic leadership. Presidents are an authoritative source of information on the economy. People assume by virtue of the presidents' institutional role and supporting expertise that they possess valuable information about the economy. Furthermore, the media broadly publicize the presidency, and especially presidential remarks about the economy. Thus, the president features prominently in the scheme whereby most Americans get most of their information about the economy.

These conditions provide the optimal context for a critical test of whether presidents' public remarks ever make a difference. The economy is highly salient to most Americans. Presidents give sustained attention to the economy. They are authoritative so that the news media provide intense coverage of administration remarks on the economy. Presidents' messages are well transmitted, and should be well received by an audience that is attentive. If presidents' remarks ever make a difference, it should be under these conditions.

Accordingly, this study has shown that presidential rhetoric on the economy alters a multiplicity of opinion- and attitude-related outcomes. These include public assessments of a president's job performance, the economic news, economic evaluations, personal consumption expenditures, business investment, interest rates, and ultimately U.S. economic performance. The combination of these effects provides abundant evidence that presidential words matter, and they matter to things of great importance to presidents and most Americans.

Presidents care about their public approval ratings and the economy. Most Americans care about the presidency and the economy. Therefore, it is likely that presidents will participate in a permanent campaign of economic rhetoric for the foreseeable future. Citizens will also continue responding to presidential words. Given the importance of this relationship to presidential power and the economy, social scientists should continue expanding understanding of how these processes work.

## DIRECTIONS FOR FUTURE RESEARCH

What should be the direction of future research on the presidency and public opinion? Debate should now end over whether presidents' words matter. We have seen definitively here that they do. With this question answered, future research should turn to other important questions relating to presidential rhetoric and public opinion.

For example, does presidential rhetoric matter to issue areas other than the economy? Does it matter for foreign policy, defense spending, healthcare, education, civil rights, and law and order? These are important issue domains, about which presidents sometimes send a sustained message. The media covers presidents' messages. The public is often attentive. Therefore, presidential words might matter for other issue domains.

More generally, future research should ask how various mediating factors affect presidents' ability to shape public opinion. For example, this study has suggested that issue salience affects how presidents are likely to affect public opinion. Can presidents alter the salience of an issue, thereby altering their own ability to shape public opinion? Past research is ambiguous on this topic. For example, Cohen (1995) and Hill (1998) examine public responses to State of the Union messages and conclude that presidents sometimes affect public attentiveness to various issues, but only for a brief period. Wood and Peake (1998) and Edwards and Wood (1999) cast doubt on this finding by showing that media coverage of particular issues is usually unresponsive to presidential rhetoric. The analysis in chapter 4, however, showed that President Clinton significantly altered public views of the importance of the federal deficit during his campaign for deficit reduction legislation. These contrasting findings require clarification with a definitive study if we are fully to understand presidential influence on public opinion.

Additionally, this study merely asserted that issue salience is important to presidents' rhetorical leadership. This assertion was not tested. Does the public's attention to an issue affect presidents' ability to shape public opinion? It seems natural that it would. If it does, then does issue salience mediate the relationship between presidential rhetoric and public opinion? Does it determine the relationship, so that presidents do not talk about low-salience issues because they think the public is unlikely to respond? Some past research has addressed this question with respect to presidential approval (Edwards, Mitchell, and Welch 1995). Social scientists, however, need to extend this work to public opinion more generally.

How do preconceptions, such as those deriving from ideology and partisanship, affect receptivity to presidents' messages? It seems likely that partisans of either political party will be less receptive to change when hearing a president's message. Opponents will typically dismiss the message, while the president's allies will typically approve of it. Undecided independents, however, may be more receptive. This implies that presidents can affect public opinion only at the margins. If this is true, then future research should be focusing on this subgroup, rather than the population at large, in exploring whether and how presidential words matter to public opinion.

How does presidential approval affect receptivity to presidents' messages? Past research has suggested that high presidential approval leads to more presidential influence in Congress, at least at the margins (Bond, Fleisher, and Wood 2003; Brace and Hinckley 1992; Edwards 1980, 1989, 1997; Ostrom and Simon 1985; Rivers and Rose 1985). This hints that presidential approval might also affect public receptivity to a president's message. Do popular presidents have an easier time convincing the public of the efficacy of their policy proposals? Do approval-enhancing events such a military interventions or foreign policy crises increase public receptivity to the president's message? Do approval-diminishing events such as scandals diminish public receptivity to a president's message?

These are all important scientific research questions that require answers if we are fully to understand how presidents' permanent campaigns shape public opinion. More broadly, future research should address these questions to enhance understanding of the role of presidents in our democracy. Presidents are key figures and receive near continuous attention from the media and public. Therefore, their activities and performance are always matters of interest to the system at large.

## WHY NOT CONTINUOUS PRESIDENTIAL OPTIMISM?

This study has shown that there are major advantages for presidents in being a rhetorical optimist. Economic optimism produces higher approval ratings. Higher approval ratings translate into political capital that presidents can spend in Congress, or with the American people for supporting policies. Moreover, higher approval ratings provide presidents with the solidary benefit of feeling popular, successful, and leaving a favorable historical legacy.

Economic optimism is also a tool that presidents can use to alter perceptions of their economic leadership, the state of the economy, economic behavior, and ultimately U.S. economic performance. These factors further influence presidential approval, and help presidents fulfill the role of institutional leader of the economy. Moreover, rhetoric is a tool that presidents can apply unilaterally, without the usual constraints from separation of powers, checks and balances, federalism, or divided government that characterize the American system. If presidents use this tool rationally, they can alter the economic tone producing positive benefits for themselves and the nation.

If presidents can positively affect their own approval ratings and a multiplicity of economic outcomes through mere words, then an obvious question is, "Why are presidents not optimistic all of the time?" A facile answer is that at least one president was. President Clinton spoke 3,730 sentences over eight years about the economy generally. Of these, this study coded 3,726 as optimistic, with only four as pessimistic, using the methodology of chapter 2. Clinton was also far more optimistic on specific dimensions of the economy, such as unemployment, inflation, and the deficit. As a perpetual optimist, Clinton enjoyed consistently high approval ratings after 1996 and did not suffer the late-term declines that characterized most other presidencies. He also enjoyed an economy with the longest period of expansion of the modern era. While Clinton did not fully determine his own public approval and these economic outcomes, the analyses in chapters 5 and 6 suggest that he certainly contributed to them.

President Clinton's mantra "It's the economy, stupid!" characterized his public rhetoric and leadership, and it would be interesting to know whether he fully understood the importance of his words to political and economic outcomes. Regardless, no other president has been so consistently positive about the economy or its various dimensions. Why have other presidents not been perpetual optimists? There are multiple reasons why a president might choose alternative strategies.

The most obvious is that presidents and their staffs have been unaware of the extent to which presidential words matter. It is clear that presidents do engage in a permanent campaign (Blumenthal 1982; Gergen 2000; Ornstein and Mann 2000). However, they have probably been running the campaign by the "seat of the pants." As social scientists, we like to characterize presidents as rational actors. They are probably not fully rational, however, and neither are their staffs. They may speculate, as President Clinton probably did, that optimistic rhetoric is an important mechanism for maintaining public approval and promoting a sound economy. Without the validation of social science research, however, presidents are merely "muddling through." A goal of this book has been to inform both social science and political actors about the importance of presidential rhetoric. If future presidents take the work reported here seriously, then they may indeed become more optimistic in the tone of their public remarks.

Yet even with this understanding, there are reasons why future presidents might not consistently use optimistic economic rhetoric. Presidents have multiple agendas. They divide their time between foreign and domestic policy. Within domestic policy, there are other areas than the economy. At times, other domains become dominant. For example, Vietnam was a dominant concern during the late Johnson administration that may have displaced the president's concern for the economy. Similarly, the wars in Afghanistan and Iraq have been dominant concerns of the George W. Bush administration, perhaps producing less rhetorical emphasis on the economy. More generally, every president enters office with an agenda that may not include such strong emphasis on economic matters. While in office, presidential attention to the economy may be "squeezed out" by a focus on foreign policy, other domestic policy issues, or even international crises. Therefore, the intensity and tone of presidential rhetoric on the economy may become secondary to other matters.

Another reason future presidents might choose not to be continuous economic optimists is that such behavior is sometimes inconsistent with the nation's economic welfare. General economic wisdom suggests that an overly robust economy can lead to high inflation. High inflation devalues people's income and diminishes their purchasing power. High inflation is especially hurtful to people on a fixed income. Indeed, the period of high inflation of the 1960s and 1970s held more serious consequences for consumers, businesses, and politicians than occur during the typical recession. Under these circumstances, it might be more prudent for presidents to "talk down" the economy. The results in chapter 6 show that economic pessimism is a potential tool for presidents to diminish economic activity. Future presidents might want to use this strategy to cool down the economy and lower the risk of inflation. Of course, there are probably political costs to this strategy, since presidential approval suffers when presidents become more pessimistic. Nevertheless, being continuously optimistic about the economy makes little sense in the context of an economy with up and down swings.

Future presidents may also choose not to be continuous economic optimists because such optimism may be inconsistent with their policy goals. For example, we observed through empirical evidence that President George W. Bush preferred to "talk down" the economy during his early years, probably to fulfill a campaign promise of lower taxes for partisan supporters. At the time that the president's campaign of economic pessimism began, there were only hints of an impending recession. Neverthe-

172 • Chapter 7

less, the president embarked on a three-and-a-half-year campaign of pessimism about the economy. His rhetoric did not turn positive until the 2004 election season. Early in the George W. Bush administration, the economy did experience a mild recession, but it was the smallest of modern times. During the last two years of Bush's tax-cutting campaign, the economy was clearly no longer in recession. The president was a continual pessimist about the economy through this period, but he achieved the largest set of tax cuts in U.S. history.

Of course, insincere rhetoric has potential costs for both the economy and a president. President Bush may have been unaware of those costs as he conducted his campaign of pessimism. Nevertheless, the analysis in chapter 6 showed that economic activity was probably lower relative to what might have occurred without the president's negativity. There were also political costs. The president lost credibility as an economic leader. Survey results show that people had little faith in Bush's economic leadership through this period, and public evaluations of his economic leadership are very weak even at this writing. This suggests that once credibility is lost on an issue, it is difficult for a president to recover. The results in chapter 5 also show that perceptions of a president's economic leadership affect Gallup and economic approval ratings. Most presidents value their credibility, the public's approval, and take seriously their role as caretaker of the economy. However, it seems clear from the case of President George W. Bush that policy goals sometimes displace common presidential values.

## THE PERMANENT CAMPAIGN AND PRESIDENTIAL LEADERSHIP OF THE ECONOMY

Past scholarship on the permanent campaign has often concluded that it is not conducive to good government. The argument has been that it is ineffective in altering public opinion or public policy. It can also be polarizing, anti-deliberative, and can lead to the gridlock that has often characterized the past quarter century of American politics. Therefore, scholars have argued that presidents should adopt other modes of governing to produce better outcomes (Brady and Fiorina 2000; Edwards 2003; Heclo 2000).

In contrast, this study has shown that at least one dimension of the permanent campaign can be a force for good. Persistent presidential attention to the economy can increase a president's approval, enabling stronger presidential leadership and a higher probability of success in achieving desired policies. It can alter the environment for economic activity, producing healthier conditions for economic growth, employment, prices, and fiscal outcomes. Used wisely, presidential rhetoric can be a tool that enables presidents better to fulfill their role as institutional leader of the world's largest economy.

Recognizing the potential of rhetorical leadership, presidents have a special obligation to use their words wisely. However, presidents have not always done so. Few presidents have exhibited economic leadership in the mold of President Franklin D. Roosevelt, who attempted to lift American spirits at the height of the Great Depression. Roosevelt spoke positively about the future in spite of the horrendous economic troubles facing the nation. In contrast, most modern presidents have tended to use their economic rhetoric for political gain.

Presidents have often spoken more positively about the economy when it is coming out of a recession than when it is entering into a recession. Their economic rhetoric has been conditional on what they think the public thinks about the economy. They have occasionally altered their remarks only when they perceive they are becoming less popular, or when the public thinks their economic leadership is weak. They also consistently shift the intensity and tone of their economic remarks for the sole purpose of achieving reelection for themselves or their political party. The image of the presidency that emerges from this study is consistent with the view that modern presidents are rational self-interest maximizers.

Yet, the founding fathers intended the presidency to be much more. The president is the sole elected official in the United States who represents the entire nation. As such, presidents should be caretakers of the national interest, instead of catering to narrow partisan or personal interests. Actions and activities of presidents should reflect their measured judgment about what is in the best interests of the nation. This extends not only to policy but also to daily activities while in office. As expressed by President Theodore Roosevelt, "My view was that every executive officer, and above all every executive officer in high position, was a steward of the people bound actively and affirmatively to do all he could for the people, and not to content himself with the negative merits of keeping his talents undamaged in a napkin" (Roosevelt 1913, 197). This "stewardship" view of the presidency suggests that modern presidents with strong rhetorical talents should use them to effect good government and the welfare of the nation at large.

Thus, the ideal rhetorical president would be one who practices credible and benevolent leadership. Credible economic leadership means that presidents should not exaggerate economic conditions for political gain. It also requires that the tone of presidential remarks be a reasonable assessment of current and future economic conditions. Benevolent economic leadership implies that presidents should attempt to create a favorable climate for economic activities in terms of policy, and the relative confidence that economic actors have about the future.

Presidential rhetoric should do more than simply mirror prevailing economic conditions or public sentiment. When the economy is in peril, presidents should try to bolster economic sentiment to give people the confidence to participate. When the economy is robust, presidents should express the degree of continuing optimism that will keep it robust. More generally, presidents should speak often and optimistically about the economy to maintain a favorable economic climate. The chief executive should be an independent force who uses rhetoric to effect a supportive environment for the nation.

It is important that presidents do so, because roughly 300 million people depend on the nation's economy. Moreover, the entire world is critically dependent on the U.S. economy due to global interdependence. While presidents do not singularly affect the state of the national or world economy, they do alter the economic environment at the margins. Therefore, future presidents should use words wisely in their continuing stewardship of the general interest.

# Notes

1. These counts contain the total number of times that the president used the phrases "the economy," "our economy," "unemployment," "inflation," and "the deficit" in public remarks. I will describe the methodology for counting the frequency and tone of presidential remarks on the economy in the next chapter.

2. This argument is the traditional Keynesian view. Because tax cuts leave households with more money, they increase their spending. With higher demand for products, there is an increase in the output of domestic business. Thus, tax cuts stimulate the economy, leading to more income, more jobs, and, under full employment, higher prices.

3. The common definition of a recession is two consecutive quarters of negative economic growth. Later adjustments to the statistics showed, however, that there were not two consecutive quarters of negative economic growth. Still, the National Bureau of Economic Research concluded that a significant slowdown in economic activity had occurred and that the period from March to November 2001 should be classified as a recession.

4. One could also claim that the process began with the Budgeting and Accounting Act of 1921, which assigned budget formulation responsibility to the president. There is little evidence, however, that presidents prior to the Great Depression viewed this obligation as contributing toward economic policy-making. Therefore, I peg the beginning at the Great Depression.

5. Under President Ford it was called the Economic Policy Board; under President Carter it was renamed the Economic Policy Group; under President Reagan it was called the Cabinet Council on Economic Affairs; under President George H. W. Bush it was renamed the Economic Policy Council.

6. Presidents have used executive orders to make policy with respect to the economy. For example, President Carter issued Executive Orders 12003, 12092, 12161, and 12185 in an effort to combat inflation.

7. One could argue that the chairman of the Federal Reserve Board is a close rival to the president for this role. However, survey evidence shows that around 23 percent of Americans either have "never heard of" or "have no opinion" of the chairman of the Federal Reserve, Alan Greenspan (CNN/Gallup/USA Today, 3-14-2003). It is undoubtedly true that citizens do not generally follow the chairman's public remarks closely. Therefore, the argument here seems valid.

CHAPTER 2

1. The master text file for this project is available on request from the author.

2. Some consideration was given to possibly weighting the sentences based on the presidential event they were associated with. For example, one could rightly

argue that sentences from a president's State of the Union Address or the economic message to Congress should be more important. I concluded, however, that any weighting scheme that could be used would be highly arbitrary. Moreover, aggregation of the sentences into larger time intervals makes weighting inappropriate since the weights are overwhelmed by the temporal aggregation process. Therefore, the sentences were not weighted prior to aggregation.

CHAPTER 3

1. The Office of Management and Budget was established in 1970 as a result of executive reorganization. From 1921 through 1970 the executive budgetary function was performed by the Bureau of the Budget.

2. President Reagan majored in economics as an undergraduate at Eureka College but was not technically speaking as an economist.

3. Mayhew developed his list by conducting two sweeps. His first sweep relied upon contemporary journalistic assessments of congressional action by the *Washington Post* and the *New York Times*. Usually at the end of every session, reporters from both newspapers write a summary of congressional action. Using these contemporary assessments as his guides, Mayhew developed a list of 211 major acts from 1947 to 1990. For his second sweep, Mayhew relied upon the retrospective judgments of scholars in individual policy areas. In total he used eighty-five scholarly sources in forty-four policy areas.

4. For example, President Kennedy first mentioned the Youth Employment Opportunities bill on June 7, 1961. He last mentioned it on November 14, 1963, just one week before his assassination. This, along with his proposal for a National Service Corps, was a failed presidential initiative to create a domestic analogue to the Peace Corps. It was finally revived some thirty years later during the Clinton administration with the passage of the National and Community Service Trust Act of 1993, which created Americorps.

5. This is reported seasonally adjusted in chained 2000 dollars.

6. For the two quarterly measures I entered data from the most recent report for the intervening monthly periods. Of course, this would be the most recent data available to presidents when assessing the economy. The surplus/deficit data were signed so as to make deficits positive and surplus negative.

7. All variables in the statistical analyses in the next two sections were stationary either through transformations contained in these descriptions, or by natural stationarity. The requirements for a time series $x_t$ to be stationary are that both $E(x_t)$ and $Var(x_t)$ are constants and $Cov(x_t, x_{t-l})$ depends only on $l$ (the lag length), and not on $t$. More intuitively, it means that the series must have a mean and variance that are constant, and the covariance of the series with lags of the series must not depend on time. Stationarity is a usual requirement for time-series analysis in levels in order to avoid the spurious regressions problem first identified by Granger and Newbold (1974).

8. The approval series was aggregated during months when there were multiple surveys using WCALC, software developed by James A. Stimson for dimensional

extraction from public opinion data. See *http://www.unc.edu/~jstimson /resource.html*.

9. This number is calculated by taking the average coefficient for Democrats (2.31) and the average coefficient for Republicans (1.32) and taking the exponentiated difference ($e^{2.31} - e^{1.32} = 6.35$).

10. To be conservative, we take statistical significance to be a two-tailed significance test with $p$-value larger than 0.05. This implies that the z-statistic shown in parentheses should be larger than about 1.96.

11. This comparison may imply a "crowding out" effect for inflation relative to general economic rhetoric. When prices are rising, the president's concern is with inflation rather than the economy generally.

CHAPTER 4

1. Inflation was higher following both the World Wars, but there was no other period of the twentieth century characterized by higher inflation than the Carter presidency.

2. As a result of deficit financing of the Vietnam War, the inflation rate began persistently exceeding the optimal rate around 1968. According to the Federal Reserve Board, the optimal inflation rate is somewhere between zero and 3 percent (Federal Reserve Bank of San Francisco 1997). Generally, when inflation persistently exceeds this target, the board takes monetary policy action.

3. Bivens (2002) provides a more detailed account of the economy during the Carter administration and the president's efforts to combat inflation.

4. The misery index is the sum of the inflation and unemployment rates. It peaked at 21.9 in May of 1980. By way of contrast, it was 12.6 at the peak of the 1990 recession and 8.9 at the peak of the 2001 recession.

5. Lowess smoothing is a data analysis technique for producing a "smooth" set of values from a time series that contains a lot of noise. A smoothing window is applied to extract new observations from a raw time series. The analyst can vary the size (bandwidth) of the smoothing window, which alters the degree of smoothing. The bandwidth is given as the fraction (0 to 1) of the data that the window should cover for each new data point. The bandwidth chosen for the Carter analysis was 0.10. The averages of the smoothed time series were also adjusted to reflect the mean of the actual data.

6. The term "trickle down" economics was coined by David Stockman, President Reagan's budget director. Stockman later revealed that the theory was a Trojan horse, actually intended to bring down the top rate for upper-income groups. See Greider (2004).

7. The bandwidth for the lowess filter producing these graphs was again 0.10.

8. The University of Michigan's Index of Consumer Sentiment was at 62 in March 1982. By way of contrast it bottomed at 51.7 in May 1980 and peaked at 112 in January 2000.

9. The bandwidth for the lowess filter producing these graphs was 0.025. The reason for the reduced bandwidth was to highlight the sharp changes following President Clinton's inauguration.

10. For a discussion of the committee's reasoning and the underlying evidence, see *http://www.nber.org/cycles/november2001*.

11. The committee's announcement of the trough is at *http://www.nber.org/cycles/july2003*.

12. These numbers come from the Congressional Budget Office as reported in Schatz (2005).

13. The bandwidth for the lowess smoothing of these graphs is 0.05.

14. The University of Michigan's Index of Consumer Sentiment fell ten points between September and October of 2001.

15. Interestingly, President Bush began his second term announcing a similar strategy with respect to Social Security reform. In a December 20, 2004, news conference the president said, "Many times, legislative bodies will not react unless the crisis is apparent, crisis is upon them. . . . And so for a period of time, we're going to have to explain to members of Congress that a crisis is here."

16. Economic growth averaged 4.4 percent in 2003 and 3.78 percent in 2004 up to the time of the election. Unemployment averaged 5.99 percent in 2003, and 5.54 percent in 2004 up to time of the election.

17. This assessment of President Bush's personal style may pertain to more than economic rhetoric. For example, VandeHei (2005) argued that Bush routinely paints his goals as "crises." He was criticized for exaggerating the danger posed by Sadaam Hussein in the lead up to the U.S. invasion of Iraq. He exaggerated the severity of economic conditions to achieve multiple tax cuts. He may also have exaggerated the terrorist threats to convince people of the need for restrictions on their civil liberties. And he began his second presidential term painting the Social Security system as in a crisis.

18. The most recent report on economic growth available to President Bush on entering office showed the economy grew in the fourth quarter of 2001 at 2.2 percent. Unemployment was at 3.9 percent. The NBER did not announce a recession had occurred until November 2001. Even then, it was classed as the mildest recession since World War II.

CHAPTER 5

1. Survey organizations have been asking citizens since 1935 whether they approve or disapprove of the president's job performance. Gallup was the first survey organization to conduct such a poll. For the first few years the poll experimented with different wording of the question. Since 1945 the approval question has read, "Do you approve or disapprove of the way [president's name] is handling his job as president?" (See Edwards with Gallup 1990, Appendix A for discussion). It was not until the Truman administration, however, that the question became routine.

2. Stationarity refers to whether a time series has a fixed mean or equilibrium state. For example, a trending time series does not have a fixed mean or equilibrium state because it is continuously increasing (or decreasing) through time. Similarly, a time series exhibiting a random walk has a mean that is non-constant due to periods when it drifts in a particular direction for a long time. When a time

series is not stationary, this causes problems with statistical inference, the so-called spurious regressions problem (Granger and Newbold 1974).

3. Engle and Granger (1987) developed the error correction approach, which applies when variables are tracking one another through time in equilibrium.

4. One minor exception to this generalization is a study by Erikson, MacKuen, and Stimson (2002), who partially evaluate the effect of media coverage of presidents on public approval. Their analysis included no statistical controls. The bivariate regression showed that media stories depicting a president as "in control" have a weak effect on the public's approval of that president's job performance.

5. Specifically, the measure used data from polls conducted by ABC, ABC/Washington Post, CBS, CBS/New York Times, Gallup, and the Los Angeles Times. The lead in to the core question differed somewhat across survey organizations. ABC, ABC/Washington Post, and CBS had no lead in, asking the question as stated earlier. CBS/New York Times, however, prefaced the question with "How about the economy—. . . ." Gallup prefaced the question with "Now thinking about some issues, . . ." The Los Angeles Times prefaced the question with "Generally speaking, . . ." It is unclear that the different lead-in for different survey organizations would in any way bias or make the survey data incompatible. Indeed, when multiple surveys were conducted in the same month, the results were substantially similar.

6. The time series for the general approval measure was initiated during the Reagan administration and terminated at the end of the first George W. Bush administration. The partial Carter administration was omitted to enable focusing on entire presidential administrations.

7. The events included in the political drama series were drawn from Erikson, MacKuen, and Stimson (2002, 52) and updated to the present. The events included the Reagan assassination attempt (April 1981), the Grenada invasion (November 1983), the Iran-Contra scandal (November 1986), the Bush-Gorbachev summit (December 1989), Iraq's invasion of Kuwait (August 1990), the budget summit (October 1990), the Persian Gulf War (January 1991), the September 11th tragedy (September 2001), and U.S. invasion of Iraq (April 2003).

8. Four separate analyses were conducted apart from the analyses reported here. Two of the analyses evaluated a president's Gallup approval ratings and two evaluated a president's economic approval ratings, each with different specifications. One specification contained unemployment and inflation and another specification contained the Conference Board's Composite Index of Coincident Indicators. Results from the analyses reported here are almost exactly the same as in the separate analyses. Therefore, the more parsimonious specifications are reported here.

9. For example, see the work by Hetherington (1996) cited previously and earlier discussion. Additionally, in a separate analysis the misery index (unemployment plus inflation) was included. As observed by MacKuen, Erikson, and Stimson (1992), the inclusion of economic evaluations "crowds out" effects from the actual economic variables on presidential approval. Note, however, that the economic news variable described and used here remains viable.

10. The five questions are as follows: (1) "We are interested in how people are getting along financially these days. Would you say that you (and your family

living there) are better off or worse off financially than you were a year ago?" (2) "Now looking ahead—do you think that a year from now you (and your family living there) will be better off financially, or worse off, or just about the same as now?" (3) "Now turning to business conditions in the country as a whole—do you think that during the next twelve months we'll have good times financially, or bad times, or what?" (4) "Looking ahead, which would you say is more likely— that in the country as a whole we'll have continuous good times during the next five years or so, or that we will have periods of widespread unemployment or depression, or what?" (5) "About the big things people buy for their homes— such as furniture, a refrigerator, stove, television, and things like that. Generally speaking, do you think now is a good or bad time for people to buy major household items?"

11. Including both separately introduces multi-collinearity and is unnecessary given the ambiguity of past research.

12. All equations in the system contained these variables. As the preceding graphs show, there are sometimes sharp shifts in the other variables that correspond to changing presidencies and other events. Therefore, it was deemed appropriate to include these variables in each equation.

13. An alternative approach would have been to use structural equations. This approach was deemed inappropriate, however, because there was no firm theoretical or empirical basis for imposing restrictions on the equation system. For example, without certainty that higher presidential approval does not cause higher economic evaluations, the corresponding restriction implied by the single-headed arrow between these two variables would be inappropriate. Similarly, there was no basis for imposing restrictions on any of the other relations on the left side of figure 5.1. Therefore, structural equation methods would require unreasonable assumptions.

14. Based on Akaike's Information Criterion (1973), two monthly lags of all variables were included in the analysis. This may seem like a short lag length. However, sensitivity testing was done to evaluate the effects of including additional lags up to thirteen. The relationships were stable and unchanged. Residuals from final analyses were non-autocorrelated, non-heteroskedastic, and normally distributed.

15. This is due to multi-collinearity.

16. For a critique of the Granger approach to assessing causality, see Lutkepohl (1993, 41–43).

17. Some past literature has suggested that Granger tests may be suspect when there are cointegrating relationships among variables in a vector autoregression (Freeman et al. 1998; Phillips 1995, 1992). Each variable was filtered using the indicators for each presidency and the events series and then evaluated for stationarity. Based on Augmented Dickey-Fuller (1979) and Sims Bayesian Unit Root (1988) tests, it was concluded we have mixed I(1) and I(0) systems. Specifically, consumer sentiment is I(1), while the news, presidential optimism, and presidential approval are I(0). Cointegration requires that at least two variables be integrated at the same order. Therefore, cointegration cannot exist here, and we report Granger tests using standard VAR.

18. Shocking a variable means successively multiplying the matrix of vector autoregressive estimates by a simulation vector containing shocks in the variable of interest. We orthogonalize the resulting innovations using Choleski factorization, because such innovations have the convenient property of being uncorrelated across both time and equations. With Choleski factorization, the ordering of the variables in the simulations can make a difference to the results if there is a high contemporaneous correlation among the variables. The only sizable contemporaneous correlation was that between the news and economic evaluations. We reordered these and the other variables in our analyses as a sensitivity check. None of the reported results changed in response to the reorderings.

19. Including multiple lags of the dependent variable also has an advantage in that omitted variables are less of a concern since *all omitted variables are by definition contained in the lagged dependent variables.* VAR models are intended to be parsimonious approximations of the true data-generation process, not complete representations. If they are good approximations, then they should have disturbances that are random with respect to the included variables and time (e.g., see Lutkepohl 1993, section 4.4). However, VAR models also require parsimony due to their high consumption of degrees of freedom. Regardless of their more parsimonious nature, the VAR approach is significantly more conservative than other approaches that do not include such strong controls for history and model misspecification.

20. This result confirms part of the analysis in DeBoef and Kellstedt (2004), whose work also suggests that economic approval affects consumer confidence. Their estimation procedures, however, ignore the joint causality shown here between consumer confidence and presidents' economic approval. Also, their analysis of the determinants of the presidents' economic approval omits economic evaluations, which have been shown by this and past research to be important (Erikson, MacKuen, and Stimson 2002; MacKuen, Erikson, and Stimson 1992; Wood 2000).

CHAPTER 6

1. This number results from dividing average U.S. personal consumption expenditure by national income.

2. Cochrane (1994) finds that "consumption shocks" account for a relatively large share of variations in macroeconomic performance through time.

3. This perspective was developed in the early work of Katona (1951, 1960, 1964, 1975), the originator of the University of Michigan's Survey of Consumers. See Curtin (1983) for an overview of Katona's contributions.

4. Nevertheless, some in the popular press still question the link between consumer sentiment and macroeconomic performance (e.g., see Maggs 2002).

5. Examination of the time series in figures 6.2 and 6.3 shows they are trending and therefore non-stationary. Doan (2004, 331) recommends that variables should not be differenced in a VAR. Therefore, the consumption variables are used in levels rather than differenced. Nevertheless, this raises the prospect that cointegrating relationships may exist in the VAR system. As noted in note 16 of

chapter 5, past literature has suggested that Granger tests may be suspect when there are cointegrating relationships among variables in a vector autoregression (Freeman et al. 1998; Phillips 1995, 1992). Cointegration tests were performed and none was found among the variables in our system.

6. The Conference Board also publishes the Composite Index of Leading Indicators and the Composite Index of Lagging Indicators. I chose the Composite Index of Coincident Indicators because the concern here is how the economy is currently doing. The Leading Indicators is used mainly for forecasting how the economy will be doing in the future, while the Lagging Indicators is used for confirmation of peaks and troughs in the business cycle.

7. An alternative to the University of Michigan Index is an index published by the Conference Board. There is controversy over which is the more accurate forecasting tool of the direction of the economy and economic behavior. For example, see Bram and Ludvigson (1998) for a literature review and comparison of the two measures.

8. The events included the Reagan assassination attempt (April 1981), the Grenada invasion (November 1983), the Iran-Contra scandal (November 1986), the Bush-Gorbachev summit (December 1989), Iraq's invasion of Kuwait (August 1990), the Persian Gulf War (January 1991), the September 11th tragedy (September 2001), and the U.S. invasion of Iraq (April 2003).

9. Based on Akaike's Information Criterion (1973), four monthly lags of all variables were included in the analysis. Sensitivity testing was done to evaluate the effects of including additional lags up to thirteen. The relationships were stable and unchanged with four lags. Residuals from final analyses were non-autocorrelated, non-heteroskedastic, and normally distributed.

# References

Akaike, Hirotogu. 1973. Information Theory and the Extension of the Maximum Likelihood Principle. Paper read at 2nd International Symposium on Information Theory, Budapest, Hungary.

Alvarez, Michael R., and Jonathan Katz. 1996. Integration and Political Science Data. Paper read at Midwest Political Science Association, Chicago, IL.

Associated Press. 2004. *Kerry: Reagan A "Great Optimist."* June 6.

Barber, James David. 1992. *The Presidential Character: Predicting Performance in the White House.* Englewood Cliffs, NJ: Prentice-Hall.

Baum, Matthew A. 2004a. Going Private: Public Opinion, Presidential Rhetoric, and the Domestic Politics of Audience Costs in U.S. Foreign Policy Crises. *Journal of Conflict Resolution* 48 (5):603–31.

———. 2004b. How Public Opinion Constrains the Use of Force: The Case of Operation Restore Hope. *Presidential Studies Quarterly* 34 (2):187–226.

Beck, Nathaniel. 1991. The Economy and Presidential Approval: An Information Theoretic Perspective. In *Economics and Politics: The Calculus of Support*, edited by H. Norpoth, M. S. Lewis-Beck, and J.-D. Lafay. Ann Arbor, MI: University of Michigan Press.

———. 1993. The Methodology of Cointegration. *Political Analysis* 4:237–48.

Berelson, Bernard R., Paul F. Lazarsfeld, and William N. McPhee. 1954. *Voting: A Study of Public Opinion Formation in a Presidential Campaign.* Chicago, IL: University of Chicago Press.

Bivens, W. Carl. 2002. *Jimmy Carter's Economy: Policy in an Age of Limits.* Chapel Hill, NC: University of North Carolina Press.

Bloom, Harold S. 1975. Voter Response to Short-Run Economic Conditions: The Asymmetric Effect of Prosperity and Recession. *American Political Science Review* 69 (4):1240–54.

Blumenthal, Sidney. 1982. *The Permanent Campaign.* New York: Simon & Schuster.

Bond, Jon R., Richard Fleisher, and B. Dan Wood. 2003. The Marginal and Time-Varying Effect of Public Approval on Presidential Success in Congress. *Journal of Politics* 65 (1):92–110.

Bosch, Adriana. 2002. Jimmy Carter. In *The American Experience.* Public Broadcasting Service. First aired November 11–12.

Box, George E. P., and Gwilym M. Jenkins. 1976. *Time Series Analysis: Forecasting and Control.* Oakland, CA: Holden-Day.

Box-Steffensmeier, Janet M., and Renee M. Smith. 1998. Investigating Political Dynamics Using Fractional Integration Methods. *American Journal of Political Science* 42 (April):661–89.

Brace, Paul, and Barbara Hinckley. 1992. *Follow the Leader: Opinion Polls and the Modern Presidents.* New York: Basic Books.

Brady, David, and Morris Fiorina. 2000. Congress in the Era of the Permanent Campaign. In *The Permanent Campaign and Its Future*, edited by N. Ornstein and T. Mann. Washington, DC: American Enterprise Institute and The Brookings Institution.

Bram, Jason, and Sydney Ludvigson. 1998. Does Consumer Confidence Forecast Household Expenditure? A Sentiment Index Horse Race? In *Federal Reserve Bank of New York Policy Review*. New York: Federal Reserve Bank of New York.

Brandt, Patrick T., and John T. Williams. 2001. A Linear Poisson Autoregressive Model: The Poisson AR(p) Model. *Political Analysis* 9 (2):164–84.

Brody, Richard A. 1991. *Assessing the President: The Media, Elite Opinion, and Public Support*. Stanford, CA: Stanford University Press.

Brody, Richard A., and Benjamin I. Page. 1975. The Impact of Events on Presidential Popularity: The Johnson and Nixon Administrations. In *Perspectives on the Presidency*, edited by A. Wildavsky. Boston, MA: Little-Brown.

Brody, Richard A., and Catherine Shapiro. 1989. Policy Failure and Public Support: The Iran Contra Affair and Public Assessments of President Reagan. *Political Behavior* 11 (4):353–69.

Brody, Richard A., and Lee Sigelman. 1983. Presidential Popularity and Presidential Elections: An Update and Extension. *Public Opinon Quarterly* 47:325–28.

Burns, James MacGregor. 1956. *Roosevelt: The Lion and the Fox*. New York: Harcourt, Brace.

Bush, George W. 2000. George W. Bush Nomination Acceptance Speech. Republican National Convention, Philadelphia, PA.

Business Cycle Dating Committee. 2003. The NBER's Recession Dating Procedure. Washington, DC: National Bureau of Economic Research, Department of Commerce.

Caballero, R. J. 1991. Earnings Uncertainty and Aggregate Wealth Accumulation. *American Economic Review* 81 (4):859–71.

Campbell, Angus, Philip Converse, Warren Miller, and Donald Stokes. 1960. *The American Voter*. New York: Wiley.

Canes-Wrone, Brandice, and Kenneth W. Shotts. 2004. The Conditional Nature of Presidential Responsiveness to Public Opinion. *American Journal of Political Science* 48 (October):690–706.

Carroll, C. D. 1994. How Does Future Income Affect Current Consumption. *Quarterly Journal of Economics* 109 (1):111–47.

———. 1997. Buffer-Stock Saving and the Life Cycle/Permanent Income Hypothesis. *Quarterly Journal of Economics* 110 (1):1–55.

Carroll, C. D., and A. A. Samwick. 1997. The Nature of Precautionary Wealth. *Journal of Monetary Economics* 40 (1):41–71.

———. 1998. How Important is Precautionary Savings? *Review of Economics and Statistics* 80 (3):410–19.

Chappell, Henry W., and William R. Keech. 1985. A New View of Political Accountability for Economic Performance. *American Political Science Review* 79 (1):10–27.

Clark, Harold D., and Marianne C. Stewart. 1994. Prospections, Retrospections, and Rationality: The "Bankers" Model of Presidential Approval Reconsidered. *American Journal of Political Science* 38 (4):1104–23.

Cochrane, J. H. 1994. Shocks. Carnegie-Rochester Series on Public Policy. 41: 295–364.

Cohen, Jeffrey E. 1995. Presidential Rhetoric and the Public Agenda. *American Journal of Political Science* 1 (February):87–107.

———. 1997. *Presidential Responsiveness and Public-Policy Making: The Public and the Policies that Presidents Choose.* Ann Arbor, MI: University of Michigan Press.

———. 2000. *Politics and Economic Policy in the United States, 2nd ed.* New York: Houghton-Mifflin.

Cohen, Jeffrey E., and David Nice. 2003. *The Presidency.* New York: McGraw-Hill.

Conference Board. 2001. *Business Cycle Indicators Handbook.* New York: The Conference Board.

Congressional Budget Office. 2000. The Budget and Economic Outlook: An Update. Washington, DC: U.S. Government Printing Office.

Conover, Pamela Johnson, and Lee Sigelman. 1982. Presidential Influence and Public Opinion: The Case of the Iranian Hostage Crisis. *Social Science Quarterly* 63 (June):249–64.

Cotton, Timothy Y. C. 1987. War and American Democracy: Electoral Costs of the Last Five Wars. *30* (December):616–35.

Curtin, Richard T. 1983. Curtin on Katona. In *Contemporary Economists in Perspective*, edited by H. W. Spiegel and W. J. Samuels. New York: JAI Press.

———. 2000. Psychology and Macroeconomics: Fifty Years of the Surveys of Consumers. In *Special Report on the Web Site of the University of Michigan Survey of Consumers.*

DeBoef, Suzanna, and James Granato. 1997. Near Integrated Data and the Analysis of Political Relationships. *American Journal of Political Science* 41 (April):619–40.

DeBoef, Suzanna, and Paul M. Kellstedt. 2004. The Political (and Economic) Origins of Consumer Confidence. *American Journal of Political Science* 48 (October):633–49.

DeRouen, Karl. 1995. The Indirect Link: Politics, the Economy, and the Use of Force. *Journal of Conflict Resolution* 39 (4):671–95.

Dickey, D. A., and Fuller, W. A. 1979. Distribution of the Estimators for Autoregressive Time Series with a Unit Root. *Journal of the American Statistical Association.* 74(1):427–31.

Doan, Thomas A. 2004. *RATS Version 6 Users Guide.* Evanston, IL: Estima.

Druckman, James N., and Justin W. Holmes. 2004. Does Presidential Rhetoric Matter? Priming and Presidential Approval. *Presidential Studies Quarterly* 34 (December):755–78.

Edwards, George C. III.s 1980. *Presidential Influence in Congress.* San Francisco: W. H. Freeman.

———. 1983. *The Public Presidency: The Pursuit of Popular Support.* New York: St. Martin's Press.

Edwards, George C., III. 1989. *At the Margins: Presidential Leadership of Congress.* New Haven, CT: Yale University Press.

———. 1997. Aligning Tests with Theory: Presidential Approval as a Source of Influence in Congress. *Congress and the Presidency* 24 (2):113–30.

———. 2003. *On Deaf Ears: The Limits of the Bully Pulpit.* New Haven, CT: Yale University Press.

Edwards, George C., III, Andrew Barrett, and Jeffrey Peake. 1997. The Legislative Impact of Divided Government. *American Journal of Political Science* 42 (2):545–63.

Edwards, George C., III, and Alec M. Gallup. 1990. *Presidential Approval: A Source Book.* Baltimore, MD: Johns Hopkins Press.

Edwards, George C., III, William Mitchell, and Reed Welch. 1995. Explaining Presidential Approval: The Significance of Issue Salience. *American Journal of Political Science* 39 (1):108–34.

Edwards, George C., III, and Steven J. Wayne. 2006. *Presidential Leadership: Politics and Policy Making.* Seventh ed. Belmont, CA: Thompson/Wadsworth.

Edwards, George C. III, and B. Dan Wood. 1999. Who Influences Whom? The President and the Public Agenda. *American Political Science Review* 93 (2):327–44.

Engle, Robert F., III, and Clive W. J. Granger. 1987. Co-Integration and Error Correction: Representation, Estimation, and Testing. *Econometrica* 55 (March):251–76.

Erikson, Robert S. 1989. Economic Conditions and the Presidential Vote. *American Political Science Review* 83 (2):567–73.

Erikson, Robert S., Joseph Bafumi, and Bret Wilson. 2001. Was the 2000 Presidential Election Predictable? *PS: Political Science and Politics* 34 (December):815–19.

Erikson, Robert S., Michael B. MacKuen, and James A. Stimson. 2002. *The Macro Polity.* Boston, MA: Cambridge University Press.

Erikson, Robert S., and Christopher Wlezien. 2004. The Fundamentals, the Polls, and the Presidential Vote. *PS: Political Science and Politics* 37 (October):747–51.

Fair, Ray C. 1978. The Effect of Economic Events on Votes for the President. *Review of Economics and Statistics* 60 (2):159–73.

Fearon, James. 1994. Domestic Political Audiences and the Escalation of International Conflict. *American Political Science Review* 88 (3):577–92.

Federal Reserve Bank of San Francisco. 1997. What Is the Optimal Rate of Inflation? *FRBSF Economic Letter,* September 19.

Fiorina, Morris P. 1981. *Retrospective Voting in American National Elections.* New Haven, CT: Yale University Press.

Fordham, Benjamin. 1998. Partisanship, Macroeconomic Policy, and U.S. Uses of Force, 1949–1994. *Journal of Conflict Resolution* 42 (4):418–39.

Freeman, John R., Daniel Hauser, Paul Kellstedt, and John Williams. 1998. Long-Memoried Processes, Unit Roots, and Causal Inference in Political Science. *American Journal of Political Science* 42 (4):1289–327.

Freeman, John R., John T. Williams, and Tse-min Lin. 1989. Vector Autoregression and the Study of Politics. *American Journal of Political Science* 33 (November):842–77.

Frendreis, John P., and Raymond Tatalovich. 1994. *The Modern Presidency and Economic Policy.* Itasca, IL: F. E. Peacock.

Friedman, Milton. 1957. *A Theory of the Consumption Function.* Princeton, NJ: Princeton University Press.

Gergen, David. 2000. *Eyewitness to Power: The Essence of Leadership.* New York: Simon & Schuster.

Gore, Albert W. 2000. Albert W. Gore Presidential Nomination Acceptance Speech. Democratic National Convention, Los Angeles, CA.

Granger, Clive W. J. 1969. Investigating Causal Relations by Econometric Models and Cross-Spectral Models. *Econometrica* 37 (July):424–38.

Granger, Clive W. J., and Paul Newbold. 1974. Spurious Regressions in Econometrics. *Journal of Econometrics* 2 (2):111–20.

Greenspan, Alan. 2001. Outlook for the Federal Budget and Implications for Fiscal Policy. In *Committee on the Budget, U.S. Senate.* Washington, DC: U.S. Government Printing Office.

Greenstein, Fred I. 2004. *The Presidential Difference: Leadership Style from FDR to George W. Bush.* 2nd ed. Princeton, NJ: Princeton University Press.

Greider, William. 2004. The Gipper's Economy. *The Nation,* June 28.

Grossman, Michael B., and Martha J. Kumar. 1981. *Portraying the President.* Baltimore, MD: Johns Hopkins University Press.

Haller, H. Brandon, and Helmut Norpoth. 1994. Let the Good Times Roll: The Economic Expectations of U.S. Voters. *American Journal of Political Science* 38 (3):625–50.

Hart, Roderick P. 1989. *The Sound of Leadership: Presidential Communication in the Modern Age.* Chicago, IL: University of Chicago Press.

Heclo, Hugh. 2000. Campaigning and Governing: A Conspectus. In *The Permanent Campaign and Its Future,* edited by N. Ornstein and T. Mann. Washington, DC: American Enterprise Institute and The Brookings Institution.

Heilbroner, Robert, and Aaron Singer. 1999. *The Economic Transformation of America: 1600 to Present,* 4th Edition. New York: Harcourt, Brace.

Hetherington, Marc J. 1996. The Media's Role in Forming Voters' National Economic Evaluations in 1992. *American Journal of Political Science* 40 (May):372–95.

Hibbs, Douglas A., Jr. 1974. Problems of Statistical Estimation and Causal Inference in Time Series Regression Models. In *Sociological Methodology, 1973–74,* edited by H. L. Costner. San Francisco, CA: Jossey-Bass.

———. 1987. *The American Political Economy: Macroeconomics and Electoral Politics.* Cambridge, MA: Harvard University Press.

Hill, Kim Quaile. 1998. The Policy Agendas of the President and the Mass Public: A Research Validation and Extension. *American Journal of Political Science* 42 (October):1328–34.

Hill, Kim Quaile, and Angela Hinton-Anderson. 1995. Pathways of Representation: A Causal Analysis of Public Opinion-Policy Linkages. *American Journal of Political Science* 39 (November):924–35.

Hinckley, Barbara. 1990. *The Symbolic Presidency: How Presidents Portray Themselves.* New York: Routledge.

Holbrook, Thomas M. 2004. Good News for Bush? Economic News, Personal Finances, and the 2004 Election. *PS: Political Science and Politics* 37 (October):759–61.

Iyengar, Shanto. 2000. In Their Own Words: Sourcebook for the 2000 Presidential Election. Palo Alto, CA: Political Communication Laboratory - Stanford University.

Jacobs, Lawrence R., and Robert Y. Shapiro. 1995a. Presidential Manipulation of Polls and Public Opinion: The Nixon Administration and the Pollsters. *Political Science Quarterly* 4 (Winter):519–38.

———. 1995b. The Rise of Presidential Polling: The Nixon White House in Historical Perspective. *Public Opinion Quarterly* 59 (2):163–95.

———. 2000. *Politicians Don't Pander.* Chicago, IL: University of Chicago Press.

James, Patrick, and James Oneal. 1991. The Influence of Domestic and International Politics on the President's Use of Force. *Journal of Conflict Resolution* 35 (2):307–32.

Jones, Charles O. 2000. Preparing to Govern in 2001: Lessons from the Clinton Presidency. In *The Permanent Campaign and Its Future*, edited by N. Ornstein and T. Mann. Washington, DC: American Enterprise Press and The Brookings Institution.

Jordan, Donald L., and Benjamin I. Page. 1992. Shaping Foreign Policy Opinions: The Role of TV News. *Journal of Conflict Resolution* 36 (2):227–41.

Katona, George. 1951. *Psychological Analysis of Economic Behavior.* New York: McGraw-Hill.

———. 1960. *The Powerful Consumer: Psychological Studies of the American Economy.* New York: McGraw-Hill.

———. 1964. *The Mass Consumption Society.* New York: McGraw-Hill.

———. 1975. *Psychological Economics.* New York: Elsevier.

Kenski, Henry C. 1977. The Impact of Economic Conditions on Presidential Popularity. *Journal of Politics* 39 (August):764–73.

Kernell, Samuel J. 1978. Explaining Presidential Popularity: How Ad Hoc Theorizing, Misplaced Emphasis, and Insufficient Care in Measuring One's Variables Refuted Common Sense and Led Conventional Wisdom Down the Path of Anomalies. *American Political Science Review* 72 (June):506–22.

———. 1984. The Presidency and the People: The Modern Paradox. In *The Presidency and the Political System*, edited by M. Nelson. Washington, DC: Congressional Quarterly Press.

———. 1997. *Going Public: New Strategies of Presidential Leadership.* 3rd Edition. Washington, DC: Congressional Quarterly Press.

Key, V. O. 1968. *The Responsible Electorate: Rationality in Presidential Voting 1936–1960.* New York: Vintage.

Kiewiet, D. Roderick, and Douglas Rivers. 1985. A Retrospective on Retrospective Voting. In *Economic Conditions and Electoral Outcomes: The United States and Western Europe*, edited by H. Eulau and M. S. Lewis-Beck. New York: Agathon.

Kimball, M. S. 1990. Precautionary Saving in the Small and in the Large. *Econometrica* 58 (1):53–73.

Kinder, Donald R., and D. Roderick Kiewiet. 1979. Economic Discontent and Political Behavior: The Role of Personal Grievances and Collective Economic Judgments in Congressional Voting. *American Journal of Political Science* 23 (3):495–527.

———. 1981. Sociotropic Politics: The American Case. *British Journal of Political Science* 11 (2):129–61.

Kumar, Martha J. 1997. The White House Beat at the Century Mark. *Harvard International Journal of Press/Politics* 2 (Summer):10–30.

Lewis-Beck, Michael S., and Tom W. Rice. 1992. *Forecasting Elections*. Washington, DC: Congressional Quarterly Press.

Lewis-Beck, Michael S., and Charles Tien. 2004. Jobs and the Job of the President: A Forecast for 2004. *PS: Political Science and Politics* 37 (October):753–58.

Lutkepohl, Helmut. 1993. *Introduction to Multiple Time Series Analysis*. Berlin, Germany: Springer-Verlag.

Machiavelli, Niccolo. 1517. *Discourses on the First Ten Books of Titus Livy*. Florence, Italy.

MacKuen, Michael B. 1983. Political Drama, Economic Conditions, and the Dynamics of Presidential Popularity. *American Journal of Political Science* 27 (2):165–92.

MacKuen, Michael B., Robert S. Erikson, and James A. Stimson. 1992. Peasants or Bankers? The American Electorate and the U.S. Economy. *American Political Science Review* 86 (3):597–611.

Maggs, John. 2002. Fear Factor: Whether the Economy Stalls Again May Hinge on Whether the Turbulence on Wall Street Sends Consumer Confidence Plunging. *National Journal* 31 (August):2294–99.

Maltese, John Anthony. 1992. *Spin Control: The White House Office of Communications and the Management of Presidential News*. Chapel Hill, NC: University of North Carolina Press.

Markus, Gregory. 1988. The Impact of Personal and National Economic Conditions on the Presidential Vote: A Pooled Cross-Sectional Analysis. *American Journal of Political Science* 32 (1):137–54.

Mayhew, David R. 1991. *Divided We Govern*. New Haven, CT: Yale University Press.

Modigliani, F., and R. Brumberg. 1954. Utility Analysis and the Consumption Function: An Interpretation of Cross-Section Data. In *Post-Keynesian Economics*, edited by K. Kurihara. Piscataway, NJ: Rutgers University Press.

Mondak, Jeffrey. 1993. Source Cues and Policy Approval: The Cognitive Dynamics of Public Support for the Reagan Agenda. *American Journal of Political Science* 37 (1):186–212.

Monroe, Kristen R. 1978. Economic Influences on Presidential Popularity. *Public Opinion Quarterly* 42 (Autumn):360–69.

———. 1979. Inflation and Presidential Popularity. *Presidential Studies Quarterly* 9 (Summer):334–40.

Mueller, John. 1970. Presidential Popularity from Truman to Johnson. *American Political Science Review* 65 (1):18–34.

Mueller, John. 1973. *War, Presidents, and Public Opinion.* New York: Wiley.

Neustadt, Richard E. 1960. *Presidential Power and the Modern Presidents: The Politics of Leadership.* New York: Free Press.

Nordhaus, William D. 2002. The Mildest Recession: Output, Profits, and Stock Prices as the U.S. Emerges from the 2001 Recession. Washington, DC: National Bureau of Economic Research.

Norpoth, Helmut. 1996. Presidents and the Prospective Voter. *Journal of Politics* 58 (3):776–92.

Ornstein, Norman, and Thomas Mann, eds. 2000. *The Permanent Campaign and Its Future.* Washington, DC: American Enterprise Institute and the Brookings Institution.

Ostrom, Charles W., Jr., and Brian Job. 1986. The President and the Political Use of Force. *American Political Science Review* 80 (2):541–66.

Ostrom, Charles W., Jr., and Dennis M. Simon. 1985. Promise and Performance: A Dynamic Model of Presidential Popularity. *American Political Science Review* 79 (2):334–58.

———. 1988. The President's Public. *American Journal of Political Science* 32 (4):1096–119.

———. 1989. The Man in the Teflon Suit: The Environmental Connection, Political Drama, and Popular Support in the Reagan Presidency. *Public Opinion Quarterly* 53 (3):353–87.

Ostrom, Charles W., Jr., and Renee Smith. 1993. Error Correction, Attitude Persistence, and Executive Rewards and Punishments: A Behavioral Theory of Presidential Approval. *Political Analysis* 4:127–84.

Page, Benjamin I., and Robert Y. Shapiro. 1985. Presidential Leadership through Public Opinion. In *The Presidency and Public Policy Making,* edited by G. C. Edwards III, S. A. Shull, and N. C. Thomas. Pittsburgh, PA: University of Pittsburgh Press.

———. 1992. *The Rational Public: Fifty Years of Trends in American's Policy Preferences.* Chicago, IL: University of Chicago Press.

Page, Benjamin I., Robert Y. Shapiro, and Glenn R. Dempsey. 1987. What Moves Public Opinion? *American Political Science Review* 81 (1):23–43.

Peretz, Paul. 1983. *The Political Economy of Inflation in the United States.* Chicago, IL: University of Chicago Press.

Phillips, P.C.B. 1995. Fully Modified Least Squares and Vector Autoregression. *Econometrica* 63 (5):1023–78.

Phillips, Peter C. B. 1992. Simultaneous Equation Bias in Level VAR Estimation. *Econometric Theory* 8 (June):307.

Pika, Joseph A., and John Anthony Maltese. 2006. *The Politics of the Presidency.* Rev. 6th ed. Washington, DC: Congressional Quarterly Press.

Quirk, Paul J., and Joseph Hinchliffe. 1996. Domestic Policy: The Trials of a Centrist Democrat. In *The Clinton Presidency: First Appraisals,* edited by C. Campbell and B. A. Rockman. Chatham, NJ: Chatham House.

Ragsdale, Lyn. 1984. The Politics of Presidential Speechmaking, 1949–1980. *American Political Science Review* 78 (4):971–84.

———. 1987. Presidential Speechmaking and the Public Audience: Individual Presidents and Group Attitudes. *Journal of Politics* 49 (3):704–36.

Ritter, Kurt, and David Henry. 1992. *Ronald Reagan: The Great Communicator.* Westport, CT: Greenwood.

Rivers, Douglas, and Nancy Rose. 1985. Passing the President's Program: Public Opinion and Presidential Influence in Congress. *American Journal of Political Science* 29 (2):183–96.

Roosevelt, Theodore. 1913. *The Autobiography of Theodore Roosevelt.* New York: Scribner's.

Rosen, Corey M. 1973. A Test of Presidential Leadership of Public Opinion: The Split Ballot Technique. *Polity* 6 (2):282–90.

Rosenstone, Steven J. 1983. *Forecasting Presidential Elections.* New Haven, CT: Yale University Press.

Rozell, Mark J. 2003. Presidential Image-Makers on the Limits of Spin Control. In *The Presidency: Classic and Contemporary Readings,* edited by J. E. Cohen and D. Nice. Boston, MA: McGraw-Hill.

Schatz, Joseph J. 2005. Revenue Down: Tax Cuts Have Put States and the Feds in a Tighter Box. *Congressional Quarterly Weekly,* February 7, 298–301.

Schlesinger, Arthur M. 1960. *The Politics of Upheaval.* Boston, MA: Little-Brown.

Schwartz, Randal L., Erik Olson, and Tom Christiansen. 1997. *Learning Perl on Win32 Systems.* Cambridge, MA: O'Reilly.

Sigelman, Lee. 1979. Presidential Popularity and Presidential Elections. *Public Opinion Quarterly* 43:532–34.

———. 1980a. The Commander in Chief and the Public: Mass Response to Johnson's March 31, 1968 Bombing Halt Speech. *Journal of Political and Military Sociology* 8 (Spring):1–14.

———. 1980b. Gauging the Public Response to Presidential Leadership. *Presidential Studies Quarterly* 10 (3):427–33.

Sigelman, Lee, and Kathleen Knight. 1985. Economic Advice to the President: From Eisenhower to Reagan. *Political Behavior* 98 (3):167–91.

Sigelman, Lee, and Carol K. Sigelman. 1981. Presidential Leadership of Public Opinion: From "Benevolent Leader" to "Kiss of Death." *Experimental Study of Politics* 7 (1):1–22.

Silvestri, Vito N. 2000. *Becoming JFK: A Profile in Communication.* Westport, CT: Praeger.

Simon, Dennis M., and Charles W. Ostrom. 1985. The President and Public Support: A Strategic Perspective. In *The Presidency and Public Policy Making,* edited by George C. Edwards III, S. A. Shull, and N. C. Thomas. Pittsburgh, PA: University of Pittsburgh Press.

———. 1988. The Politics of Prestige: Popular Support and the Modern Presidency. *Presidential Studies Quarterly* 18 (4):741–59.

———. 1989. The Impact of Televised Speeches and Foreign Travel on Presidential Approval. *Public Opinion Quarterly* 53 (1):58–82.

Simon, Herbert A. 1947. *Administrative Behavior.* New York: Free Press.

Sims, Christopher A. 1980. Macroeconomics and Reality. *Econometrica* 48 (January):1–48.

———. 1988. Bayesian Skepticism on Unit Root Econometrics. *Journal of Economic Dynamics and Control* 12 (2):463–74.

Sims, Christopher A., and T. Zha. 1999. Error Bands for Impulse Responses. *Econometrica* 67 (5):1113–56.

Smith, Renee M. 1993. Error Correction, Attractors, and Cointegration: Substantive and Methodological Issues. *Political Analysis* 4:249–54.

Souleles, Nicholas S. 2001. Consumer Sentiment: Its Rationality and Usefulness in Forecasting Expenditure-Evidence from the Michigan Micro Data. National Bureau of Economic Research Working Paper W8410.

Stimson, James A. 1991. *Public Opinion in America: Moods, Cycles, and Swings.* Boulder, CO: Westview.

———. 1999. *Public Opinion in America: Moods, Cycles, and Swings.* 2nd ed. Boulder, CO: Westview.

Stimson, James A., Michael B. MacKuen, and Robert S. Erikson. 1995. Dynamic Representation. *American Political Science Review* 89 (September):543–65.

Tenpas, Katherine Dunn. 2000. The American Presidency: Surviving and Thriving amidst the Permanent Campaign. In *The Permanent Campaign and Its Future*, edited by N. Ornstein and T. Mann. Washington, DC: American Enterprise Institute Press and The Brookings Institution.

Thomas, Dan B., and Lee Sigelman. 1985. Presidential Identification and Policy Leadership: Experimental Evidence in the Reagan Case. In *The Presidency and Public Policy Making*, edited by George C. Edwards III, S. A. Shull, and N. C. Thomas. Pittsburgh, PA: University of Pittsburgh Press.

Thomas, L.B. 1999. Survey Measures of Expected U.S. Inflation. *Journal of Economic Perspectives* 13 (4):125–44.

Tufte, Edward R. 1978. *Political Control of the Economy.* Princeton, NJ: Princeton University Press.

Tulis, Jeffrey. 1987. *The Rhetorical Presidency.* Princeton, NJ: Princeton University Press.

United States Energy Information Administration. 1997. *World Oil Market and Oil Price Chronologies: 1970–1996.* Washington, DC: Department of Energy.

VandeHei, Jim. 2005. Bush Paints His Goals as "Crises." *Washington Post*, January 8, p. A01.

Weller, Christian. 2001. What the Crash Means for Your Retirement. *Economic Policy Institute Issue Brief* (156).

Western Standard Publishing Company. *American Reference Library* [CD-Rom]. Western Standard Publishing Company, 2000 [cited]. Available from *http://www.OriginalSources.com.*

Will, George F. 2004. An Optimist's Legacy. *Washington Post*, June 6.

Williams, John T. 1993. What Goes Around Comes Around: Unit Root Tests and Cointegration. *Political Analysis* 4:229–36.

Wlezien, Christopher. 1996. Dynamics of Representation: The Case of U.S. Spending on Defense. *British Journal of Political Science* 26 (January):81–103.

Wolf, Julie. 1999. *The American Experience: The 1982 Recession*: Public Broadcasting Service On-line.

Wood, B. Dan. 2000. Weak Theories and Parameter Instability: Using Flexible Least Squares to Take Time-Varying Relationships Seriously. *American Journal of Political Science* 44 (July):603–18.

Wood, B. Dan, and Jeffrey S. Peake. 1998. The Dynamics of Foreign Policy Agenda Setting. *American Political Science Review* 92 (March):173–84.

Wood, B. Dan, Roy Flemming, and John Bohte. 1999. Attention to Issues in a System of Separated Powers: The Dynamics of American Policy Agendas. *Journal of Politics* 61 (February):76–108.

Wright, Gerald C., Robert S. Erikson, and John P. McIver. 1987. Public Policy and Policy Liberalism in the American States. *American Journal of Political Science* 31 (November):980–1001.

Zaller, John R. 1992. *The Nature and Origins of Mass Opinion*. Boston, MA: Cambridge University Press.

# Index

Annual Economic Report of the President, 39

approval of president's job performance: average across presidencies, 110; base level of support, 112, 113, 116–17, 122; Blumenthal on, 109; congressional influence and, 169; direct vs. indirect influences on, 117, 118–19, 120, 131–34; dramatic events and, 12, 110, 111, 112, 113, 114, 122, 169; economic leadership and, 9, 43, 162, 165; economic news as influence on, 116–20, 122–23, 127, 128, 132–35; economic performance linked to, 8, 112, 113–14, 119; expectations of future economy and, 115–16; graphs of, 122; inertia and, 112–13; inflation linked to, 115; issue salience and, 115–16; measurement of, 121–24, 133; military interventions and, 111, 169; news media and, 109, 120 (see also news, economic); objective economic indicators and, 113–14, 115, 116, 123, 163; perceived economic performance and, 163–64; policy success linked to, 8–9, 43, 109; political behavior and, 112–17; as political incentive, 43–45, 51, 53–54, 59, 111; presidential influence on, 10–13, 117–20, 126–35, 165; presidential response to, 43–45, 53–54, 62; retrospective vs. prospective formation of, 114–15, 124; rhetoric and (see also economic rhetoric and *under this heading*); rhetoric as influence on, 10–13, 109–10, 111, 119; scandals linked to drop in, 113, 114; single-speech impacts on, 12–13, 111–12, 134, 166; statistical analysis methods, 124–26; tone of economic rhetoric and, 118, 119, 124, 127–34, 164, 165; unemployment levels linked to, 114

audience: as attentive to economic issues, 13–14, 62, 167; partisanship and receptivity to presidential rhetoric, 169; receptivity of, 18, 167, 169; responses of, 18; simplification of economic message for, 19

Balanced Budget and Emergency Deficit Control Act of 1985, 88

Barber, James David, 36, 37

Barrett, Andrew, 40

base level of support and public approval, 112, 113, 116–17, 122

behavior, economic: aggregation of, 138, 139, 140, 141, 158; business investment as, 139, 145–46, 149–51, 153, 154–57, 159; expectations and, 138–40, 155, 157–59; heard economic news and, 140–43, 145–48, 150–51, 154–57, 159; life cycle theory of, 138; passive model of presidency in scholarship, 116; permanent income theory of, 138; presidential rhetoric as influence on, 138, 142–49, 154–58; public approval as focus of research, 112–17; tone of presidential rhetoric as influence on, 16, 143, 155–58, 169–72; uncertainty and, 138–40. *See also* consumer confidence

Blumenthal, Sidney, 11, 109, 121

Brace, Paul, 44, 111

budgets: balanced (see deficits); public approval and budget allocations, 44–45

Bureau of the Budget, 7

Bureau of Economic Analysis, 39

Bureau of Labor Statistics, 39

Bush, George H. W.: approval levels of, 110, 116; average intensity of economic rhetoric, 29; average tone of economic rhetoric, 31; communication style of, 36–37; deficits and, 32, 88; economic leadership or stewardship of, 9, 32; inflation as issue for, 56; intensity of rhetoric, 27–28; personal style of (presidency-specific effects), 36–37, 49, 55; quoted rhetoric samples, 25, 26; tone of economic rhetoric, 25, 26, 32, 56; unemployment as issue for, 27–28

Bush, George W.: approval levels of, 1, 81, 110; average intensity of economic rhetoric, 29; average tone of economic rhetoric, 31; credibility of, 33, 160, 172; deficits and, 3; economic leadership or stewardship, 1, 3, 34, 44, 92–105, 172–74; economic policy-making under, 7; as